The massac
the innocents

Infanticide in Britain
1800–1939

Lionel Rose

Routledge & Kegan Paul
London, Boston and Henley

First published in 1986
by Routledge & Kegan Paul plc

14 Leicester Square, London WC2H 7PH, England

9 Park Street, Boston, Mass. 02108, USA and

Broadway House, Newtown Road,
Henley on Thames, Oxon RG9 1EN, England

Set in Baskerville 10/11pt
by Columns of Reading
and printed in Great Britain
by St Edmundsbury Press,
Bury St Edmunds, Suffolk

© *Lionel Rose 1986*

Library of Congress Cataloging in Publication data

Rose, Lionel, 1944-
The massacre of the innocents.
Bibliography: p.
Includes index.
1. Infanticide—Great Britain—History—
19th century. 2. Infanticide—Great Britain—
History—20th century. I. Title.
HV6541.G7R67   1986   363.4   85-19596

British Library CIP Data also available

ISBN 0–7102–0339–X

Contents

List of illustrations

Acknowledgments

I wish to record my especial appreciation to the following for advice, co-operation or service in the preparation of this book:

Miss Sally Sainsbury of the Department of Social Science and Administration at the London School of Economics; Dr Michael Rose of the History Department, Manchester University; Mrs Katharine Clark of Lewes, Sussex, who allowed me to use material from the diary of her ancestor, Edward Watson, in the preparation of Chapter 6; Miss G. Jones of the (now defunct) library of the Royal Society of Health; Mrs Doreen Elwell, for an efficient and speedy job of typing; Rona and David Gottesmann for the indexing.

In connection with the illustrations I would like to thank:

The Librarians of the NSPCC for their helpful assistance, in particular Miss Christine Smakowska, Chief Librarian, who went out of her way to assist me, and for permission to reproduce figure 5; The Wellcome Institute Library for figure 1; The British Library (Newspaper Collection) for figures 4, 6 and 9; The Public Record Office, Kew for figures 7 and 8; The Institute of Heraldic and Genealogical Studies at Canterbury for permission to use their Middlesex Parish Boundaries map as the basis for my diagram of the Middlesex coroners' jurisdictions in Chapter 7.

My thanks also to Havering Education Authority for the leave of absence that enabled me to complete the book.

And finally the warmest thanks to Mr Andrew Wheatcroft of Routledge & Kegan Paul, who saw potential in this work and was instrumental in rescuing my initial research potterings from years of oblivion in a drawer.

1 Setting the scene

In January 1984 a baby's body was found in a plastic bag, deposited in a litter bin in Sutton, Surrey. In March came news of the discovery of a badly burned body of a new-born baby in a field at Bramford, Ipswich. A few weeks later the mutilated body of a baby was found in a refuse skip on a factory site at Misterton, Doncaster.[1]

Such accounts received only a brief paragraph in the press, and, of their type, form only a fraction of all the stories of babies killed in rage, or under stress by parents or parents' lovers, that periodically crop up in the press. More commonly come accounts of live babies abandoned in places where the desperate parents intend that they should be found and taken care of: outside a police station, in a phone box, in a hospital lavatory – these are a few instances in recent times; and the police approach generally is to regard the mother as needing psychological and social help rather than to think of her as a criminal.

Babies under 1 year old today are four times as likely as other age groups to be victims of homicide (murder, manslaughter, infanticide) and even this figure is a very pale reflection of a phenomenon that once stained the social record of Christian Europe, which tended both figuratively and literally to sweep the problem under the rubbish tips and dung heaps where so many babies' bodies were hidden. This book starts in 1800, but its theme can be traced back through the ages; and indeed forms an integral part of the foundation myth of many great cultures: Romulus and Remus, the abandoned babes suckled by a she-wolf, as originators of the Roman civilisation; Moses, the foundling in the bullrushes, as the Biblical deliverer of the Jews; and the baby Jesus who was saved from Herod's soldiers.

Leaping the centuries, we find that such was the prevalence of infanticide in Stuart England that a draconian law passed in 1624 automatically presumed that the mother of a bastard was guilty of murder if she had tried to conceal the birth by secreting its corpse;

1

and it was for her to prove otherwise, for example that it was stillborn or died naturally. The law, be it noted, applied only to unmarried mothers, as legitimate babies were assumed not to be at risk. In Scotland, the fear of a public shaming in the Kirk drove many single girls to kill their offspring and in 1690 a law there made it a capital offence for a woman to conceal her pregnancy, should the baby be subsequently found dead or missing (circumstantial proof of a secret birth would have included signs of lactation, the mother's overnight change of weight, or stained bed linen). As the misogynistic Puritan influence that inspired such laws wore off in the eighteenth century, their very severity made them more and more unenforceable in an increasingly understanding climate of opinion. The Scottish law was the theme of Sir Walter Scott's *The Heart of Midlothian*, set in 1736, in which Effie Deans was capitally convicted of concealment of pregnancy (the baby had disappeared, though in fact it was not dead), but she was subsequently pardoned. The last hanging under the 1690 Act was in 1776; thereafter, under a peculiar Scottish procedure, an accused woman could avoid trial by electing to be 'banished' instead.[2]

In the eighteenth century the subject of infanticide and 'baby dropping' (the dumping of anonymous babies in exposed places) revolves round the efforts of the former sea captain Thomas Coram to establish a Foundling Hospital where desperate women could bring their babies. He faced much prejudice from people who thought that the existence of such repositories would encourage sexual irresponsibility and increase the problem of unwanted births. Coram's intention was to confine admissions to the infants of innocent, deceived girls (I shall dub them 'first-time lapsers' in this book) whose lives would otherwise be ruined. The London Foundling Hospital was founded in 1739, and after a very chequered history, it followed Coram's principles of selection only from 1801. But its relief was only a drop in the ocean, for in the nineteenth century it was taking in about 40 babies a year.[3] Despite its emotively appealing name, it was not strictly a foundling institution, as the mothers had to come for prior interviews. Such charity did not by any means necessarily conserve infants' lives, as the crowding of babies in institutions, especially when deprived of breast-milk, could produce a frightful mortality rate. Ecclesiastical foundling hospitals in Catholic countries could have infant death rates as high as 80 per cent in Paris and 90 per cent in Dublin just prior to 1800.

The London Foundling Hospital adopted a system of boarding babies out to wet-nurses and managed to reduce the death rate to 52 per cent, set against the average death rate of 70 per cent for

Figure 1   *This allegorical engraving c. 1740 shows 'dropped' babies to the right. A penitent mother who has abandoned her infant is being reassured by Thomas Coram. He carries the Charter of the newly founded London Foundling Hospital, which he points towards, preceded by a beadle bearing the rescued baby to its portal. At the left are clustered the hoped-for future fruit of the Hospital's nurture. The girls carry symbols of the domestic occupations they are intended for. The seascape towards which the boys are turned, clutching navigational instruments, signifies the naval careers they will be encouraged to follow.* (Source: John Brownlow, Memoranda or Chronicles of the Foundling Hospital, *1847. Courtesy:* Wellcome Institute Library, London.)

infants under 2 in the London of the 1750s.[4] The great exponent of boarding-out was the eighteenth-century businessman-turned-philanthropist, Jonas Hanway. In the six months from December 1758 he counted 2,271 foundlings under a year old in the streets of London; the general receptacle for unwanted bastard babies was the workhouse, from which they were farmed out to local nurses, who let them die off in droves. Hanway's efforts secured the passage of an Act in 1767 which obliged the workhouses to board babies out in rural homes where the survival chances were higher. But it is a moot point whether the totality of infant deaths was reducible by this expedient alone, for the wet-nurses, by suckling strangers' babies for money, were denying their own babies, and so prejudicing their survival chances.

If infanticide is related to the level of illegitimacy, then it is quite likely that it was increasing as the eighteenth century wore on, for there was apparently a rise in illegitimacy during the century;[5] this was aggravated by the domestic dislocations caused by the Napoleonic Wars, and early nineteenth-century newspapers were sprinkled with stories of babies found dead or abandoned, with the occasional trial of some wretched girl for murder.[6]

2   Infant mortality: 'the waste of infant life'

Historically, the value of infant life is determined by the forces of supply and demand, and contemporary attitudes to the inevitability of death. Dead babies were quickly replaceable when the birth rate was high; and an ignorance of the means to prevent death bred a helpless, resigned mentality – 'it's God's will', 'perhaps it's for the best' and so forth – which compounded the cheapening of infant life.

When babies became relatively scarce and as improved medical and sanitary understanding eroded the fatalism, so infant life started to become more precious, and we see the beginnings of this change at the end of the nineteenth century. An important element in the equation, too (more notably in the case of illegitimate babies), was the economic status of women: the more desperate the plight of the unsupported mother, the greater the compulsion to abandon the child. This will be examined in the next chapter.

The later eighteenth and early nineteenth centuries were marked by an unprecedented population explosion; in the period 1801 to 1851 the population of England and Wales doubled from 9,000,000 to 18,000,000. This was due not to an increase in the rate of procreation but a decline in the infant death rate from the late eighteenth century. Primitive contraceptive devices were not altogether unknown, but rarely used.[1] The average number of surviving births per family in the mid-Victorian period was about six. The lower down the social scale one went, the greater the number of pregnancies a woman tended to have. However, there were marked variations among the working classes. In the textile districts like Lancashire, where there was a tradition of independent earnings by girls in the mills, the birth rate was almost as low as among the middle classes; in mining and agricultural districts, however, the birth rate was very high, and remained well above average, even when the working classes were evidently taking to family limitation at the beginning of this century.

From around 1880 the birth rate began to decline perceptibly, and this trend began among the middle classes; their average family size fell by about 30 per cent between 1851 and the early 1880s;[2] textile workers and artisans were not too far behind, but unskilled workers did not show an appreciable fall till nearer the end of the century. Dock labourers married between 1861 and 1881 would have about 7.5 children on average, but those marrying between 1881 and 1891 would produce an average of 5.7.[3] This decline is attributed to an increased interest in contraception from the late 1870s, as indicated by the spread of contraceptive advertising and retail outlets but there was also evidence of a growing use of abortifacients. Working-class women from the 1890s were becoming more determined to limit family size.

The trend of infant mortality between 1800 and 1939 reveals two striking landmarks, coinciding with the turn of the nineteenth and twentieth centuries. The death rate of 0–1-year-olds in England had been falling sharply from the mid-eighteenth century; in the 1790s it is estimated at about 24 per cent; in the early nineteenth century at 20 per cent, and from the time when civil registration of births, marriages and deaths began in 1837 (in England and Wales) it hovered around 15 per cent until 1900.[4] The reason postulated by M.W. Beaver[5] is the increased availability of all-the-year-round cow's milk for infants, as the agricultural revolution made possible a storeable winter fodder and permitted the expansion of urban cowsheds. However contaminated and un-hygienic this milk was, he argues, it probably saved more infants' lives than it killed. The infant death rate[6] remained obstinately static till 1900, despite improvements in public sanitation, and a progressive fall in death rates among all ages above 1 in the last quarter of the century. However, after 1900 it began to fall as well – to 10.5 per cent in 1910 and 6.5 per cent in 1930.[7]

Beaver proposes his milk theory to explain this phenomenon. Greater attention was being paid to milk hygiene and its suitability for infants at the end of the century, as the falling birth rate, among other economic and political considerations, was making infant life more precious. With the municipal milk depôt movement for mothers of infants starting in 1899, and the consolidation of dairies into modern, better-managed and more hygienic combines proceeding apace from 1900, the improvement in milk quality enhanced infants' survival chances.

The average infant mortality rate hid dramatic social contrasts. Dr John Brendon Curgenven explained before the National Association for the Promotion of Social Science[8] in 1867, in a notable address on 'The Waste of Infant Life', that while the death rate of 0–5 year-olds among the 'educated and well-to-do' ran at

11 per cent, the equivalent figure among the urban working class ranged from 35 to 55 per cent, and this concealed, even more shockingly, an estimated 60–90 per cent among illegitimates.

Within the 0–5 age group it was the 0–1s whose lives were overwhelmingly at risk. In 1860, of the 167,000 children in England and Wales who died in this age range, 101,000 alone were 0–1, and fewer than 33,500 were 1–2.[9] The 0–1s, who in 1890 formed about 2.4 per cent of the total population, accounted for just under a quarter of all deaths that year (131,000 out of 562,000),[10] and the figures for this group conceal a startling variation within those first twelve months of life. A third of all deaths within the first year took place in the first month,[11] and a fifth in the first week![12]

There were also striking geographical variations. The infant death rate among farm labourers was closer to that of the urban middle classes; country air and wider dispersal in villages assisted survival chances. The industrial cities, especially those of the Midlands and Lancashire, had the worst record; Leicester and Liverpool vied with each other as the blackest of black spots, with an infant death rate (0–1) hovering around 22–24 per cent in the 1870s,[13] compared with the national average of 15 per cent. Until 1926 stillbirths were not entered in the official returns, and these figures exclude an untold number of infants born dead, or born alive but dying so soon afterwards that they were casually treated as if stillborn (see Chapter 14).

What, then, were the listed causes of this frightful mortality? We are at the mercy of Victorian inaccuracy and wooliness in medical terminology: 'Wasting Diseases' (such as 'congenital defects', 'injury at birth', 'want of breast milk', atrophy, debility, 'marasmus' and prematurity) led the way, followed by 'Diarrhoeal Diseases' including gastritis and enteritis, and then respiratory disorders, like bronchitis and pneumonia. 'Convulsions' took a fair number, but this blanket-term could cover a variety of causes – such as gastritis, acute indigestion and teething. The 'common infectious diseases', such as smallpox, measles, scarlet fever, diphtheria and whooping cough, accounted for only a small proportion of all infant deaths. We can see why it was the new-born who were so vulnerable. Most infant deaths were due to nurtural deficiencies: maternal exhaustion and malnutrition producing sickly offspring; and unhygienic conditions; wrong feeding, and a damp, foetid atmosphere producing respiratory infections; whilst maternal venereal infection, and contamination of the bloodstream with alcohol or poisonous abortifacients would have been responsible for many of the 'congenital defects' as vaguely classified in the official returns. For a mother so inclined, it would not have been difficult to will death upon her infant by neglecting it and inducing one or other of the symptoms described. Such causes were so common anyway that the child's death was unlikely to attract any suspicion, and we can never know how many child-murders were concealed under these generalised symptomological terms in the Registrar's tables.

Now, there was a separate category called 'Violent Deaths', covering burns, cuts, scalds, falls, poisonings (from opiate 'soothing' medicines), suffocations (chiefly in bed), drownings, and the like, but they formed only a tiny percentage of all recorded causes of death. In 1864, for example, of 113,000 deaths of 0–1 year olds, 1,730 were attributed to 'violence'[14] of which 192 were classed as 'homicides' (murder and manslaughter). This gives some idea of how remote the chances were of detecting a suspected murder or manslaughter among the welter of infant deaths – let alone of proving it against the defendant at the Assizes. The more helplessly infant you were, the greater the chances of dying a 'violent death'. Figures for 1871–80 show that a 0–1-year-old was two and a half times as likely to die a 'violent death' as a 1–2-year-old, and more than four times as much at risk as a 4–5-year-old;[15] and within the first year, we can safely assume that those in the earliest weeks of life were the most vulnerable of all, for suffocations and overlying, as we shall see in Chapter 19, were the predominant causes of infantile violent death.

The 'homicide' figures for infants, grotesque understatement as they were, still revealed that they were disproportionately at risk to a prodigious degree as the following table will show.

Total deaths from homicide in England and Wales 1863–1887[16]

Age	Total
Under 1	3,225
1–2	106
2–3	70
3–4	54
4–5	40
All ages over 5	1,789

Thus the under-1s formed 61 per cent of all homicide victims, at a time when they constituted 2.5–3 per cent of the population.

There was a widespread Victorian assumption that the practice by working-class women of continuing to work in the mills after

giving birth contributed to the high infant mortality rate. Domestic
duties were neglected, and the mothers' daily separation from their
infants, it was claimed, engendered an indifference to their
survival. This has been well established as misleading and
exaggerated to the point of fallacy, and prompted by male fears of
economic competition from women.[17] Most women, in fact, left
factory work upon marriage, and two classic Victorian 'proofs' of
the adverse effects of female factory employment upon the infant
survival rate have other explanations. The fall in infant deaths in
Lancashire from over 18 to 16 per cent during the 'cotton famine'
of the American Civil War period 1861–5 was ascribed at the time
to mothers who were laid off now staying at home to breast-feed
their babies, instead of leaving them in the hands of incompetent
daily minders. Now, the half-starved unemployed mothers would
scarcely have been able to produce adequate breast-milk, and the
real cause of their infants' improved survival chances was the
decline in maternal alcohol consumption during this depression.[18]

A comparison of infant death rates in Staffordshire between 1882
and 1892 showed that in the pottery districts of the north, where
women commonly worked, it averaged 18.2 per cent, whilst in the
mining areas of the south, where women did not work, it averaged
15.8 per cent. Now, mining areas had the worst record for
alcoholism in Britain at that time; the Potteries' worse infant death
rate was due not to working mothers' supposed indifference to their
babies, but poisoning from the lead that the pottery workers
handled.[19]

Mid-Victorian public health reports paint a picture of mill-girls
depositing their babies with local minders on their way to work
each morning; and how the minders fed the infants with
indigestible 'pap' (bread or other cereal sopped in diluted milk or
water and sweetened) and dosed them on babies' opiate soothing
mixtures like 'Godfrey's Cordial' or alcohol to quieten their
squalling – not infrequently with permanent results. This was
based on an exaggerated impression of factory working among
married workers. As Virginia Berridge has pointed out,[20] child-
minders in fact only cared for a 'minute proportion' of infants in
the factory areas; while Dr Jessie Duncan deduced from her socio-
medical researches in Birmingham between 1909 and 1911 that the
case against mothers' factory employment was inconclusive:

It seems pretty certain that industrial employment has a bad
effect on the infantile mortality, principally because it interferes
with breast-feeding. . . . But the influence of industrial
employment is quite small when compared with the influence of
acute poverty. It would seem therefore that in so far as the

mothers' employment reduces the acuteness of poverty, it may
tend to improve the infant mortality.[21]

However, the alleged effects of one area of female employment
on child death have not been explained away by modern
historians. Along the east side of Britain, from the Humber down
to East Anglia, the universal ganging system of farming (whereby a
contractor would hire gangs of labourers to farmers for short-term
seasonal tasks) was blamed for the excessive infant mortality rate,
and was made the subject of an official enquiry by Dr Julian
Hunter for the Privy Council in 1864.[22] Whilst the typical rural
infant death rate was 12 per cent or less, in the ganging districts it
exceeded 20 per cent. Hunter attributed this to the long periods
mothers spent away from home, as gang labour was peripatetic,
and they were too exhausted to breast-feed their babies on their
return home at night. The work was unremittingly hard and
coarsening. Immorality among gang workers was rife, and there
was an exceptionally high illegitimacy rate. The root source of
rural promiscuity was cottage overcrowding; where family privacy
was unknown, physical and sexual restraints were broken down
when the girls were still young, and gang labour was more
probably the opportunity for than the underlying incitement to,
sexual licence. An addiction to opium in East Anglia, traditionally a
palliative against the once widespread fenland malaria, led to
overlying on their infants, with fatal consequences. Hunter found
little concern among female gang workers for the death of their
infants, especially the bastards, and the spectrum of degradation
ranged from comparatively innocent girls 'seduced' for the first
time in the fields to hardened women who had produced a
succession of bastards, the survival chances of the latest of whom
was commonly a subject of 'jocular gossip' in the village. Among
his local medical informants the 'degree of criminality attributed to
the women varied from a sympathising excuse for their ignorance
to a downright charge of wilful neglect with the hope of death – in
fact, infanticide'. Some doctors, he said, whose suspicions had been
aroused by a series of infant deaths in the same household, had, by
reporting cases to the coroner, forestalled more tragedies.

Overcrowding at home, then, was a key factor in the infanticidal
element of infant mortality, for overcrowding promoted immorality,
and the story of infanticide is primarily an account of the fate of
illegitimate babies.[23] Dr Lyon Playfair's report on the sanitary
state of large towns in Lancashire for the Health of Towns
Commission in 1845[24] highlighted the degradation with case
studies. For example:

D.M., with his family makes 30s a week; his daughter, with a
bastard child about two years old, a son about 16, another of 12
and a daughter of 10 years old, making with his wife seven in all,
sleep in the same room with two beds. . . .

   D.F., a widower, slept in one apartment with his son and
daughter: The latter has a bastard child, which she affiliates on
the father, he upon his son, and the neighbours upon both.

And a survey in Preston of 442 slum dwellings showed an
average of nearly three persons sleeping to a bed.
   As Hunter's report reveals, ignorance and negligence shaded
into a conscious death-wish upon the unwanted child. The degree
of negligence in fact considered necessary to secure a manslaughter
verdict would depend on the standards of the age. In the case of
Regina versus *Nicholls* in 1874, in which a baby died of malnutrition,
the legal standard as judicially defined made proof almost
impossible: 'Mere negligence is not enough. There must be
negligence so great as to satisfy a jury that the offender has a
wicked mind in the sense of being reckless and careless whether
death occurred or not.'[25]
   In Victorian social conditions ignorance and poverty were the
legal saving graces against any manslaughter (let alone murder)
charge. Improper feeding loomed large in this context; 'pap' was a
necessity where mothers could not breast-feed for one reason or
another, and no one could blame a mother if the lethality of the
mess was due to the frequent adulteration of the ingredients by
traders: for example, with alum added to bread, sand to sugar, and
chalk to the cowshed milk, which also stood a good chance of being
infected with typhoid, scarlet fever, bovine TB, and other
contaminants from the cows' droppings and tail-flickings.[26] When
condensed milk, like Nestlé's, became available from the 1860s, and
when manufacturers were legally free to make unwarranted and
dangerous claims that their products were 'fit for infants' even
around 1900, who could conceivably impute criminal motives to
benighted working-class mothers for using them? Indeed, the
ignorance extended to the higher social classes and to the general
run of doctors, for, as we shall see when we turn to wet-nursing
later, the proliferation of expensive but nutritionally unsuitable
branded baby foods from the 1860s testified to the fashionable
classes' eagerness to clutch at anything but their own breasts to
feed their infants.
   Who could make a charge against a mother for dosing her baby
with 'Godfrey's Cordial' or laudanum, when they were freely sold
as soothers? Since opium was a traditional and valued analgesic in

an age when few medicines could cure complaints, its sale for babies was in no way seen as sinister, and until the Poisons and Pharmacy Act of 1868[27] any grocer or market trader could purvey it. The Act applied only to 'neat' opium, and limited it to sale by qualified druggists, subject to purchasers' signing the poisons book. Branded commercial 'soothers' containing opium were still unrestricted, and even the Food and Drugs Act of 1875, which required the statutory merchandise to be 'of the nature, substance and quality demanded', exempted proprietary medicines; customers bought branded drugs whose strength and composition could quite legally vary from batch to batch, so who under these conditions could prove murder against a mother or baby-minder who claimed to have accidentally overdosed a baby? The 'poisoning' figures for babies in the Registrar General's mortality columns appear but a drop in the ocean of infant deaths – 235 under-1s were so recorded in the five years 1863–7, and even these small figures were going down as the century wore on – 46 in 1868, and 10 in 1898. Dr George Newman's authoritative study 'Infant Mortality, a Social Problem' in 1906 did not even mention opiate-dosing as a cause of death. Yet very many cases of poisoning must have been concealed under more physically obvious symptoms of death like 'debility' and 'atrophy', listed in the Registrar's tables. At the turn of this century an Australian Royal Commission estimated that 15,000 infants a year were killed by proprietary medicines.[27] But opium itself from 1900 was going out of fashion as a baby soother, as manufacturers found alternative ingredients – not necessarily more beneficial – like potassium bromide.[28] The Dangerous Drugs Act of 1920 which made opiates like laudanum available only on doctors' prescription must have killed off any lingering practice of dosing babies.

Alcohol was another threat hanging over babies. Like opium, it served as a potentially lethal baby-soother – the cartoons of sodden mothers pouring gin down their babies' throats is one of our stock images of Victorian Britain. Yet this practice was also on the way out by 1906, according to Newman: 'Here and there one has come across such cases, but they are happily few and far between. . . . There is no ground for believing that any perceptible portion of the infant mortality is now due to this cause.'

But alcohol was more pervasively dangerous to babies through its degenerative effects on their parents. Alcoholism was the most corrosive social disease of the nineteenth century. Scotland and the large urban areas had the worst record, and rural areas the least bad before 1900.[29] Parental drunkenness was a crucial factor in the deaths of infants from overlying, as we shall see in Chapter 19.

Drink-besotted parents inflicted all manner of suffering on their infants, and it was said on behalf of the NSPCC in 1901 that half the cruelty cases it dealt with had a drink background.[30] In 1898, for instance, a mother received twelve months' hard labour for neglecting two children. Six children in her family of thirteen had died. A witness to her drunken conduct testified that 'she had seen her so regardless of the baby's life as to be using it as a pillow on the floor when dead drunk'. In December 1899 a Bradford coal-hawker was convicted for mistreating his 10-month-old son. After coming home drunk, he poured rum down the baby's mouth 'causing it to roll its eyes and go black in the face. . . .'[31]

Alcoholism severely impaired mothers' ability to care for their offspring. A study at Liverpool prison during 1899 and 1900 showed that among alcoholic female inmates the infant death rate (including stillbirths) was 55.8 per cent; among non-alcoholic inmates it was 23.9 per cent. Medical research at this period was bringing out the harmful physiological effects of alcohol on women's nurtural capacities – its contamination and shrinkage of breast-milk for instance – and the injuries to the foetus caused by uterine impregnation, which increased the chances of miscarriage, and congenital debility.[32]

As we shall see in Chapter 19, it was almost impossible to pin a manslaughter charge on a drunken mother who overlaid her baby, for certainty of 'wicked negligence' against any inebriate woman where her own offspring was concerned, in a society where inebriation was commonplace, was very hard for a gallant middle-class, male Victorian jury to accept. The Prevention of Cruelty to Children Acts of 1889 and 1894 (the latter Act making it a specific offence for parents to cause a child suffering by virtue of their drunkenness) became the NSPCC's real weapons, and as its net widened so it was able to intervene more and more frequently before drink-inflamed cruelties proved fatal.

In the years before the First World War there were signs of a decline in alcoholism. In 1911 proceedings for drunkenness in England and Wales were 78 per cent of what they had been in 1890. Spirits consumption in 1911 was 65 per cent of what it had been in 1890.[33] But it was the War itself, which brought stringent emergency controls over pub hours and liquor strengths to lay low the 'enemy within', namely Drink, that had the most dramatic and beneficial long-term impact on the nation's drinking habits. Beer consumption in 1918 was just over a third of what it had been in 1914, and spirits a half – and the nation remained sober throughout the 1920s and 1930s; drunkenness convictions which hovered around 200,000 a year before 1914 in England and Wales, were

30–40,000 a year in the 1930s. The improvement that inter-war sobriety accorded to infants' survival chances will emerge later in the book.

3 The economic and sexual vulnerability of women

The motives that could impel a woman to dispose of an unwanted infant can only be appreciated against the setting of women's economic and social vulnerability.[1] The prevailing assumption about women's earnings throughout the period covered by this book was that they were only supplemental to the male breadwinners' earnings and should be justifiably depressed; this presumption held true even if the woman was single and unsupported, or had dependent children as a respectable widow. A woman's true place was in the home, it was felt, and in the world of work they must never be allowed to compete with men. The quiet desperation of the unsupported woman was described by a sympathetic male observer in 1870:

> . . . from the restriction of female labour to the more servile
> departments of industry, from injurious competition with the
> young, and from other causes, the wages earned by every adult
> woman are reduced to the lowest scale; and with the small
> earnings she has too often little command even over the
> necessaries of life. Her food is scanty and innutritious; her wages
> are forestalled; her clothing for the weekday is pawned to relieve
> that for Sunday; she can only procure the shelter of a roof by
> clubbing with a few of her companions to rent an attic room or a
> cellar.[2]

The five main areas of employment for women in the mid-nineteenth century were domestic service, factory work, needlework, agricultural work and domestic industries, such as lacemaking. As I have noted, working women were predominantly single or widowed. At the 1851 Census, just under half the females over 10 were in paid employment.[3] Over a quarter of all employed women were in domestic service alone, and this was to remain the biggest single employer of women by far throughout the Victorian and Edwardian periods. Around 1870 there were about 1,300,000 female domestics, the circumstances of their employment dictating that they remain unmarried.

Among factory workers, the cotton mill girls of Lancashire were the élite earners, but they were confined to less skilled grades of work. 'Needlework' covered, at the supposedly more refined and fashionable end, millinery and dressmaking, recruiting the hapless daughters of decayed gentlefolk now forced to scrape a living in vile sweatshops and lodging rooms; the trade descended through shirt-making to slopwork at the bottom. The number of female farm labourers was to fall sharply by the early 1900s, but in the later nineteenth century there was to be an increase of openings in 'white collar' occupations, as we would call them today – notably as shop assistants, but with also a steady growth in the number of office workers (especially after the advent of the typewriter in the 1880s), nurses, and teachers. In 1861 5 per cent of all working women were 'white collar'; by 1891 it was over 11 per cent, and in 1911 16.4 per cent.[4]

Large numbers of women were employed full or part time in home-work at starvation rates; seamstresses blinded themselves working morning to night to earn a pittance in their garrets. Slopworkers could earn as little as 3 to 4 shillings a week around 1850[5] (compared with a working man's wage of about £1); umbrella covering, paper flower-making, matchbox packing, label-sticking, laundrywork, and for that matter baby-minding and baby-farming – all provided marginal incomes.

By 1914 there was more diversity of manual employment for women – opportunities were opening in light engineering, the stationery, food and drinks industries, for example – but the 'traditional' occupations (apart from farm labour) still accounted for two-thirds of female jobs. During the First World War there was a temporary dislocation of this pattern, as women filled vacancies left by men at the Front, but after 1918 – especially as the depression took hold – women were being forced back into detested domestic service; however, decades of mass education, and the postwar emancipation, were achieving an unparalleled advancement. By 1931 a fifth of all female employees were 'clerks'.[6]

Generally, women's earnings in the nineteenth and early twentieth centuries were about half of men's. An official wage census in 1906 showed that the average wage for women in industry was about 11 shillings to 13 shillings and 6 pence a week. Research showed, however, that a single woman supporting herself alone needed 15 to 17 shillings a week to keep herself at a tolerable subsistence level.[7] Mrs Beeton had reckoned on a range of £9 to £14 a year for a general maid in 1861,[8] with cooks commanding up to £30 a year, to which, of course, food and keep must be added.

It is against this background of female hardship that prostitution – 'the Great Social Evil', as it came to be openly recognised from the 1850s – flourished,[9] and with this recognition there came a vogue for philanthropic 'rescue' work and, subsequently, schemes for assisting first-time lapsers whose prospects would otherwise be blighted by their infant burdens (see Chapter 6). But rescue work was only a conscience-salve for the charitable, and did not touch the heart of the problem. It was infanticide that Mr Frederic Hill was referring to at a meeting of the NAPSS in 1873 when he blamed the 'practical monopolising by the male sex of all the more lucrative branches of employment as one of the great causes of the present evils'.[10]

Women's economic vulnerability was compounded by their extraordinarily poor prospects of marriage. It is true that females outnumbered males throughout the nineteenth and early twentieth centuries – in 1891 out of a population of 29,000,000 in England and Wales, women outnumbered men by 900,000, but many of these would have been girls under the marriageable age, and older women, who have always tended to outlive men. This surplus alone does not explain the phenomenon. As the Victorian female social reformer, Frances Power Cobbe, pointed out in a rather unkindly-headed article 'What Shall We Do With Our Old Maids?' in 1862,[11] while women were in surplus by some 4–5 per cent, statistics indicated that 30 per cent of them would remain unmarried.

The 1851 Census showed that 41 per cent of all women between 20 and 40 in England (and 48 per cent in Scotland) were spinsters, and if we add the widows in the same age bracket, roughly half the women in the prime of life were unsupported by a husband! (Official figures must, however, be qualified by the fact that unknown numbers of working-class women were living in a state of more or less stable 'concubinage' without going through the forms of marriage.)

The cause of this Victorian female crisis was men's preference for late marriage or permanent bachelorhood. In 1851 30 per cent of all men over 20 in England, and 35 per cent in Scotland were bachelors. In 1891 there were 2,000,000 bachelors in England and Wales between 20 and 44 alone, out of a total adult male population of less than 10,000,000.

Broadly speaking the further up the social ladder a man was, the later he married. In 1886 the average marriage age for a working man was just over 24; for the tradesman class it was 27, and the professional class, over 31.[12] Among the middle classes there was a rigid convention that a suitor must be able to keep his intended 'in the manner to which she is accustomed' and so had to wait until he was prosperously established before her father would consent to the match. Moralists were apt to blame the prevalence of 'seduction' and the downfall of working girls on inveterate tom-catting by these bachelor-roués.[13] And in 1864 John Brownlow[14] wrote of the particular susceptibility of downtrodden seamstresses and servants

> looking to marriage as a relief to all the difficulties and hardships of their condition, real or imaginary. This weakness (if weakness it be) is too well-known to the seducer, and 'marriage' therefore is the bait with which he entices and deludes his victim.

Now, Dr William Acton, the eminent venerologist and authority on prostitution, adduced figures in 1859 showing that only a tiny proportion of the imputed fathers of illegitimate children born in St Marylebone workhouse in 1857 was middle class. Of the 180 children, the two largest groups of fathers were male servants (25) and 'labourers' (20); only 8 middle-class fathers were cited, namely 6 'gentlemen', plus a surgeon and a solicitor. The remainder were a working- or lower-middle-class assortment: carpenters, painters, shoemakers, tailors, bricklayers, clerks, and so forth.[15] A later survey by the Revd G.P. Merrick, the Chaplain to Millbank Prison, in 1890 revealed that of 16,000 'fallen women' only 700 attributed their initial ruin to 'seduction' by a 'gentleman'.[16] The vast majority of single mothers owed their predicament to one of their own class, but there was a persistent belief that servants were especially vulnerable to 'seduction' and betrayal by their social superiors. J.D. Milne[17] showed in 1870 that the surplus of females over males was greatest in towns which had received a large influx of country girls to work as servants; in manufacturing centres the balance was more even. The implication was that servants faced more competition for a husband and were therefore more susceptible to false charmers.

Servants appeared as the overwhelmingly predominant recipients of aid among Rescue Societies. Daniel Cooper, Secretary to the Society for the Rescue of Young Women and Children, told the Select Committee on Infant Life Protection in 1871 that 95 per cent of the women his society had helped were servants, the victims 'in large numbers of instances' of sexual exploitation by their employers. But Dr Alfred Wiltshire told the Committee that he believed that the term 'servant' was often a camouflage used by girls 'in difficulties' to hide their backgrounds:

I have known cases of young ladies, people in very high positions indeed, who were put in the registration books as domestic servants. And therefore the servants get, as a class, taxed with crimes which they are not altogether more prone than other people.

It was inevitable that servants should figure so frequently as unmarried mothers, as they formed the largest female occupational group. The 1911 Census showed that servants were responsible for 46 per cent of all illegitimate births, but an analysis showed that their *rate* of illegitimacy was by no means the highest among employed women:[18]

Occupation	Rate of illegitimate births per 1,000 women
No occupation	5.7
Average for all occupied	8.9
Charwomen	43.6
Agricultural workers	35.7
Women surface workers at mines	29+
Rag gatherers	29+
Hemp and jute mill workers	15.3
Laundry workers	15.2
**Domestic servants	14.9**
Clerks/nurses	2.1
Schoolteachers	0.7

Servants were particularly vulnerable if they became pregnant, as it would mean instant dismissal without references; for this reason they figure so prominently in the story of infanticide; a factory girl could deposit her baby with a daily minder, and her employer need not know, less care. But one should not imagine that a pregnant servant, however tragic and desperate her circumstances were, was a 'seduced' innocent. Girls who had come from the country, where poverty and overcrowding and rustic earthiness relaxed moral inhibitions, were quite likely to be sexually experienced already; no shame was attached to premarital pregnancy in many rural districts[19]; while the illegitimacy table just cited shows that farm girls were carrying on this tradition in 1911. Evidence like Acton's indicates that servants were most at risk of pregnancy through dalliances with tradesmen and male servants. As early as 1743 a servants' etiquette book, *A Present for the Servant Maid*,[20] warned her not only against advances from the master, but forwardness from fellow male servants, 'for the most part pert and saucy where they dare and apt to take liberties on the least encouragement'. If her employer was the father of the child, she was indeed likely to be a little better off. While dismissal must follow as a matter of form, she probably received a sum to pay for the child's 'adoption', for, as will emerge, there was frequently a shadowy male figure negotiating with the baby-farmer or midwife, and the sums involved were often beyond a servant girl's own means. In conclusion, servants were no more 'easy' than other girls of the same class, but their employment situation in the event of pregnancy was much more endangered than that of factory or farm girls, hence their readier resort to desperate means for disposing of their burdens, or to Rescue Homes when dismissed without references; and I would hazard that they were no more specially at risk from their employers' advances than factory girls were from their foremen or gangers from their gangmasters.

At this point I ought to balance the picture: I have dwelt exclusively on the vulnerability of working-class girls as the source of illegitimacy and infanticide. As will become apparent, numbers of upper-class ladies 'in difficulties' went through surreptitious channels to dispose of their embarrassments, but had the money and protection of the Victorian class system to cover their tracks. Servants worked and lived in the better-off neighbourhoods where crude attempts to dispose of a baby were more likely to be discovered than in the teeming slum habitations of other lower-class girls. So the upper classes had money to conceal their shame; the very poor had the camouflage of the slums, while the servant, between-worlds, occupied an exposed and unenviable position.

Middle-class sympathisers with the plight of the 'fallen woman' were fixed on the notion of 'seduction'. The woman was seen invariably as the victim of men's wiles, and Victorian fiction dwells repeatedly on the theme of the remorseful 'Magdalen' as an object to be pitied, yet whose slate can only be wiped clean, in mawkish literary convention, in tragic death, emigration or a self-sacrificing devotion of the rest of her life to good works.[21]

In reality working-class girls were not at all irrevocably blighted by sexual lapses. The *Saturday Review*, a journal very hard-headed about the morals of working-class girls,[22] poured scorn on sentimental middle-class illusions, and in 1866 reminded its readers that among the working classes sexual intercourse 'is regarded as an incident of honourable courtship and is – or at least used to be – followed by the solemnization of marriage'. This loss of chastity 'does not imply the loss of every other virtue' and even if the man deserts her 'she does not lose her self-respect, or become either a drunkard or prostitute. Unless her neighbours are very puritanical or cruel, her lapse does not prevent her from getting a situation, or discharging its duties with fidelity.' Such a statement echoes the findings of William Acton in his 1857 study on prostitution that the notion of the 'fallen woman' sliding deeper and deeper into the mire of vice, ending in VD-racked death, was a myth. Prostitution was usually a temporary expedient in a girl's life, and did not ruin her social recovery later. The *Saturday Review* held that the main cause of illegitimate births was not 'seduction' but young people's self-indulgence and frivolousness. Even in rural Scotland, the prospect of a public shaming by the Kirk Elders does not seem to have been effective as a sexual discipline. In the 1850s the illegitimacy rate in parts of rural Scotland reached 16 or 17 per cent, double the official average for the country.

Thus, for a working-class girl an illegitimate child was less of a social stigma than an economic liability; and provided it was cast out of sight and out of mind of society she might hope to recover her station. Indeed, the whole business of wet-nursing depended on the availability of 'fallen women' whom the higher classes took under their roofs to queen it among the servants.

Why, then, were the upper classes so fixed on this notion of 'seduction'? The answer lies partly in a reaction to the severity of the new bastardy laws in 1834.

4 Bastardy and the Poor Law in mid-Victorian England

Official statistics of the rates of illegitimate births under the English and Scottish Civil Registration Acts of 1836 and 1854 respectively must be treated with caution. Until 1874 registration of births in England was not even compulsory; in 1867 the proportion of non-registrations in parts of London alone was estimated at anything between 15 and 33 per cent,[1] and as the local Registrars had to depend on their informants' word, many illegitimates were in fact being registered as legitimate.[2] Country districts showed a higher bastardy rate than towns. In the late 1850s, while London was estimated to have a rate of 4.2 per cent, for example, Cumberland, Westmorland and Norfolk revealed rates of over 10 per cent, and Scottish rates could go much higher. Country customs, as I mentioned in the last chapter, were earthier, but in the towns, we must remember, there was more scope for concealing illegitimate births. The *British Medical Journal* in 1867[3] sceptically compared the official bastardy rates for some wealthy London West End parishes – like Marylebone at 9.1 per cent and St Pancras at 5.1 per cent – with poor East End parishes like Whitechapel at 3.3 per cent and Stepney at 1.6 per cent, and invited readers to question whether the denizens of the slums were really more chaste, or more misleading. The Registrar General believed there was a 10 per cent underestimate in the official returns of illegitimate births, but the Infant Life Protection Society (see Chapter 12) in 1870 put it as high as 30 per cent.[4] Even when the 1874 Registration Act made registration of births compulsory this could still be widely evaded, either by pretending that a dead baby was stillborn (this did not have to be registered) or by exploiting the six-week period of grace allowed by the law before registration, and decamping untraceably from the district. I shall, however, use the official returns for England and Wales, unless otherwise stated.[5]

As noted in Chapter 1, the illegitimacy rate appeared to be rising in the eighteenth century and this seems to have continued into the early nineteenth century – a reason, as we shall see, for the radical changes in the Bastardy Law in 1834. Despite hopes, this law proved ineffective to check the trend, for the Registrar General acknowledged a continuing rise in illegitimacy to the mid-1840s where it peaked at 7 per cent. Thereafter it began falling steadily to 5.8 per cent in 1869 and 4 per cent by 1900. (Scottish returns from 1855 were consistently higher at 8–9 per cent to the 1890s.)[6]

Although the *rate* was falling in England after 1845, the absolute number of illegitimate births each year held steady at 40,000 to 44,000 a year, owing to the rapid growth in population, and only after 1890 did it fall below 40,000,[7] until the First World War. If we accept the 30 per cent underestimate figure, it means that up to 65,000 unwanted children were being born each year in mid-Victorian England. The official statistics (in England) did not distinguish illegitimate death rates, but sample local estimates indicate a frightful holocaust. Dr Bachoffner, the Superintendent Registrar for Marylebone, found in the 1860s that the death rate of *registered* illegitimates under 1 ranged from 46 to 93 per cent in his constituent districts. Dr John Brendon Curgenven told the 1871 Select Committee on Infant Life Protection[8] that 90 per cent of the infants born in St Giles workhouse and subsequently removed by their mothers did not see the year out, and generally 60–90 per cent of illegitimates (two-thirds of whom, Curgenven believed, were put into the care of dry-nurses) died under those nurses' care.[9]

Later nineteenth-century figures indicate that the illegitimate death rate was double that of legitimates under 1. For example, in Glasgow between 1881–90 the figures were 27.5 and 13.7 per cent respectively, and in Manchester between 1891–4 39 and 17 per cent respectively.[10] Whilst all infant death rates fell after 1900, this ratio held true until the mid-1930s when the gap started narrowing: in 1915, for example, the rates were 20.3 and 10.5 per cent.[11]

Official circles were perturbed in the early decade of the nineteenth century by a growing burden of poor law relief and a rise in illegitimacy which was reckoned to be contributing to that burden, as unmarried mothers threw themselves on to the parish. Aspects of poor law 'generosity' and its alleged stimulus to a 'population explosion' among the unworthy and shiftless elements of society[12] came increasingly under attention. Thomas Malthus, whose '... Principle of Population', first published in 1798, established him as the high priest of the 'dismal science' of population economics, believed that population growth was self-regulating, as cycles of war, famine and disease eliminated the surplus. A high infant death rate was therefore, however regrettable, a biological necessity:

. . . we shall be compelled to acknowledge that, if the number
born annually were not greatly thinned by this premature
mortality, the funds for the maintenance of labour must increase
with much greater rapidity than they have ever done hitherto in
this country in order to find work and food for the additional
numbers that would then grow up to manhood.

Birth control only dimly entered his mental firmament[13] but the
existing bastardy laws seemed to him a pernicious stimulus to
unnecessary births.

Under laws of 1733 and 1809[14] if an unmarried girl became
pregnant, she had only to name the putative father – with no other
evidence required – and the parish poor law authority would haul
him before the magistrates, where he would have to undertake to
pay maintenance at the court's discretion (usually 2 to 3 shillings a
week) or go to prison. The House of Lords Select Committee on
the Poor Law in 1831, and the great Poor Law Royal Commission
of 1834 were regaled with accounts of all the mischiefs this caused:
blackmail of eligible, but innocent, bachelors by girls, 'arm-
twisting' of accused men by the parish to marry the girl (for the
parish did not want to be left supporting the girl and her child at
ratepayers' expense); flight by men to distant parts, or even a
preference for prison by some – for a completed sentence discharged
all further obligations to the parish, which was left 'holding the
baby'. The bastardy laws were accused of encouraging 'profligacy'
in girls. Edward Simeon, an Oxfordshire magistrate, told the 1831
Select Committee: 'I feel convinced that three fourths of the women
that have bastard children would not be seduced if it were not for
the certainty that the law would oblige the man to marry.'

Economic desperation must have played a big part in prompting
such scheming by girls; the fear of a destitute spinsterhood
evidently outweighed the prospect of marital misery at the hands of
the men they hooked.

Inspectors' reports told the 1834 Commission how parishes were
giving up the prosecution of putative fathers, as the legal
proceedings and the pursuit of defaulters still left them out of
pocket. And laws, whose antecedents dated back to Elizabethan
times, for imprisoning mothers who produced a succession of
bastards as a burden to the parish were not worth enforcing, as
women came out harder than they went in, and the children still
had to be supported. Women were alleged to be cold-bloodedly
producing bastards for the net profit from parish relief, and that
single mothers were by and large treated more generously than
needy widows with legitimate children! Captain Chapman, an

inspector, reported from the West Country that the widow 'can be obliged to work, her earnings are inquired into, and even her child may be taken from her into the workhouse whilst the mother of a bastard has only to receive her weekly stipend, liable to no control, subject to no inquiry.' Now, the Commission did acknowledge that some parishes were strict with unmarried mothers, but its Report leaves the impression that on balance they were having it easy. However, other research has shown that women *were* being imprisoned for producing bastards, and were being offered minimal relief. At Leeds in 1822, for example, relief was limited to 1 shilling a week by the parish, even if the father contributed nothing; at Sheffield unmarried mothers were only given indoor relief (i.e. they had to live in the workhouse) and at Halifax no relief at all was given.[15] The Commission's report was swayed by a Malthusian dogma, yet there is a possible juristic reason why unmarried mothers were exempt from the means test in the illustrations cited in the Report. Under the ancient legal doctrine of *Filius Nullius*,[16] a bastard was technically 'nobody's child' and not part of the family; it was a community responsibility, and, apart from prosecuting a woman for producing it under the aforementioned laws, the parish could not impose the family responsibility tests applicable in the case of a widow. This is the only sense I can possibly make of the anomalies revealed by the Report of 1834.

Malthus had argued that bastardy could be checked by shifting the responsibility on to the mother, and denying her the support of the Poor Law. He recognised that this would work hardship on the woman by freeing the father, but this regrettably was 'the invariable law of nature', and it was for the woman to take care for her chastity. This was the view adopted in the 1834 Poor Law Report, and against the argument that this would lead to more desertions of infants and infanticide, the Commissioners readily seized on the rationalisation submitted by Inspector Walcott, from Wales. He argued that the bastardy rate would fall, so

> abortion and infanticide would be less frequent, not only from
> there being fewer cases to give rise to them, but because the man
> who in most instances is now the first to suggest these crimes,
> especially that of abortion, and to assist in their execution, would
> no longer have an interest in doing so, and the female, left to
> herself, from maternal feelings and natural timidity, would
> seldom attempt the destruction of her own offspring.

The argument was a tissue of unproven but convenient assumptions: infanticide was male-instigated, and women, left to their own devices, would never kill their child from poverty alone: 'we do not believe that infanticide arises from any calculation as to expense. We believe that in no civilised country, and scarcely any barbarous country, has such a thing been heard of as a mother killing her own child in order to save the expense of feeding it.' This was considered justification enough for the recommendations duly implemented in the 1834 Poor Law Act.[17] Under section 71, all poor relief granted to a bastard child 'while under the age of sixteen shall be considered as granted to [the] mother'. The 'family allowance' principle for single mothers (to use modern analogies) was now categorically and universally replaced by the same means test as was applied to widows. The single mother could not dump her child on the parish and go her own way.

The Affiliation Law, under sections 69 and 72, was transformed. The object was to make maintenance proceedings against the putative father so awkward that actions would wither away, and as girls came to realise the harsh consequences of sexual delinquency, they would guard their chastity and bastardy would decline. Proceedings could only be started on their behalf by the local Poor Law unions, and were to be held before magistrates only at Quarter Sessions; these were held four times a year at the county town, and involved delays and much travelling – far less convenient than if held before a single justice at the frequent local petty sessions. The claimant now required 'corroborative evidence' of the defendant's paternity; this loose phrase, designed to protect innocent men from false accusation, left much to the justices' discretion as to the circumstantial evidence sufficient to establish paternity, and was to prove a major bugbear in affiliation proceedings into modern times.

Before the Act was even passed, these provisions were coming in for impassioned objection as tilting the balance too sharply against women. In the debate on the Bill in the Lords, the Bishop of Exeter warned:

> If you pass the bill you must be prepared to find every woman who can manage the thing at all – I will not say ready to destroy her child, – but ready to try every expedient which it is possible for her, to place the poor babe . . . out of her own hands into the hands of others. These children will be carried in baskets nicely wrapped up . . . and laid at the . . . workhouse door, or at the door of the clergyman. . . . In short, you will find that every workhouse will become an hospital for foundlings, and the least deplorable of the proposed measure, if it is adopted, will be that injury to morals of which hospitals for foundlings have been invariably found productive.

Thus the affiliation proposals would be self-defeating as attempts to improve public morals, especially as men would now be free to 'seduce' the weaker sex with impunity: 'You will', he protested, 'release men, especially in the humbler walks of life, from all temporal restraints on their licentiousness' and 'harden the heart of man and increase his selfishness to an intensity of which we have never yet believed him capable.'[18] Similar sentiments were expressed by others at this time, including *The Times* and the poet Coleridge.

From the new Poor Law's own narrow angle, however, an early success was claimed under the first impact of the Act: the number of bastards on poor relief in England and Wales fell from 71,298 in 1835 to 61,826 in 1836, and affiliations fell from 12,381 to 7,686 in the same period.[19] However, as we have noted, the level of bastardy in society was not decreasing, and local poor unions felt impelled, as time went on, to pursue putative fathers into the Quarter Sessions notwithstanding the cost, as a vengeance for loading them with bastards. Affiliations were not withering away as the Malthusian exponents hoped,[20] and in 1839 the government had to bow to local pressures and pass an act transferring proceedings to the cheap and convenient petty sessions. The Bishop of Exeter could say 'I told you so' in 1839, when he told the House of Lords of 'a large increase in the number of illegitimate children registered as baptized'. The *Halifax Guardian* in 1837 stated that in the year from March 1834, thirty-two bastards were baptised in Halifax, while in the year from March 1836 the figure was seventy-two.[21] Statements from MPs and letters to the press from individual parishes by 1840 were confirming the same impression:[22] bastardy was increasing, and the Poor Law was feeling the pressure despite the more stringent principles of section 71.

The severity of the new Poor Law in general, and the bastardy provisions in particular, swung sympathy strongly towards the unmarried mother: she was seen as the innocent victim of 'seduction' now reduced to desperation by a flinty-hearted Poor Law. The *Merthyr Guardian* of December 1840 reported the case of one Ann Davis, a servant girl whose child was fathered by a 'low vagabond fellow' from a neighbouring parish in South Wales. She left the child at the father's door and for this was imprisoned for a month. She pleaded with local magistrates to help her, saying that since her release 'she had passed the previous night under a hedge with her infant, which she did not wish to murder, but which she could not support! The father neither would nor could support her or it. She would be glad to be sent to gaol to keep them from perishing.'[23]

Now stories were circulating of an increase in infanticide due to the new law, and George Wythen Baxter's *Book of the Bastiles* (1841), a broadside against the inhumanity of the 1834 Act, contains several references to this alleged phenomenon. He quoted for example a letter from a Mr Jonathan Toogood of Somerset to *The Times* of 2 March 1841:

> I cannot forbear remarking, in reference to the Bastardy clause that, in late conversation with the coroner for the western division of this county, I learned that he had held seven inquests on newly-born children within the space of eight months in his district. He admitted that he attributed this enormous increase of infanticide to the operation of the New Poor Law, and that notwithstanding a reprimand he had received from the Commissioners, he had repeated his conviction to the jury.

The situation was aggravated by the economic depressions of the 'Hungry Forties', and the government learned that the poverty riots, the so-called 'Rebecca riots', in South Wales in 1844 were in part provoked by the new bastardy provisions. Sir James Graham, the Home Secretary, accordingly spoke in the Commons of proposed reforms to the bastardy law, to 'relieve the Poor Law of an immense weight of odium, and on the whole be conducive to the welfare of the poorer classes'.[24] The Poor Law Amendment Act of 1844[25] roughly assimilated the English affiliation procedure to the Scottish one: women were to have a direct right of proceeding to petty sessions without going through the Poor Law. And in fact the Poor Law was expressly prohibited from assisting in any action, or taking any resulting maintenance money as reimbursement for poor relief accorded the woman. In my judgment the government's real objective was not humanitarian at all, but designed really to dissociate a heartily detested Poor Law from one of its most reviled aspects at a sensitive time: for the Act, if anything, made the woman's position worse.

Poor ignorant girls were now left entirely to their own devices to start proceedings. The 'corroborative evidence' rule remained. A maintenance limit was now set, regardless of the father's means, at a miserable 2 shillings and 6 pence a week, and if he defaulted, he could only be forced to pay a maximum of thirteen weeks' arrears. Maintenance was payable till the child was thirteen, but if the mother married another man in the meantime, the father's obligations ceased. (The curious anomaly under the Act that, if a woman in receipt of an inadequate maintenance subsequently went into the workhouse, the Poor Law could not touch her income, was rectified under the 1868 Bastardy Act.[26] The principle of 1844 remained, but the Poor Law could now attach such income as a set-off against the costs of relief.)

Allegations of an increase in infanticide, now blamed on the 1844 Act, were to mount sporadically but noticeably into the 1850s, and then reached a crescendo in the 1860s. *The Times* as early as 1847 opined that 'the murder of children has ceased to be murder in England. It is beginning to be thought as little of as braining a process-server, or shooting an in-coming tenant, in Ireland.'[27] And in July 1853 *The Times*[28] quoted Mr Justice Coleridge at Oxford Assizes where he had presided over three cases with female defendants involving the deaths of new-born infants:

'He had reason to think that crimes of this character were on the increase. . . . No one could tell how many lives of innocent children were sacrificed by the hard-heartedness of mothers, in endeavouring to hide their shame.' And in the same *Times* issue was the report of a manslaughter case against two women at York Assizes for the death of a child.

Affiliation was a daunting prospect for a poor and unassisted girl. She had to pay 2 shillings for a summons, and additional costs entailed in its service,[29] and Justice Coleridge's somewhat blinkered view prompted a 'Clerk to Magistrates' to write to *The Times* a few days later[30] to explain the tribulations of affiliation as a reason for the reputed increase in infanticide:

'Nothing, I assure you is of late more common than for the putative father to be off 100 miles or so by one of the many railways which now-a-days facilitate such migrations. . . .' The constable follows, and even if he succeeds in serving the summons, the troubles are just beginning:

The day arrives; he does not appear and an order is made in his absence. The constable, or some one, is despatched to serve him personally, in this instance with the order. A month follows, and he disregards it. A warrant is then to be issued and a constable started off in search of him, and to apprehend him for disobedience of the order. He is, or is not, found. He has had a full six weeks to make another removal and with more secrecy than before.

In 1864 John Brownlow,[31] in condemning the bastardy law, also made a point of the withering humiliation felt by basically decent girls in making application in open court before the gawping male audience. Exactly the same point was to be made by Miss Mary James of the Bethnal Green Poor Law Union before the 1909 Select

Committee on Bastardy Orders.[32] Decent girls recoiled at the prospect, so that 'the worst cases where a really innocent girl is led astray under a promise of marriage is just the very one where a man gets off altogether; and it is a well-known fact that unworthy men trade on this. . . .'

The wonder is that the affiliation procedures were used at all after 1844, when one considers the long daily hours of labour and little time that girls would have to attend court; servants at this time could only expect half a day off a month.[33] Perhaps the applicants tended to be unemployed girls already subsisting on poor relief – but then where would they get the money for court costs, when the Poor Law was now forbidden to get involved? Yet figures show that the Act was being used. Between 1845–59 inclusive, of 157,485 summonses issued, 107,776 ended in the issue of orders.[34] However, officially there were over 600,000 illegitimate births in this period, and more than 800,000 if we allow for a 30 per cent understatement, so that only a sixth to an eighth of single mothers had orders made on their behalf, and many of these would have had subsequent difficulties in making the men pay up. In 1857 alone 5,816 men were taken into custody for disobeying bastardy orders, of whom 2,956 were convicted.

Sympathy for 'betrayed' victims of the post-1834 Bastardy Law prompted Mr Miles M.P. to introduce a Seduction Bill in 1840[35] to tilt the balance back against male 'seducers'. In civil law a girl who had lost her chastity under promise of marriage had an action for damages for 'a breach of promise' if the man renegued. Pregnancy was not necessary to the case, but if she did become pregnant her parents or employers could independently sue for 'loss of services' caused by her indisposition. Legal costs in practice restricted this to the middle classes, and Mr Miles's proposal was to create an alternative cheap process in the magistrates' courts, allowing a maximum of £30 damages to bring it within range of the working classes.

Opposition to the bill had a definite class bias – it was all right for the middle classes evidently, but said Sir Edmund Head, Assistant Poor Law Commissioner (and staunch supporter of rigid application of the 1834 Act's principles): 'Weapons capable of being fearfully abused are placed [if the bill were passed] within the reach of a far greater number of persons; some of whom will be constantly ready to avail themselves of them for the purposes of extortion and speculative profligacy.'[36] The bill failed to pass, and the idea of a 'seduction' law was not to be taken up again until the 1870s as part of the Infant Life Protection Society's battery of proposals to check infanticide.

Unmarried mothers and the poor law

Suppose that an unmarried mother or mother-to-be was jobless, destitute and unable to obtain maintenance: was the condition of Poor Law relief likely to ease or intensify the impulse to dispose of her infant? The aspiration of the 1834 Poor Law was to deter scrounging by making conditions in them 'less eligible' than those of the poorest paid worker outside, and (an aspiration never to be fully achieved) to restrict the able-bodied paupers to the more degrading in-house relief where they would have to perform labour-tasks for their keep. A parturient woman would be classed as 'not able-bodied' and placed in the lying-in ward, and then for a very short time, perhaps, in the nursery ward, but within days she would (if she elected to stay in the workhouse) be transferred to the 'able-bodied' ward and virtually lose contact with the baby, which remained under the care of the pauper 'nurse'.

The whole idea of going 'on the parish' filled the average person with horror and shame. In George Eliot's *Adam Bede*, set in 1799 but evidently expressing the attitudes of the time it was published in 1859, the 'seduced' country girl Hetty Sorrel was prompted to abandon her baby to its doom partly out of fear of the workhouse:

> 'The parish!' You can perhaps hardly understand the effect of
> that word on a mind like Hetty's brought up among people who
> were somewhat hard in their feelings even towards poverty . . .
> and had little pity for want and rags . . . but held them a mark of
> idleness and vice – it was idleness and vice that brought burdens
> on the parish. To Hetty the 'parish' was next to prison in
> obloquy. . . .

An unmarried mother, whose condition was wrought by her own 'vice', could expect little sympathy. The extreme form of Puritanical censoriousness was expressed by the Reverend Herbert Smith, Chaplain to the New Forest Workhouse in 1838.[37] He did not distinguish between types of unmarried mother, who might range from some pathetic betrayed girl to hardened wantons, but between *all* unmarried mothers (who should be kept together in a separate ward) and the married paupers. The former were all alike 'fornicators', and 'adulterers' in his eyes, and their babies the misbegotten 'offspring of sin and profligacy'; the women should properly be the objects of a cold charity, to be scripturally harangued, and from whom submission and gratitude were to be expected as a matter of course. Usually, the first-time lapser could expect to be confined in the 'black ward' for refractories.[38] As late as 1909 the Royal Commission on the Poor Law was criticising the lack of classification and segregation of unmarried mothers by type.[39] It was only in 1914 that the Local Government Board formally encouraged local Poor Law unions along these lines, with a recommendation to remove the first-time lapser to some voluntary home (in part subsidised by the local unions) away from the workhouse atmosphere,[40] though some of the more progressive unions had already been doing this for some time.[41]

One must judge workhouse standards by the standards of the prevailing social conditions of the day,[42] but the fact remains that married women, however poor, avoided the workhouse lying-in ward if they could; it was seen as a dump for bastard births. About 75 per cent of babies born there were illegitimate,[43] and unmarried mothers tended to leave the place with their babies less than a month after delivery right into the early 1920s.[44] The workhouse baby's survival chances in this month were no worse than those of a legitimate baby born outside, since this was the extent of the nursing period, when the mother was allowed to breast-feed him:[45] but once removed, his chances in the nineteenth century were, as we have seen, very slim, and his prospects could not have been better if his mother had stayed longer, for the denial of breast-milk after her transfer, and the disgraceful conditions of the workhouse nurseries, conspired to seal his fate. Dr Joseph Rogers, a London workhouse medical officer, described the nursery at the Strand workhouse which he joined in 1856 as a 'wretchedly damp and miserable room nearly always overcrowded with young mothers and their infants' where epidemics spread like wildfire. Single mothers in the lying-in ward were kept on a diet of gruel 'as a deterrent against the use of the workhouse as a place in which to be confined', and the Guardians looked on him as an 'irreconcilable fellow' for protesting about this.[46] The dry-nurses were feeble and ignorant old pauper women, 'grannies' unfit for other work, and such conditions were still prevalent enough in 1909 to shock members of the Royal Commission, who learned that many of them were mental defectives. One witness told of a nursery as being 'under the charge of a person actually certified as of unsound mind, the bottles sour, the babies wet, cold and dirty'. In another instance, a subnormal woman washed a baby in boiling water and caused its death.[47]

In 1871 nearly two-thirds of the illegitimate children born in London workhouses were the mothers' first births,[48] so the large majority were first-time lapsers. But even among single mothers-to-be there was an overwhelming preference to stay outside the workhouse if they possibly could. In 1909 illegitimate workhouse births formed 18 per cent of *all* illegitimate births in England and Wales.

Suppose a single woman applied to the Poor Law not for a lying-in place, but sustenance for herself and her child: what treatment could she expect? If she had no 'settlement' in the parish (that is a claim through legal roots there) the union had no obligation to give her any help. George Wythen Baxter in 1841 cited a case from Morpeth, involving one Elizabeth Scott who applied for relief for herself and her illegitimate child, both on the edge of starvation: she was given an interim allowance of 1 shilling and sixpence a week, pending determination of her place of settlement. One shilling of this went in rent, and the woman was left with sixpence a week to feed herself and her child![49]

For women with a settlement, in the early decades of the new Poor Law there was a good chance that they would be allowed outdoor relief; in 1836, with the new arrangements settling in, at least three-quarters of single mothers were on outdoor relief among those unions sending early returns.[50] At the beginning of 1849 just under half the 14,639 illegitimate pauper children under 16 (from which we can deduce the same proportion of mothers) were getting outdoor relief,[51] but once the 'Hungry Forties' were over, and more space became available in the workhouses, indoor relief became increasingly the rule (especially after the government instigated a tightening-up against outdoor relief generally from 1871). By mid-1870 of 11,179 pauper illegitimate children, only 2,894 were on outdoor relief.[52] (Various statistics suggest an average of 1.2 to 1.5 illegitimates to each mother applying.)[53] By the end of the century the number of unmarried mothers on outdoor relief was down to about 250 for the whole of England and Wales.[54] Now from the late nineteenth century there had been a relaxation of the indoor relief rule for 'deserving' classes of pauper, so that by 1920 over 97 per cent of pauper widows were on outdoor relief, but only 20 per cent of unmarried mothers.[55] The unmarried mother remained at the back of the queue for the advancing range of Poor Law welfare services between the wars.[56]

We must not identify Victorian outdoor relief as the generous antithesis of indoor relief towards the mothers. It must have been more economical in many cases to dole out some pittance to a woman than shelter her in the workhouse. In 1859 Marylebone, for example, was awarding only 1 shilling a week out-relief for the child of a single woman.[57]

In conclusion, therefore, we can judge that in the nineteenth century at least the Poor Law remained a bogey to the single mother, and must have prompted many cases of child destruction or desertion. Strictly speaking, she was not permitted to leave her baby in the workhouse while she went out to find work, for this would have amounted to a return to the licence of the pre-1834 Poor Law; but one authority has stated that there is evidence of 'plenty' of women managing to leave their children there.[58] Whether the babies stayed, or whether the mothers took them out with them, was all the same to their survival chances.

5   Infanticide and the mid-Victorian conscience 1830–70 (I)

In the context of the high infant mortality rate, the periodic discovery of a baby's body in the street or river was shrugged off as a grim inevitability. In the early nineteenth century infant life was held cheap, especially bastards. As the fictional evil midwife Nancy Drury put it: 'Them chance-children have a bad life on't. They're best out of the world.'[1]

In his *Principles of Population* (1822) Francis Place, the radical trade union law reformer, wrote:

> Neither do I regard a new-born child with any superstitious reverence. If the alternative were complete I had rather such a child should perish in the first hour of its existence than that a man should spend seventy years of life in a state of misery and vice.

And the Reverend Herbert Smith was expressing a common half-wish of death on the illegitimate workhouse nursling when he wrote in 1838:

> Then, what are we to expect will be the training of such an unfortunate offspring? If the example of the parents has been so evil, can we anticipate much benefit from their instruction? Humanly speaking there is nothing to be expected but misery and woe, in time and throughout eternity, as the fruits of such profligacy.

Before the 1834 Poor Law there was general complacency about the incidence of infanticide in Britain. When in 1824 Dr Gordon Smith, an early British author on forensic science, canvassed his colleagues to send him data relating to new-born babies to promote better diagnoses in cases of suspicious deaths, over a three-year period he received not a single reply.[2] And in 1831 Dr Charles Severn's *First Lines in the Practice of Midwifery* claimed that infanticide 'is a crime in this country rarely committed' and he shared the common assumption of the time, that it was to be identified with the pagan cultures of China, India and the South Seas where it was institutionalised,[3] but apart from exceptional circumstances, was foreign to the instincts of Christian womankind. Yet it was apparent enough at home to merit a special provision in the 1836 Birth and Death Registration Act, for under s.19 Overseers of the Poor and Coroners had to notify local registrars of infants found exposed or dead in the streets, to add to the national birth and death statistics.

Less than thirty years later the complacency – most particularly the complacency in the medical profession – was shattered. Over the years, the hardships inflicted on women by the new bastardy laws were to become a running theme; the comprehensive official returns of births and deaths from 1837 paraded the annual holocaust of infants; and the judicial statistics from 1857 provided indications, deficient as they were, as to the numbers of infants whose deaths were suspicious enough to invite inquests. And it was the growing interest in public health (stimulated by the Asiatic cholera epidemics of 1832, 1848 and 1854) that finally brought the problem home. The first priority of sanitarians was public cleansing, drainage and water supplies; and the focus was to shift to infant survival in the 1860s, once public cleansing programmes were under way. The awareness filtered through unevenly. Benjamin Disraeli was fully alive to the problem as early as 1845 when he wrote ironically in his novel *Sybil*: 'Infanticide is practised as extensively and legally in England as it is on the banks of the Ganges; a circumstance which apparently has not yet engaged the attention of the Society for the Propagation of the Gospel in Foreign Parts.' From 1840, as we shall see in Chapters 15 and 16, the question of suspected murder of infants enrolled in death clubs for the burial money was to engage the attention of successive Select Committees on the Friendly Societies. Most tellingly, John Brownlow, the Secretary of the London Foundling Hospital, was to change his tune dramatically on the subject between 1847 and 1864. In his *Memoranda or Chronicles of the Foundling Hospital* of the former year, he discounted the frequency of infanticide through destitution 'for the wise and systematic provision which has been made for the relief of indigence, by the institution of poor laws, takes away from poverty the desperate alternative to which it might otherwise be exposed'. Yet his booklet signed 'J.B.' of 1864 on *Thoughts and Suggestions having Reference to Infanticide* is a tract eloquently protesting the scale and causes of the problem.

Between the 1830s and 1850s there was statistical evidence of an increase in infanticide from official sources. Between 1832 and 1837 the number of inquest homicide verdicts (that is, of murder and manslaughter) on illegitimate children was very small. Middlesex recorded 5, Lancaster 13 and the Midlands Assize circuit area 6 in this period.[4] The Registrar General reported 76 murders of infants under 1 in the period 1838–40, averaging 25 a year. But the annual average for 1852–6 was 146.[5] However, official statistics in this context, as the *Saturday Review* cautioned its readers in 1856, 'are, of course, evidence of the vigilance of the police than of the actual amount of crime', and policing had improved markedly in those two decades. In 1839 Borough police forces had been instituted on the model of Peel's Metropolitan police in 1829; and county constabularies became mandatory in 1856. And, as we shall see in Chapter 7, the tenure of Dr Thomas Wakley as Coroner for West Middlesex from 1839 to 1861 was to mark a vitalisation of the coroners' court system to be pursued by his eminent successor, Edwin Lankester, with comparable vigour.

The growth of a popular press following the repeal of the Stamp Duty on newspapers in 1855 helped to highlight the problem, as accounts of discoveries of babies' bodies now received a wider coverage. The *Marylebone Mercury*, for instance, founded in 1857, regularly reported the inquests, and a sample will show what readers were being regaled with:

26/12/1857: a heavily drugged infant was found in a basket by two lads in Regent's Park; alive when discovered, but it died soon after. . . .

22/5/1858: Elizabeth Clarke, a housemaid, was attending a service at the Roman Catholic Chapel in Manchester Square, and 'while kneeling in the pew she found something obstructing her feet, which she pushed aside at the time. . . .' She informed the pew-opener of the parcel as she left the chapel, and this led to the discovery of a baby's corpse inside. . . .

9/10/1858: A charwoman, cleaning a house in Bryanston Square, climbed into the attic and 'on looking into the cockloft, saw a bundle, which curiosity prompted her to open'; inside was the mummified body of a baby. As there had been a succession of occupants in the house, each having servants, it was impossible to trace the parentage. . . .

3/9/1859: The body of a baby boy was found floating in a water-butt of a house in Upper Boston St. Attention had been alerted when the wife of a tenant noticed a peculiar taste in the water. . . .

And so on: accounts of a skeleton dug up in a garden, or of fresh bodies thrown into people's gardens, or left inside entrances or on doorsteps; of babies found in Kensington Gardens, Regent's Park, the Regent's Canal and Primrose Hill. They were not sensational-ised, but tucked away on inside pages, occupying one or two paragraphs of close print.

There was much speculation about the numbers of bodies being dumped in this way; and interest was intensified by the detailed statistics of inquests which Edwin Lankester was to provide for Central Middlesex after 1862. In 1861 *The Times*, citing the Registrar General's report, stated:[6]

> In the last five years within the metropolitan district alone, at least 278 infants were murdered; above 60 were found dead in the Thames or the canals or ponds about London and many more than 100, at all events were found dead under railway arches, on doorsteps, in dustholes, cellars and the like.

Other estimates for London ranged from 1,200 a year down to Wakley's moderate guess of 300 a year, based on the assumption that for every body found there was at least one undiscovered, and Lankester agreed with this figure.[7] The London police furnished a precise figure of 276 infants' bodies found exposed in the capital during 1870[8] (the police area then covered about three and a quarter million people). Other parts of the country are less well documented, though Lancashire received some mention. Edward Herford, the coroner for Manchester, told the 1871 Select Committee on Infant Life Protection that Lancashire was relatively less beset than London with baby-dropping,[9] and claimed that 'there is much less infanticide with us'. But Herford, as we shall see in Chapter 7, was probably complacent. Certainly the mill towns of Lancashire would have continued to provide employment for unmarried mothers, and the demise of unwanted babies would have taken place semi-accidentally through the ministrations of daily minders, obviating the need to dump babies surreptitiously about the streets. But Manchester itself was not a mill town, and Liverpool's experience should not have given Herford grounds for complacency about Lancashire. Frederick Lowndes, the Liverpool police surgeon, told the NAPSS in 1873[10] of his experiences in examining the bodies of abandoned babies. Liverpool, as a port with a shifting seafaring population, had a more than average share of immorality, bastardy and hence child-murder, he said, and told of the near-impossibility of tracking the perpetrators. Decomposition in many cases prevented a satisfactory autopsy:

In all the cases I have had brought to my notice there has been
literally no clue by which the police could trace the crime;
generally, the body has been found wrapped in a rag or piece of
sacking; often naked; *never* in any properly made garment. . . .
Most usually they are found at night or early in the morning, by
scavengers, policemen, etc.; more rarely when deposited in fields
or pits they are discovered in the daytime by children at play, or
labouring men on their way to work. The localities, also, show
that all calculations have been made for preserving secrecy,
being generally those parts of town which are badly lighted; or, if
thoroughfares, those least frequented by passers-by in the night
time. . . .

But even allowing for different levels of police endeavour and
coroners' vigilance around the country, could London's apparently
more conspicuous baby-dropping problem have had a basis in fact?
London was the great centre for lying-in houses where ladies 'up
from the country', to use a Victorian euphemism, would come to
be delivered of their embarrassments in secret[11] and disposing of
the baby was part of the deal with the midwife. As the wealthy
metropolis, it had the biggest single concentration of servants, and
it was servants, as we have seen, who had the strongest motive for
disposing of illegitimate babies in this way. The stories of pregnant
servant girls concealing their condition, and giving birth secretly in
their bedrooms to babies that were either wilfully killed in the
mother's panic or died as an inevitable consequence of a botched
self-delivery, were a hardy perennial. William Hunter's *Essay on the
Uncertainty of Signs of Murder in the Case of Bastard Children* in 1783
told of tragic instances of girls – not just servants – concealing the
infants' bodies in their bedrooms ready for disposal, and being
accidentally discovered; and John Brownlow in 1858[12] wrote of
such secret births taking place even where girls shared beds. Such
discoveries must have rocked the households behind the genteel
façade of Victorian villas. In 1858, for example, a nurse who had
been called in to attend to a 'sick' housekeeper at 39 Crawford St,
St Marylebone, found the body of a baby she had secretly given
birth to in a box while she was searching the housekeeper's room
for clean linen.[13] In April 1863, when a doctor was called in at
5 Gordon St, St Marylebone, to attend a sick servant, he suspected
that she had just given birth; a search of her room uncovered a
new-born baby in a box with a ligature round its neck.[14] Such
episodes were still occurring late in the century. In October 1895
one Julia Moss, a servant at Kennington Rd, London, was
convicted of manslaughter at the Old Bailey. She had given birth

secretly in her bedroom, and put the baby, still alive, in a box; out of fear of discovery she threw it onto a roof from her window, and when another servant heard the crying, Moss said it was cats on the roof. The baby's corpse was later found with a fractured skull. Moss received three months' prison.[15]

Edwin Lankester believed that such baby-dropping in the wealthier districts could be traced back to nearby houses, as servants would not venture far from their places of employment at night for fear of being spotted.[16] I have one intriguing speculation to offer as to why baby-dropping stories were becoming an almost daily occurrence in the London press in the 1860s. The sewerisation and water-closeting of London in the 1850s and 1860s deprived women of a traditionally standard place for concealing babies, namely the privy. This could have been a factor in the apparently disproportionate amount of dumping within some of the more prosperous and better closeted parts of London, whereas the persistence of the privy in provincial industrial towns and the countryside may have continued to provide some measure of concealment.

What evidence is there of increasing sensitivity to the problem in government circles? From 1844 and possibly earlier, the Home Office had been made aware of the fraudulent burial of live-borns as stillborns and its possibilities as a cover for infanticide. Viscount Palmerston in 1853, as Home Secretary, was convinced that parents were murdering their babies for the burial insurance money, but could not obtain conclusive proof. There was an increase in the tempo of abandoned baby stories emanating from Middlesex between 1859 and 1860 (the *Marylebone Mercury* for example contained a new local story in each of its weekly issues in January 1860 alone); and the St Marylebone Medical Officer of Health's report for the parish in October 1860 lamenting at the unsolved cases of abandoned babies 'which form the opprobrium of our parish month by month', prompted the Home Secretary, Sir George Cornwall Lewis, to seek more information in 1861.[17] Coroners Wakley and Humphreys, for the western and eastern divisions of Middlesex respectively, both confirmed an increase in infanticide, but the Commissioner of the Metropolitan Police, Sir Richard Mayne, was more dubious, and supplied figures for 'infanticides' (he did not define the term) in the Metropolitan Police District as a whole to counter any impression that the problem was getting out of hand. In the last ten months of 1859 there were 213 'infanticides', and 251 in the first ten months of 1860. However, as we shall see in Chapter 7, the constituent districts revealed some interesting comparisons. In 1861 the government announced its readiness to offer rewards for the discovery of persons who abandoned babies, but without result.[18]

Public sensitivity to infanticide was to reach its height during the 1860s. The National Association for the Promotion of Social Science, a prestigious forum for discussion of social problems, was formed in 1857, but the beginnings of its focus on infanticide, the affiliation laws and the means of caring for the offspring of working single women did not come till 1864,[19] and it thereafter became a recurring subject throughout the 1860s and 1870s. The best-informed contributors were to be doctors like Lankester, Lowndes and John Brendon Curgenven: the new consciousness of infanticide was not unconnected with the enhanced self-image of the medical profession. Medical breakthroughs such as anaesthesia in the 1850s, and the successful use of quinine in the Crimean War, would have helped its standing. Doctors like John Simon, and John Snow (with whom Edwin Lankester collaborated in confirming his water-borne theory of cholera arising out of the Broad Street Pump episode of 1854), were among many medical men making invaluable contributions to public health reform at the time. The passing of the Medical Act of 1858, by establishing a register of doctors qualified through accredited training institutions, set the seal of social responsibility on the profession.

From the early nineteenth century a multiplication of medical societies, like the Hunterian Society, the Obstetric Society and the Medical Society of London, promoted learned exchanges;[20] and it was the Harveian Society, formed in 1831, that was destined to carry the torch in relation to infanticide during the 1860s. Dr William Burke Ryan's classic socio-medical study of the subject, *Infanticide, its Law, Prevalence and Prevention* published in 1862, had originated as a prize-winning thesis for the Medical Society of London in 1856.[21]

In the provinces, the only evidence of an organised expression of professional concern over infanticide appears to have come from Lancashire. In 1863 Dr George Greaves, a Manchester obstetrician, addressed the Manchester Statistical Society on 'Observations on Some of the Causes of Infanticide', and in 1867 both this Society and the Manchester and Salford Sanitary Association independently appealed to the Home Secretary to reform death registration procedures (see Chapter 14), to prevent the fraudulent burial of live-borns as stillborns.[22]

In 1865 a horrific criminal case involving Charlotte Winsor, the wife of a West Country farm labourer, was to highlight the popular indifference to illegitimate infant life. Mrs Winsor, three-times married and with a local reputation as a low-life, was living near

Torquay at this time.[23] Police had been pursuing inquiries following the discovery of a number of murdered infants in the surrounding countryside, and by following up any cases of babies missing since their births had been registered, they tracked down one Mary Jane Harris, a farm servant. Her illegitimate baby son Thomas, born in 1864, had disappeared. It transpired that she had approached Charlotte Winsor to board-nurse him, for 3 shillings a week, so she could find work again. In February 1865 a baby's body wrapped in newspaper was found on the road between Torquay and Torre and subsequently identified as Harris's. Both women were taken into custody; Harris was deeply agitated, whilst Winsor stayed cool and brazen. The women accused each other of the murder, and both were tried at Exeter Assizes in March 1865. The evidence, largely based on the testimony of Winsor's 7-year-old granddaughter as to the timing of the baby's disappearance, was not firm enough, and the medical evidence of the cause of the baby's death was hedged and tentative: he *might* have died of some disease before being abandoned, the doctor testified, or else it might have been exposure or immersion in water that killed him.

The jury was divided, and a new trial was ordered for the next Assizes in July. In the meantime Harris turned Queen's Evidence, and it was her story at the July Assizes that secured Winsor's conviction. Winsor had boasted to Harris that she made money out of killing unwanted babies – at £2 to £5 a time – by compressing their jugular vein, and persuaded Harris to let her dispose of Thomas for £5. This she did in February by smothering the baby under a mattress at her cottage while Harris waited in the next room.

Winsor escaped the gallows, however, over protracted legal argument, which took over a year to go through the courts, as to whether Winsor should have been tried a second time; the Home Secretary decided in 1866 that execution would be cruel after so long a delay, so her sentence was commuted to life imprisonment.

Two more cases of lesser notoriety in the 1860s were to bring the term 'baby-farmer' into popular usage.[24] Mrs Chard of Oxford was discovered when the local Registrar had become suspicious at the succession of death certificates she had applied for on babies boarded at her establishment. A coroner's inquest on the illegitimate baby of 'a respectable person' that she was caring for revealed that the infants at Mrs Chard's house were 'scarcely recognizable as human beings'. The jury's verdict was based on the immediate symptoms of death – 'debility' – and not on the neglect that caused it; Mrs Chard was censured, but no charges followed.[25]

The case of Mrs Caroline Jaggers of Tottenham, London, in

1867 received wide press coverage.[26] Mrs Jaggers advertised in the *Daily Telegraph* as a foster-mother and ran a very extensive baby-farm. In the three years prior to 1867 she had had the care of 40 infants. The current inquest – this was the third held on infants from her establishment – was on an illegitimate infant daughter of 'a young lady of wealth and position' who had arranged the delivery through a firm of solicitors; her name was withheld at the inquest at the request of her solicitor, who told the jury that she would otherwise commit suicide. A doctor summoned by Mrs Jaggers at a very late stage in the infant's decline diagnosed glandular disease and emaciation. Mrs Jaggers admitted having eight infants on her premises at the time of the inquest, but there was a cryptic allusion to other infants 'upstairs that are never seen' by the coroner that sent Mrs Jaggers into convulsions at the hearing. The jury's finding was again purely symptomological – glandular disease – and Mrs Jaggers was censured for failing to call a doctor earlier. It transpired later that she used a 3-year-old boy as a 'ganger' to look after younger infants in the house, and when removed to the workhouse for safety, the medical officer found that his legs were 'like drumsticks', and his belly 'like a drum'; he had a burn scar on his cheek and a contracted arm; and there was evidence that Mrs Jaggers was drunk with gin on one occasion when he had a serious accident.

The case throws two sidelights on the contemporary social etiquette to women that militated against justice for their infant victims: a greater willingness to protect the identity of the high-born mother than to make her account for the disposal of her unwanted infant; and inquest juries' reluctance to return a criminally culpable verdict against a female witness.

A leading light in the effort to bring home to the Legislature the scandal of infanticide in general and baby-farming in particular was Dr John Brendon Curgenven (1831–1903).[27] Hailing originally from Cornwall, he worked as a doctor at the Royal Free Hospital, London, till 1854 and subsequently served as a military surgeon during the Crimean War. When Florence Nightingale fell ill with fever in the Crimea, it was Curgenven who attended her on her sea journey back to Scutari. After the war he resumed private practice in London and in 1862 became Honorary Secretary of the Harveian Society. Like the venereologist William Acton, he was a strong supporter of the Contagious Diseases Acts of 1864 and 1866 to 'regulate' prostitution in certain garrison and naval towns, and shared Acton's belief in the power of legislation to improve human conduct. From 1866 he began devoting his attention to the possibilities of legislation to check infanticide. In May 1866 the

Harveian Society resolved, on a motion by Curgenven, to set up a Committee to investigate the issue and make recommendations.[28] The Committee, which included Curgenven, received help from the Foreign Office in obtaining information about Continental law on the subject, and Curgenven was impressed by French and Belgian systems of municipal foundling hospitals and hospices from which babies could be distributed to registered and officially inspected wet-nurses. And in Belgium no midwife was to receive an unmarried woman in her establishment without notifying the police.[29] Historically, be it noted, much of this system had an authoritarian origin, inspired by Napoleon I, who wished to develop state foundling homes as nurseries for future soldiers and sailors. The Prussian infanticide law, which recognised a distinction between maternal infanticide (where prompted by psychological disturbance) and murder, was particularly admired (see Chapter 8).

In January 1867 the Committee produced its report (which was sent to the Home Office) with twenty recommendations.[30] In summary:

all births, and in particular stillbirths to be compulsorily registered;
a non-capital offence of infanticide to be created, with abolition
of the 'separate existence' rule (see Chapter 8);
the Poor Law to give destitute women improved pre- and post-
natal facilities;
liberalisation of the affiliation laws;
a 'colonising system' of boarding out of workhouse children to be
adopted (see Chapter 6);
registration of foster-nurses who take in illegitimate children
with the Poor Law unions, and their subjection to regular
inspection by Poor Law medical officers;
the prohibition of burial insurance on infants (see Chapters 15
and 16).

The Committee also drew attention to the social conditions that promoted illegitimacy, singling out domestic overcrowding and the rural ganging system specifically.

Curgenven's thinking, which involved faith in a higher degree of state intervention (and expenditure) than was really practical politics in the age of *laissez-faire*, can be seen behind these recommendations. He followed them up with his address in March 1867 to the NAPSS on 'The Waste of Infant Life', a comprehensive survey of the causes of infant mortality which produced a resolution calling for the registration of foster-nurses; and in 1869 the Society sympathetically received his draft of an Infant Life Protection Bill[31] in his address on baby-farming; in the same year, following an address by Dr Lankester,[32] the Society passed resolutions calling for registration of stillbirths, the creation of a non-capital offence of infanticide and a more informative presentation of inquest returns on infants in the judicial statistics.

The fact is, however, that infant life protection was not a vote-catcher. In 1867 Parliament was absorbed in Parliamentary reform manoeuvrings; and Gladstone's new administration in 1868 was preoccupied with the problems of Ireland and education reform.[33] The 1868 General Election, however, had brought to Westminster the new Conservative member for Salford, William Thomas Charley, who was to give the infanticide protagonists the energetic and single-minded Parliamentary spokesman they badly needed; for Lord Shaftesbury the subject of infanticide was only one of his multifarious social concerns, and his involvement was more peripheral.[34] The government had no intention of acting; the Home Office even mislaid its copy of the Harveian Society's report![35] Ernest Hart, the crusading medical journalist and himself a member of the Harveian Society, had recently been appointed editor of the *British Medical Journal*. Annoyed at the government's inertia, he decided in 1868 to commission an investigation that would take the lid off the netherworld of midwife-abortionists and baby-farmers, and this will be examined in Chapter 9.

6 Infanticide and the mid-Victorian conscience (II): the milk of human kindness

A related area of heightening social conscience was the economic plight of the first-time lapser, the 'ruined maid', reduced to unemployability with her infant burden. As mentioned in Chapter 3, there was to be an upsurge of philanthropic rescue mission activity from the 1850s. However, on the whole its priority was to rehabilitate the 'fallen woman', not to preserve her illegitimate infant.

Outside the workhouses there was a severe dearth of charitable institutions where the single girl could go to have her baby. In the 1860s only two Lying-In Hospitals, Queen Charlotte's and the General Lying-In Asylum, allowed in unmarried women,[1] and Queen Charlotte's restricted this concession to first-time lapsers.[2] Rescue agencies had an enormous gap to fill, and in fact could only make the most marginal contribution. By 1890 London's 269 Rescue Societies could accommodate over 4,000 women, but only a 'small proportion' of them specialised as lying-in homes for unmarried women.[3] By 1908 there were some 300 of such lying-in homes in the whole of England and Wales; these were concentrated in a few towns, and could still only meet a fraction of the need.[4]

Some homes worked closely with the Poor Law, and took deserving girls and their infants from workhouse lying-in wards. A notable mid-Victorian example was Miss Broughton's 'Home for Deserted Mothers and Infants' at Pimlico. Lambeth Board of Guardians, for example, during 1870 sent her twenty-nine inmates, and for each gave a 5 shillings a week subsidy for a period of eight weeks.[5] Such schemes were to expand in the late nineteenth and early twentieth centuries, as Poor Law authorities began subsidising local voluntary homes regularly, to get the more innocent type of girl out of the workhouse atmosphere.[6]

Other homes worked independently. The two most notable in London were Daniel Cooper's 'Society for the Rescue of Young Women and Children' (the 'Rescue Society') founded in 1853,[7] and Mrs Jane Dean Main's 'Refuge for Deserted Mothers and

Children' of Coram Street, founded in 1864. By 1871 the Rescue
Society had taken in 7,000 women, though it had turned away
10,000 applicants in that time. It permitted mothers to suckle their
infants for a time, but then found them jobs, usually in domestic
service; they made their own arrangements for a dry-nurse without
interference from the Society, which subsidised payments by
sixpence to 1 shilling and sixpence a week. The Society's prime aim
was the rehabilitation of the mother, not the welfare of the child,
and the effect of this and similar agencies was simply to re-channel
the circumstances of the infant's death. *The Lancet* in 1882 lamented
the fate of these infants, who were generally suckled for a month
and then passed to a nurse, who fed them cornflour, boiled bread,
and sour milk from dirty feeding bottles. It added: '. . . the
responsibility of benevolent but misguided people who insist upon
the weaning of an illegitimate child with a view to getting the
mother back into a respectable situation is very serious indeed.'[8] In
fairness, however, one should remember that such charities must
have operated on a shoestring, and laboured under a prejudice that
any relief for unmarried mothers would encourage immorality.

Mrs Main's Refuge, however, described by W.T. Charley M.P.
in 1877 as the 'most admirable of all refuges in London',[9] did take
greater pains for the infants' welfare. Up to 1868, the infants were
left in her institution when the mothers were found jobs, but the
death rate through this concentration was so unsatisfactory that
thereafter the babies were dispersed to foster homes. However, the
mothers were allowed to suckle their babies for up to five months,
and the foster homes had to be approved by the Refuge.[10] So
dramatic had been the fall in the death rate that infant funeral
expenses in 1869 were less than a fifth of what they had been in
four years before,[11] despite a rapid growth in its operations. In
1869 it assisted 76 women, and in 1876 200, but such numbers
scarcely scratched the surface of the problem. Mrs Main had her
imitators: a similar home was opened in Glasgow, and experience
showed, it was claimed, that such rescue agencies did not
encourage immorality, and the maternal bond was preserved.
Over four-fifths of the expenses of the infants' upkeep were met
from the mothers' own earnings, and a similar 'House of
Compassion' at Oxford stated in 1869 that three-quarters of the
mothers sent regular payments for the children's upkeep while only
5 per cent ever 'lapsed' again.[12]

Philanthropic attention was also directed towards day-minding
for these women whose jobs did enable them to retain daily contact
with their children. The ordinary day-minders, as we have seen,
were notoriously ignorant, and some charitable effort was made

from 1850 to establish crèches or day-nurseries where babies could
be properly looked after, but growth was very slow. Philanthropy
was prejudiced against them as bolsters to sinful motherhood, and
in the neighbourhoods where they were established they were often
resented as savouring of patronage; moreover people felt that they
were taking the bread from the mouths of poor neighbours who
customarily took in babies at 2 shillings and sixpence to 3 shillings
and sixpence a week[13] to supplement their incomes. Unlike France
and Germany, where crèches were widespread and closely
regulated, the scheme never really caught on in Britain. In 1871
Manchester and Salford had 3 centres;[14] in 1874 Glasgow had 3,
but they were shunned by the lowest classes, and one of them, at least,
was highly selective about its intake of illegitimate children.[15]
Different estimates for London after 1900 are given. George
Newman in 1906 said there were 55, half of which refused
illegitimate children;[16] the Poor Law Commission of 1909[17] gave a
figure of 70 to 80, with a total accommodation for only 2,000
children out of London's 1,000,000 families. Both stated that the
majority of the country's crèches were in London, but while
Newman thought their standards were good, the Commission's
Minority Report found otherwise: 'Many of them were overcrowded, ill-ventilated, dark, dirty and foul-smelling. The babies
were in the charge of totally inexperienced women. The milk and
bottles were often wholly unsuitable.'

Some nineteenth-century observers believed that a public crèche
system, where the baby would be kept while the mother worked to
support it, and would be encouraged to maintain contact with it,
would put the baby-farmers out of business, but they were
whistling in the wind.[18] Government would do nothing. So was
there an alternative? The infant life protectionists of the 1860s
urged the registration and inspection of all private baby-minders,
boarding and day alike, but, as we shall see, proposals for the latter
was to be howled down, and compulsory registration of day-
minders was not to come until 1948![19]

The Harveian Society had pinpointed one indirect source of
illegitimacy in the demoralising effects of workhouse life on pauper
children, who grew up to leave the institutions unsocialised,
misfits and ready prey to 'seducers'; within a few years the girls
returned to have their pauper bastards, and an hereditary cycle of
vice was perpetuated.[20] In 1859, of the 100,000 people on indoor
relief in England and Wales, 51,000 alone were children, and
12,000 of these were orphans.[21] If infants were removed to private
homes and fostered till their teens, they would escape the

workhouse taint and be able to stand on their own two feet; this was a theme of Frances Power Cobbe's weighty article *The Philosophy of the Poor Law* first published in 1864,[22] that was to influence Curgenven, the Harveian Society and the Infant Life Protection Society. (The Scottish Poor Law, unlike the English, had always preferred boarding-out, but one might recall that the Scottish bastardy rate was still higher.)

In the 1840s the London Poor Law unions had adopted a crude form of 'boarding-out', but for reasons of economy only, by concentrating their children in a private institution, namely Mr Bartholomew's 'Baby-Farm' at Tooting; this became notorious in 1848 during the cholera epidemic, for 155 of its 1,300 inmates died in the appallingly crowded and insanitary conditions that were uncovered there.[23] However, the reformers' objective was to disperse children into country homes, on Foundling Hospital lines, and this is one measure the British government did espouse. By a regulation of the Poor Law Board in November 1870 English unions were empowered to board children over 2 years old outside their boundaries – that is into rural districts, and fosterings were to be supervised by local voluntary 'boarding-out committees', which themselves functioned under the oversight of a local government board inspector.

Space does not permit a full history of boarding-out, but the general judgment on it by the early twentieth century was that while good in principle it could lead to abuses in practice – such as the exploitation and neglect of the children – without vigilant inspection. In this respect 'in-union' boarding-out (that is, within the union boundary), where there was no local government board oversight, was compared unfavourably with the 'out-union' arrangement. Boarding-out in England, however, was not widely practised. In 1897 there were only 1,957 'out-union' cases; in 1909 there were 6,000 'in-union' cases, compared with a similar number for Scotland alone in 1903.[24]

Another area of conscience-stirring from the late 1850s – at least in the medical world – was the ethics of employing wet-nurses.[25] Breast-milk was the only truly appropriate food for infants, and for fashionable ladies unwilling to spend the time or fearful of losing their figures, the wet-nurse was traditionally indispensable. But there were other reasons for employing them, if one had the money: the mother might have been too frail to breast-feed her child, perhaps through repeated child-bearing, or she might have died after the delivery. Such was the problem for the recently bereaved Mr Dombey in Dickens's novel, and occasioned his hiring Mrs

Toodles to wet-nurse his new-born son.

So necessary were wet-nurses that their hirers shut out all thought for the consequences for the wet-nurse's own offspring, or at most yielded to some passing twinge of regret.

An extract from the diary of Edward Watson, a nineteenth-century merchant, was kindly supplied to the author by Mrs Katharine Clark, his great-great granddaughter of Lewes, Sussex. His wife bore him eight children, but she had been an invalid since the first birth, and he had employed a succession of wet-nurses. On the 10th of July 1848 he records the hiring of a Mrs Webb to feed his latest arrival. On the 26th of July he notes the death of Mrs Webb's own infant 'which occurred about a week ago' – so its demise without breast-milk was very rapid. Mr Watson has conscience to observe: 'It is a very melancholy reflection that our own infant should be sustained, as it were, at the expense of the life of another infant', but retreats into this comforting thought: 'In this case the same thing might have happened had we not engaged Mrs Webb as a Wet Nurse, as she had made up her mind to wean her infant, even if she had not secured a situation with us, being under the necessity of doing so to enable her to go to service to support herself and two children.' And in the same entry he mentions the death of the child of a Mrs Cooper, an earlier wet-nurse he had employed.

Mr Watson was very selective about his wet-nurses: they were poor but respectable married women, some or all evidently widowed. The fictional Mr Dombey was likewise very choosy. He had Mrs Toodles's family paraded before him to establish the health of her children, and was particular about testimonials. But while employers ideally preferred to house a reputable woman under their roof, it was unmarried mothers who provided the main supply of wet-nurses, and it was the medical profession that aided and abetted this supply. Dr C.H.F. Routh's authoritative *Infant Feeding and its Influence on Life* (1860) urged women to breast-feed their own babies, and only to resort to wet-nurses in extremity, adding: 'It is usual in our profession to select a fallen woman.' Dr George Greaves, in his address to the Manchester Statistical Society in 1863, alluded to doctors' habit of recommending wet-nurses to their wealthier clients, and said his own investigations had shown most to be unmarried. Dr Curgenven informed the 1871 Infant Life Protection Committee likewise, adding that Queen Charlotte's Lying-in Hospital, 80 per cent of whose intake was unmarried, was the major source of wet-nurses for London.[26] They were, of course, second best to respectable married women, very few of whom, said Curgenven, were willing to neglect their own children for the job. Nineteenth-century manuals recommended women who had produced previous healthy offspring and were experienced in child-rearing. A single woman with a history of bastard-bearing was obviously an undesirable character to have in the house, and there was a risk of her passing on undetected syphilis to the infant, quite apart from the deluded but still lingering notion that her 'immoral milk' would pass on undesirable traits to the child.[27] A first-time lapser, as Routh pointed out, was better, but by definition had no experience of child-rearing. The family doctor would inspect the applicant first, but so keen were unmarried women to get the work that some were past-masters at lying about their backgrounds.

The great attraction of the job was the life of ease and plenty that attended it. Wet-nurses were fussed over right royally in the household; they had the choicest food, and plenty of rest and fresh air to encourage a copious milk supply. Suckling, and hence employment, periods lasted anything from three to seven months,[28] and unscrupulous women, it was believed, were tempted to beget bastards deliberately, and leave them to their fate while they enjoyed sybaritic employment as wet-nurses.[29] Curgenven reckoned that (in London at least) a wet-nurse could earn over £50 a year in 1871,[30] which would put her on a par with the best-paid cooks of the period, and Dr Walter Whitehead, the eminent Manchester obstetrician, gave a figure for the provinces of up to £25 a year plus perquisites.[31] Since it cost 3 to 5 shillings a week to have her own infant dry-nursed, for as long as it survived, the profit was very alluring. Other servants, whose general wage levels we have noted, resented the intrusion of this privileged and often demanding 'Hen Cuckoo', and there was some apprehension that 'virtuous' female servants would be tempted to copy her example to reap the evidently comfortable wages of sin; while Dr Routh hints obliquely at other illicit temptations this fallen woman could present to the master of the house. Employers were warned to keep an eye on the wet-nurse, for whom the sudden access of plenty could lead to over-indulgence in food and liquor to the detriment of the quality of her milk. And Dr Thomas Bull's *The Maternal Management of Children* in 1861 typically cautioned:

> A wet-nurse should never be allowed to have medicine of any kind at her command to administer to the child, whatever she may think fit, and it is right that a parent should be made aware that an unprincipled woman will give laudanum in one or other of its preparations to quiet a restless child and secure for herself a good night's rest.

Dr Edmund Cautley in 1897 mentioned how wet-nurses sometimes even rubbed the opiates on their nipples to escape detection. Yet single women had certain advantages: they were vulnerable, so their wages could be forced down; and they did not have the distractions of family life to interrupt their nurture.

Despite all the headaches, wet-nurses were seen as an unavoidable necessity, and advertisements for them regularly cropped up in the press; according to Jonathan Gathorne Hardy, an advert appeared in *The Times* once every six days on average in 1873.[32] Family doctors would contact midwives or the local lying-in hospitals for any interested applicants, and the hospitals kept registers for their benefit.[33]

Medical men were only too ready to pander to their rich clients' desire, despite its consequence as a 'quick but effectual means of infanticide' as one conscience-troubled doctor called it in 1861.[34] The average Victorian – and even Edwardian – doctor was fairly ignorant of paediatrics, a low-status speciality, which as late as 1913 was described as 'neither medicine, surgery nor midwifery, and [which] has received scant attention in the medical curriculum'.[35] He was disinclined to advise on proper infant-feeding, and tended to leave it to the monthly nurse's judgment. (A monthly nurse attended a woman prior to and after birth, and might help in the delivery, but, as distinct from a midwife, only as the doctor's assistant.[36])

The medical profession had a lot to answer for, and a few doctors had made early attempts to mitigate the evils of wet-nursing. Dr Thomas Denman (1733–1815), an eminent obstetrician, was one of a small minority of professional men who were way ahead of their time in their concern for the deserted children of wet-nurses; he helped set up an asylum for such infants, but it had to close through lack of funds.[37] But it was not until 1857 that the columns of the *British Medical Journal* were to start giving space to the subject in a phase of agonising that lasted to 1871. Parallel to this was the propaganda against wet-nursing conducted by the Ladies Sanitary Association,[38] which was formed in 1857 and based in London and Brighton. It published and distributed educational tracts relating to hygiene and domestic management, including infant-feeding. One of its leading members was Mrs Mary Anne Baines, who addressed the NAPSS against 'The Practice of Hiring Wet-Nurses, especially those from the Fallen' in 1859, in which she exhorted the upper classes to breast-feed their own infants. An early LSA tract on *The Evils of Wet-Nursing*[39] castigated upper-class female humbugs who dabbled in good works, whilst contributing to the very social problems they deplored by employing wet-nurses; it rhetorically rounded on 'the fashionable mother, who lives a butterfly life at the ball, concert and theatre and leaves her little ones to die through neglect' while spectating at the trial of 'some poor downtrodden dupe of a seducer' who in shame and misery had made away with her infant. One wonders how much of this reached home to the high-born ladies who figureheaded the patron's committee of the LSA. Mrs William Gladstone was one such member, yet her husband hired a wet-nurse for his son, and purged himself with a fleeting fit of conscience for the fate of the nurse's own child![40]

Mrs Baines was keen to see statistical data on wet-nursing built up, for she believed that many infants' deaths recorded as due to 'want of breast milk' or 'convulsions' in the registrar's tables could be traced back to the mothers' employment as wet-nurses; her idealistic suggestions for collecting such data, which involved enlisting the active co-operation of local registrars, medical officers of health and obstetricians, were presented before the International Statistical Congress in 1860.[41] Yet while wet-nurses were so expedient to the ruling classes, they were hardly likely to be officially monitored in a way that would confirm the evils of their use.

Much was owed to Dr C.H.F. Routh for stimulating medical debate on the subject, following his address on the 'Disadvantages of Employing Fallen Women as Wet-Nurses' before the Medical Society of London in April 1860. Nearly all the discussion it generated in *The Lancet* and the *British Medical Journal* supported his opinions. In January 1861 the latter published an editorial under the heading 'Child Murder: Its Relation to Wet-Nursing',[42] stating what the true ethical position of the profession should be:

> We are bound, by every right principle, to consider the health of the wet-nurse's offspring just as much as the health of our lady patient's who is able to pay for the luxury of hiring another to feed her child. . . . What becomes of the children of the wet-nurses. . . .? Are not numbers of their lives yearly sacrificed as a direct result of wet-nursing? Is our profession justified in recommending the use of wet-nurses in any case? If so, is it justified except in those urgent cases in which the life of the patient, mother or child, may be endangered by suckling?

And in May 1871, a doctor's letter to the *BMJ*,[43] inspired by the simmering scandal over baby-farming arising from the Margaret Waters affair (see Chapter 11), reminded subscribers that while baby-farming was branded as disreputable, wet-nursing, which indirectly caused far more infant deaths, was still orthodox while it remained patronised by royalty, nobility and gentry, because the medical profession 'as a body, do not hesitate to sanction largely the general practice, thereby throwing over it the prestige of the Hippocratic mantle'.

One eminent medical figure spoke out against this transforming ethical view. Dr William Acton, through his social study on prostitution in 1857, was convinced that wet-nursing was the necessary, and indeed the only, available means to rehabilitate the betrayed 'fallen woman' who would otherwise sink to the streets.[44] At the Medical Society of London's debate in 1860 following Routh's address[45] Acton stood his ground: if a girl saddled with a baby could not earn a living, he argued, the child would die anyway, and it was the lack of a means of livelihood that drove girls to commit infanticide. In sum, wet-nursing did not worsen infant mortality overall, which always found its own set level in a given state of society, whatever palliatives were tried.

Acton's argument was very cogent and the *BMJ* offered no answer. Indeed, one of the standard employment outlets for 'fallen women' found by the Rescue Agencies springing up since the 1850s was that of wet-nurse, and their infants' lives were usually of secondary importance. Only Mrs Main's Refuge, and the London Foundling Hospital, in their different ways sought to protect the infant; and even in the case of the latter, it seems that the tragedy was just shifted along the line, for even the carefully selected country wet-nurses they employed were reckoned to be neglecting their own legitimate offspring for the money they earned suckling a stranger's child, so that 'scarcely any of them live long' according to the conclusion of the 1871 Infant Life Protection Committee. When Lady Jane Taylor opened a home near Watford for the infants of wet-nurses, the *British Medical Journal* gently chided her for unwittingly encouraging wet-nursing, yet it offered no solution to the problem posed by Acton.

A superficial palliative had been suggested by *The Lancet* in 1858: wet-nurses should be officially registered (as they could be in France) and only those medically certified as free of disease and posing no danger to their own children's lives should be eligible.[46] This begged the question, however, that in Britain wet-nurses resided with their employers, who would certainly not tolerate the presence of the woman's own child in the house competing for milk and attention!

Under the suasions of Mrs Baines, the British Lying-In Institution, of which she was a governor, from September 1859 required all applications for wet-nurses to be accompanied by a doctor's certificate attesting to the mother's unfitness to suckle her own child[47] – but given doctors' readiness in general to do their patients' bidding it is questionable how truthful such certificates would have been.

Now, there was a definite decline in wet-nursing during the last twenty years of the nineteenth century. In 1882 *The Times*, according to Mr Gathorne Hardy, was advertising for wet-nurses on average once every twelve days, half the frequency of nine years before. In 1897 Dr Edmund Cautley remarked that in Britain 'the employment of a wet-nurse is rarely advised, much less insisted upon' by the medical profession, but the Foundling Hospital was still using them at least as late as 1890.[48] As a contrast, moreover, whilst the 1871 Infant Life Protection Committee has several references to their prevalence, the Department Committee on Physical Deterioration, in reviewing the nation's health in 1904, contained not a single reference to wet-nursing.

The cause of this decline had little to do with public conscience. It was the expanding range of branded baby foods, from the 1860s, starting with Ridge's in 1862 and von Liebig's 'Malted Milk Extract' in 1867 that was gradually to oust the wet-nurse. Advertisements for 'Mellin's', 'Frame's Food', 'Horlicks', 'Allenbury's', 'Savory and Moore', 'Benger's' and many others were a familiar sight by 1900. They were cereal-based and really unfit for babies, but so persuasive were the manufacturers' promotional slogans that the middle classes readily took to them, and the average doctor, in his ignorance of dietetics, readily prescribed them: they seemed to have descended like manna, to do away with all the domestic botherations connected with wet-nurses. Their use must have contributed to the refusal of the infant mortality rate to go down despite a general improvement in public health at the end of the century.[49]

It is probably no accident that the emerging ethical aversion to wet-nursing coincides with the advent of the so-called artificial feeds and, relatedly, innovations in feeding bottle design; the French 'biberon' was displayed at the Great Exhibition in 1851. Rubber teats appeared in 1856; various 'patent' improved bottles appeared in the 1850s, and Dr C.H.F. Routh did his practical bit to displace the wet-nurse by marketing his 'Mamma' bottle in 1869.[50] One popular but quite lethal device that reinforced the preference for artificial feeding in workhouses, orphanages and the like was the long-tube feeding bottle; this allowed a busy nurse to leave the infant, while the feed was siphoned automatically from the bottle, which rested on a ledge. The tubes were notoriously difficult to clean properly, but despite condemnation were still being used in 1906.[51]

By 1900 expert dieticians were scathing about the quality of branded baby-foods but they had come up with what they fondly hoped was the perfect answer – 'humanised' or 'modified' cow's milk. This entailed re-balancing the milk and cream proportions and adding other ingredients to simulate mother's milk. Meigs's Formula, for example, was published in 1885, and according to Dr James Knight at the Infantile Mortality Conference in 1906 was 'much used in the houses of the well-to-do in this country', though it needed elaborate preparation. The wet-nurse was by now a very rare bird.

7 Coroners, inquests and the exposure of infanticide

The inquest system as employed by a handful of Victorian coroners became a lantern that uncomfortably illuminated the dark recesses of society's guilt over infanticide. Through the coroner's court were channelled the cases of babies found abandoned, or who had otherwise died in suspicious circumstances, and it was the coroner who, of all public officials, received week by week the most concentrated insight into infant death at its most harrowing.

The inquest system – a quasi-judicial inquiry with jury and witnesses to determine the cause of death – is peculiar to England and Wales. In Scotland a local public prosecutor, the Procurator-Fiscal, performs the equivalent task administratively, and whereas the expert medical opinions are given as open evidence in the coroner's court, in Scotland the doctor commissioned by the Procurator-Fiscal to examine the body makes out a confidential report.[1] The coroner has (within statutory limits) discretion whether to hold an inquest on a reported case; and in the nineteenth century the inquest by no means necessarily entailed an autopsy, though by law the body had to be 'viewed' by coroner and jurors before the proceedings. The frequently decomposed body of the infant was kept in the deadhouse of the local workhouse (though municipal mortuaries began to be built under the Sanitary Act of 1866) and the principals then usually repaired to the local tavern for the hearing in a distinctly beery and sometimes ribald atmosphere, as purpose-built coroners' courts did not come till late in the century; the use of pub venues was not abolished until the 1910 Licensing Act.

Coroners were appointed through election by the county ratepayers, and then held office for life, until the 1888 Local Government Act substituted appointment by the County Council. No professional qualification was required until the Coroners Act of 1926, but the post was long established as a lawyer's preserve. Thomas Wakley, a radical MP, and founder of *The Lancet*, was elected for West Middlesex as the country's first medically

qualified coroner in 1839, but despite this breakthrough doctors
formed only a sixth of all coroners in 1892, and the proportion was
no higher in 1936.[2]

Lawyer-coroners varied widely in quality. Mr Hollins, the
coroner for Stockport in 1840 at the time of the Sandys poisoning
case (see Chapter 15), was described by Henry Coppock, the town
clerk, as 'past the prime of life and in fact perfectly incompetent to
conduct the investigation'.[3] At the other end of the scale was
Athelstan Braxton Hicks, the S.W. London and Surrey coroner in
the 1880s and 1890s, whose vigilance and conscientiousness earned
him the nickname 'The Children's Coroner'[4]: he gave no
suspicious death the benefit of the doubt, but invariably held an
inquest,[5] and made a public contribution in the controversy
surrounding infant life insurance (see Chapter 16). More commonly,
however, they were abysmally ignorant of medical matters, and a
police surgeon, Horatio Nelson Hardy, in 1893 told of one coroner
who had even asked him what *rigor mortis* meant![6]

Coroners were perennially handicapped by the law's imprecision
over the circumstances under which they were entitled to hold
inquests, and the parsimoniousness of the county justices of the
peace (who ran the counties until County Councils were created in
1888). The costs of inquests came from the county rates, and
coroners were always conscious that they might be disallowed.
Justices held that inquests should only be held in cases of violent
death, and breathed fire at those coroners, like Thomas Wakley,
who sought to extend them to cases of 'sudden' and 'unexplained'
deaths. Although a Parliamentary Select Committee of 1860
advocated this wider interpretation, it was not legally enshrined
until the Coroners Act of 1887 obliged coroners to hold inquests
where there was 'reasonable cause' to suspect that the subject had
died 'either a violent or an unnatural death, or has died a sudden
death of which the cause is unknown'. Now up to the 1880s the
proportion of inquests to (all) deaths had hovered around a
constant 50 per 1,000; from 1885 there was a rise, as registrars
were instructed by the Registrar General to refer a wider class of
doubtful cases to coroners, and this was reinforced by the 1887 Act,
after which there was a sustained trend upwards to 70 per 1,000 in
1907.[7] However, the effects of the Act must not be overstated. The
1893 Select Committee on Death Certification learned that many
coroners were still very reluctant to antagonise their local
authorities by holding unnecessary inquests and the wording of the
Act offered many let-outs: 'reasonable cause' allowed wide
discretion, and if the sudden death was accompanied by a doctor's
certificate, however unreliable or untruthful it might in fact be, the

cause was *not* technically 'unknown'. Furthermore, an inquest could be done on the cheap by avoiding an autopsy, even if it made a nonsense of the proceedings. There was a parallel problem in Scotland. Sir Charles Cameron MP told the 1893 Committee how doctors commissioned by the Procurators-Fiscal were 'instructed to "stare" at a body and deduce the causes of death without a post-mortem' to save the dissection fee![8]

A coroner's refusal to hold an inquest sometimes had disastrous consequences. The Sarah Freeman case of Somerset in 1845 is just one instance.[9] Sarah was the wife of a farm labourer, and had a bad reputation for immorality. In November 1843 her 7-year-old son died with stomach pains after eating bread and butter. The local doctor, called in to attend the child, was suspicious and notified the coroner, who refused to hold an inquest as the magistrates would not like the expense. As a result, the boy was buried without analysis of the contents of his stomach, and Sarah was able to poison three more people – her husband, mother and brother – until brought to justice and hanged in 1845.

Even where inquests were held, coroners often steered the juries towards expedient or meaningless verdicts, partly through their own ignorance, and partly to justify the decision against holding a post-mortem. Not that juries needed much steering; their chivalrous members were notoriously reluctant to return verdicts in infants' cases indicating culpability on the mothers' part. One egregious case prior to 1815 will illustrate this. A servant was found dead in a hayloft of the house where she worked. Her throat was slit with a razor and a handkerchief was found round her new-born baby's throat. In the face of all logical conclusions, the jury decided that she had taken the razor 'for the purposes of delivery' and had wound the handkerchief round the child's neck to assist in the delivery. Their verdicts were 'lunacy' on the mother and 'found dead' on the infant.[10] The source of this account surmises that a 'suicide' verdict on the mother was avoided as, under the law at that time, she would have had to be buried at a crossroads with a stake through her heart.

A selection of typical coroners' verdicts on infants in the early 1860s shows just how shallow and uninformed the inquests were:[11]

In Birmingham, almost invariably 'Visitation of God' or 'Accidental Death'.
Elsewhere:

Accidentally suffocated in bed
Accidentally burnt
Accidentally choked

Accidentally poisoned
Found dead; illegitimate; cause unknown
Found dead in basin of a gasworks; cause unknown
Found dead in a dust hole, without marks
Falling from mother into pan of water-closet at time of birth;
concussion of the brain
Suffocated in privy; no evidence how it got there. . . .
. . . and so on.

It was rare indeed, except in Edwin Lankester's jurisdiction of
Central Middlesex, for juries to return frank verdicts of manslaughter or murder. Dr George Greaves of Manchester in 1863,
while acknowledging the pressures coroners were under to skimp
their inquests, commented on the wide variation in the proportions
of murder verdicts among inquests on infants under coroners
outside Middlesex; to him it reflected the comparative rigour of
those coroners.[12] At the top was Westminster with 10 per cent; at
the bottom, Bristol with 1 per cent. Manchester had a low 2.5 per
cent, and its coroner, Edward Herford, must therefore be viewed as
rather complacent in the favourable impression he gave of the level
of infanticide in Lancashire before the 1871 Infant Life Protection
Committee.

The disproportionately high number of 'illegitimates or un-
knowns' in the judicial statistics on infant inquest subjects should
itself have suggested that there was something gravely unsatisfactory
about the prevailing neutral verdicts, since illegitimates were far
and away the most at risk from infanticide or something
approaching it. In 1869, for example, of the 3,979 inquest subjects
under 1, 1,251, or nearly a third, were 'illegitimate or unknown',[13]
at a time when the official return of illegitimate births was 5.8 per
cent or at the most 8.3 per cent on unofficial estimates. Intriguingly
the picture for 1–7-year-olds is very different: of the 1,905 inquest
subjects, only 193 were 'illegitimate or unknown'; this contrast
applies throughout the nineteenth century, and it is no wonder that
to observers like Edwin Lankester it suggested that a wilful
holocaust of illegitimates after birth was leaving few unwanted ones
above twelve months old. The comparison of total inquest figures
on the under-1s and the 1–7s is itself very revealing.

When it came to allocating time and money to inquests, it was
the babies who lost out most, as their deaths were least regarded,
so many being illegitimate. Infants under 1 were accounted for
about a quarter of all the deaths each year, but even though
overwhelmingly the age group most vulnerable to 'violent deaths'
(see Chapter 2) let alone 'sudden' and 'unexplained' deaths, they

formed between a fifth and a sixth of all inquest subjects.[14] As inquests in general became more frequent from the later 1880s, infants fell under this trend, too. In the early 1860s about 1 infant death in 31 was subject to an inquest; in 1890 the ratio was roughly 1 to 21.[15] But there was no improvement, it seems, in the scientific thoroughness of those inquests; they were still being got through hurriedly as a matter of form. Dr Hardy, the Dulwich police surgeon, told the 1893 Select Committee:

> Infanticide is a crime which seems to me to be lamentably frequent, and owing probably in part to the disinclination of coroners to pay for the medical evidence at inquests upon these cases, one which is but rarely traced home to its perpetrator. During the whole seven years, out of a number of cases of infanticide to which I have been called at East and West Dulwich Stations, I have only, I find, in one case made a post-mortem examination or given evidence at an inquest on a body of a newly-born infant.[16]

However, certain points must be made in the defence of coroners. They were dependent for information about suspicious deaths upon the initiative of local doctors, registrars of births, deaths and marriages and police: if these were not vigilant, there was nothing the coroner could do. Their 'why bother?' attitude towards inquests and post-mortems in the case of infants was induced by the workings of the judicial system. Even if an autopsy *was* held, and a verdict of 'murder' *was* returned, leading to the mother's trial at the assizes, the chances of a suitable conviction (assuming the police bothered to prosecute in the first place) were very remote, as we shall see in Chapter 8. In 1861 in Manchester and surrounding districts, out of 176 inquests on 0–2-year-olds, coroners recorded only three murder verdicts, and police prosecuted in none of these as they felt they had insufficient evidence.[17]

Another consideration is the generally poor calibre of medical evidence given at inquests and trials. 'Medical jurisprudence' as it was then called required specialised experience and real experts were few and far between in the nineteenth century. The law governing the summoning of medical witnesses at inquests was laid down in an act of 1836.[18] Any doctor selected by the coroner was legally obliged to give expert evidence and to conduct an autopsy, if so required. For this he received a flat fee of one guinea, however long the inquest lasted, plus a guinea for the autopsy – and these fees remained fixed until the 1926 Coroners Act! It was to be an abiding criticism of coroners that they indiscriminately picked the doctors who last attended the subjects, or those who were geographically convenient, regardless of their inexperience in pathology, with the result that they ended up covered in confusion at the hearing.[19] The average doctor hated the experience: the thought that his evidence might lead to the trial and conviction of the pathetic unwed mother of the infant made him hedge his evidence about to a degree that sank the prosecution's case; while the 'proof of completed live birth', essential to a conviction for infanticide in England, was so often impossible in the rudimentary state of Victorian forensic science.[20] We can understand some case-hardened coroner regarding the whole thing as a waste of time, taking the easy way out with findings like 'found dead' or 'stillborn', and letting sleeping babes lie.

Middlesex and its coroners 1839–74

The emerging issue of infanticide was primarily centred on London; with Middlesex, whose densely populated south-eastern corner was organically part of the metropolis, as the focal point. Middlesex (excluding Westminster) was divided into three coroners' divisions before 1862, the largest of which by far was West Middlesex, to which Dr Thomas Wakley was elected in 1839. After his death in 1861 the new division of Central Middlesex was carved from it, no doubt because of a rapidly growing population, and it was this that Dr Edwin Lankester was elected to in 1862. Wakley, as we have noted, was the country's first medically qualified coroner, and the first of an unbroken line of medical coroners for Central Middlesex (Central London from 1888[21]) up to the 1890s, at least. It was Wakley, and then much more emphatically Lankester, who were to be the national oracles on infanticide; and Lankester's tenure was marked by a series of statistically detailed Annual Reports,[22] reflecting the analytical rigour of this eminent scientist. From modest Suffolk origins Lankester had risen to become a distinguished botanist and biologist, and lecturer on anatomy and physiology. His contribution to understanding the water-borne nature of the spread of cholera in association with Dr John Snow in 1854 earned him the appointment as Medical Officer of Health for Westminster in 1856, a post which he combined with that of coroner till his death in 1874.[23] Wakley's epic and victorious struggle with the mean-natured Middlesex justices in 1840 over the exercise of his powers probably paved the way for the bold interpretation Lankester placed on his duty to hold inquests.

Figure 2   *Middlesex: showing selected parishes and coroners' divisional boundaries 1860s. (Sources: PP 1861 vol. 51, PP 1862 vol. 44, NAPSS-Sess. 1866–7 p. 158, and Middlesex Parish map, published by Institute of Heraldic and Genealogical Studies, Canterbury.)*

It was the dramatically increasing number of suffocation, 'found dead' and murder verdicts on infants in West and East Middlesex between 1859 and 1860 tha tprompted the Home Secretary's request for statistics for the whole of London in 1861, as we saw in Chapter 5. The Metropolitan Police return, however, showed that *south* of the Thames the number of 'infanticides' had actually fallen between 1859 and 1860 that prompted the Home Secretary's 9[24] – and that the *overall* increase for London was not alarming. It was in Middlesex that the statistics were alarming: in East Middlesex alone, comparing the last nine months of 1859 with the first ten of 1860 the number of inquest verdicts on infant deaths in suspect circumstances had risen from 66 to 170.[25] There can scarcely be any sociological reason for the contrast between Surrey and Middlesex; after all, attention was to switch passingly to the alleged prevalence of lethal baby-farming in *south* London following the Waters affair in 1870 (see Chapter 11). The contrast must reflect more on the comparative vigilance of the relevant authorities north and south of the river, but the impression was to be firmly fixed in people's minds in the 1860s that Middlesex was the national hotbed for infanticide, and that the Marylebone and Paddington parishes of central Middlesex were, as the *British Medical Journal* put it in March 1861, 'especially infamous as seats of such massacres of the innocents'.[26]

Central Middlesex at Lankester's accession comprised about a third of London's population, and was growing rapidly. Of its 800,000 rising on 900,000 people in the early 1860s[27] most were concentrated in the five parishes of St Pancras (199,000), St Marylebone (162,000), Islington (155,000), Paddington (76,000) and Clerkenwell (66,000).[28]

Now I have mentioned that the form of juries' verdicts was largely influenced by the coroner. Wakley appears to have been readier than his (non-medical) East Middlesex colleague, John Humphreys, to return candid murder verdicts on infants. In 1861 out of 316 inquests on 0–2-year-olds in West Middlesex 39 murder verdicts were returned, compared with 17 out of 421 inquests in Humphreys' division. However, even at Wakley's inquests the truer figure must have been depreciated under non-inculpating verdicts like 'Found dead in a tub of water: drowned', and 'Killed by accidental burns',[29] for within Lankester's truncated division murder and manslaughter verdicts were to leap in the 1860s, fluctuating around 58 to 70 a year. If we take his Fourth Annual Report, covering the year ending 31/7/1866, as an example, we see a typical statistical pattern for Central Middlesex in the 1860s.

Of 1,294 inquests for all ages, 361 were on 0–1-year-olds (of these 105 less than a week old): only 144 were on 1–5-year-olds. He classified the verdicts by causes of death. Under 'Natural Causes', which included stillbirths and premature births, most of the infants' corpses had been picked up off the streets – overwhelmingly, however, showing suspicious signs, such as torn umbilical cords (which caused haemorrhaging) and neglect.

Under 'Accidental Deaths', which included burns, scalds and suffocations, of the 136 inquests on 0–1-year-olds 108 were 'accidentally suffocated in bed'.

But it was the astounding proportions of 'Murder and Manslaughter' verdicts allied no doubt to the man's own intellectual charisma, that made Lankester an object of press attention. Of the 361 infant inquests, 79 'murders' and one 'manslaughter' were returned; and 75 of the 79 murders were on 'new-borns', less than a week old.[30] If we compare the other age groups: on the 1–5-year-olds there was only 1 'murder' and 1 'manslaughter'; and for all remaining ages there were only 4 'murders' and 7 'manslaughters'. Thus 94 per cent of all murder victims were under 1 year old.

Now the judicial statistics show that in 1867 there were 149 inquest murder verdicts on 0–1-year-olds in the *whole* of England and Wales, so that Central Middlesex alone was responsible for over a half of all 'infanticides' that year according to official returns! In fact Central Middlesex alone accounted for an average of over a third of the nation's inquest murder verdicts on infants between 1864 and the early 1880s, though declining somewhat to over a quarter in the later 1880s before the division was redrawn in 1888.[31] The disproportion thus continued beyond Lankester's tenure. One must remember, however, that Central Middlesex was possibly unique in having an unbroken succession of medical coroners to 1888, and the Central London division continued with Dr Danford Thomas in the 1890s.

Within Central Middlesex it was Marylebone and Paddington, as we have noted, that gained particular notoriety for the numbers of infants' bodies found in their streets and squares from the late 1850s. Lankester's Fourth Report shows that of the 93 murder and manslaughter verdicts in the year 1865–6 for all ages in Central Middlesex, 34 corpses came from St Pancras, 16 from Islington, 15 from Marylebone, 14 from Paddington and 4 from Clerkenwell. Islington, well away from the West End of London, had a bad record of baby-dropping but seems to have attracted less press

attention. Curgenven told the 1871 Infant Life Protection Commit-.
tee that Islington's record was due to the high proportion of houses
taking in nurse-children, in which it had a long tradition, and he
quoted Lyson's history of London in 1796: 'The present number of
houses in Islington parish is about 1,200; the burials in this place
very much exceed the baptisms on account of the number of nursed
children who die here.'[32] The police returns of London's 'infanticides', comparing 1859 and 1860,[33] showed that in West Middlesex
Islington had a much bigger jump than Marylebone, from 24 to 43,
compared with Marylebone's rise from 20 to 25. But in East
Middlesex the parish of Stepney, which got no press attention in
the 1860s, showed a leap from 25 to 47.

I show Marylebone's area and social structure in the 1860s in
Figure 3. Babies' bodies were found in the streets and fashionable
squares south of Regent's Park, and occasionally in the Park and
on Primrose Hill to the north. It comprised a cross-section of social
classes and neighbourhoods, but in its most fashionable areas had
a high proportion of multi-servanted households, and Lankester
saw this as the reason for such a prominent amount of baby-
dropping: for a pregnant servant's condition was more likely to go
unnoticed by her employers under such conditions than in a more
modest establishment, and she had a better opportunity of secretly
delivering and then 'dumping' the body,[34] which Lankester believed
never took place far from her place of employment. It is a plausible
theory, but the figures I have cited for the slum district of Stepney,
which in 1861 had at most 73,000 inhabitants, less than half
St Marylebone's, indicates that plenty of infanticide was going on
here as well without the glare of publicity. Now, the notorious
criminal slum parish of St Giles in Lankester's jurisdiction, with a
population of 54,000 in 1861, made a negligible contribution to
inquest murder returns.[35] Are we to believe that an area like this
was more caring about its illegitimate offspring? This contrast
reminds us of the distortions in the official illegitimacy rates in the
1860s which would have us believe that London's West End was
far more immoral than the slum denizens of the East End (see
Chapter 4). Just as the slums were better able to conceal their
bastardy, so I believe they were better able to hide their infanticide
in an environment where an inordinate infant death did not arouse
suspicion and there were few doctors to inspect the dead children;
where perhaps the persistence of the cess-pit provided more hiding
places for dumped bodies, and where local Mrs Drurys could
'produce' stillborns and arrange for infants to be surreptitiously
buried by their undertaker accomplices. The West End parishes
came in for attention because the infanticide was taking the more

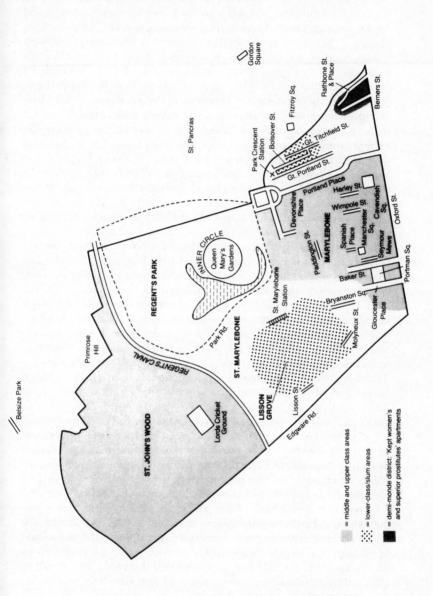

Figure 3   *Marylebone: social composition 1860s. (Source: Gordon Mackenzie, Marylebone: Great City North of Oxford St, Macmillan, 1972.)*

conspicuous form of 'dropping', literally, on the upper classes' own doorsteps. Lankester strongly resisted any notion that Central Middlesex was uniquely wicked for some reason. He pointed out to the 1871 Select Committee that a third of the 276 abandoned babies' bodies found in London during 1870 came within his division, that is just proportional to its share of London's population. The meaningless verdicts accepted by the general run of coroner, he maintained, grossly under-represented the true extent of infanticide; if all were as thorough and forthright as he, then a more realistic national figure could be gained by extrapolating Central Middlesex's verdicts of murder, and in this way he estimated a minimum of 1,420 infanticides for England and Wales as opposed to the official figure of 166 for 1866![36] And even this, he believed, was a substantial underestimate because of the numbers of corpses that never came to light, the burials of live-borns as stillborns, and decomposed subjects on whom a conclusive verdict was impossible.[37]

Lankester believed that an improved presentation of inquest verdicts in the judicial statistics would bear him out. They showed the total number of inquest verdicts on 0–1-year-olds, but the only specific verdict they listed was murder. If they showed all the verdicts of 'found dead and exposed' – the favourite non-committal verdict among coroners – this would serve as a pointer to the true extent of infanticide, since there appeared to be an inverse relationship between 'murder' and 'found dead' verdicts, according to coroners' predilections. He showed, for example, that the Central Middlesex and Westminster jurisdictions, both with a high proportion of 'murder' verdicts, had a small number of 'found dead' verdicts: the latter, for example, had 28 murder verdicts (all ages) and only 8 'found dead' in 1866, whereas East Middlesex had no 'murder' verdicts and 96 'found dead'.[38] Lankester underlined his case by looking at the north, and contrasting the performance of Clarke Aspinall of Liverpool, with other provincial coroners. In 1869, for example, of the national total of 165 infants returned as 'murdered' at inquests, 81 came from the whole of Middlesex and 15 from Liverpool. Since Liverpool's population was then about 500,000 in a total national population of 21,000,000, its contribution was disproportionately high; Frederick Lowndes in 1873, as we saw in Chapter 5, was to put some blame on the city's social peculiarities as a seaport, but Lankester gave Aspinall the credit for revealing the truth. In 1868 Liverpool returned 20 murder verdicts on 0–1s, and Lankester commented sharply:

We can hardly suppose that in Lancashire, with its teeming

population, that independent of Liverpool, there should be only two cases of infanticide in the whole county; that in Staffordshire there should be only seven and in Yorkshire only five.[39]

Thus, in the 1860s it was only in a few divisions like Central Middlesex, Westminster and Liverpool that the inquest became a crucible of criminal exposure. A generation later the numbers of socially concerned coroners had expanded and the Coroners Society was to become a useful lobby for drawing attention to the incidence of suspicious child deaths. But it was Wakley and even more outstandingly Edwin Lankester who deserve all honour as the pioneers.

8 Infanticide and the law 1803–70

We saw in Chapter 1 that the Stuart laws against infanticide both in England and Scotland were becoming unworkable by 1800 through their very severity. They were reformed after 1800 to bring them more into line with modern sentiment. Lord Ellenborough's Offences Against the Person Act 1803[1] decreed that infanticide was to be proceeded with like any other form of murder: the mother was innocent till proven guilty, thus reversing the presumption of the 1624 Act; and where a murder charge failed the jury could instead return a verdict of 'concealment of birth', with a penalty of up to two years' imprisonment.[2] In Scotland an Act of 1809[3] reduced the penalty for concealment of pregnancy to two years' prison (and the law still applies![4]).

Now that the prosecution had to prove murder in England, they had first to establish that the infant victim was an independent human being, a 'reasonable creature in being and under the King's peace'[5] according to the legal definition; and it was early established by the courts that a child still emerging from the womb had no 'separate existence' to qualify as a 'creature in being'; and could not be the subject of a murder charge – even if, say, only a foot remained lodged in the mother's passage at the time it was killed. In Scotland no such proof of a separate existence is necessary to a murder charge.[6]

The Offences Against the Person Act of 1828,[7] however, made it clear that the separate existence rule did not apply to 'concealment of birth': the child could have been stillborn, say, and the mother still be liable for hiding its body. The killing of an emergent child was not covered by the abortion law either, as judges felt this properly applied only to babies in the womb.[8] The 1861 Offences Against the Person Act allowed the prosecution to bring an independent charge of concealment of birth, while leaving it also as an alternative verdict to a murder charge. 'Concealment of birth', it should be remembered, applied only to cases of infants found dead. For those found alive an exposure charge would have been appropriate under the 1861 Act.

Now, quite apart from the near impossibility of convicting mothers for murder, owing to the separate existence rule in England, both the English and Scottish 'concealment' laws themselves were vitiated by the courts' notorious aversion to convicting mothers. In England, if the jury was convinced that the body had been only temporarily placed out of view pending a final burial, it was not (until the 1861 Act) legally a 'concealment'; if the concealment was so inept that the baby was likely to be discovered, or placed on the public highway where passers-by were likely to see it, then there was no 'concealment',[9] and Dr Frederick Lowndes was of the opinion in 1876 that mothers were getting wise to this technicality and that there was a trend away from concealing bodies on private premises and instead dumping them in the streets.[10] It was held that where a mother cried out at the time of birth, but was so inconveniently located that no help could reach her before the baby died, she could not be found guilty of 'concealment of birth'.[11] In Scotland, if the girl had told anyone in confidence, even her lover, of her condition, she was not guilty of 'concealment of pregnancy'; in *The Heart of Midlothian* it was suggested to Effie's sister Jeanie that she could save Effie by testifying that she had known of her pregnancy, but Jeanie refused to perjure herself.

But perhaps the most striking anomaly of all was that wilful failure to prepare for an imminent birth, so that the child was born dead, or dies soon afterwards, was not manslaughter;[12] 'murder by omission' of an unborn child (as opposed to active abortion) was not unlawful, and it was only the concealment of the body afterwards that attracted the legal penalty![13]

If a murder indictment was brought in an English court, what would the prosecution have to show to establish an 'independent existence'? Victorian judges were often divided among themselves and out of step with the latest medical thinking,[14] and I showed in Chapter 7 that the quality of evidence by the average medical witness usually failed to clinch the prosecution's case. Scientific tests were crude and uncertain, and could be torn apart by a good defence counsel, much to the secret relief (if public discomfiture) of the doctor, who was a most reluctant prosecutor of some wretched girl on a capital charge.

The prosecution had the almost impossible task of showing not only that the child had lived, even if momentarily, but that it did so separated from its mother; some judges held that the descent of the after-birth was a legal requisite of separate existence, under the misconception that the umbilical cord transmitted the mother's blood circulation through the child. But by 1846 most judges recognised that the foetus had an independent circulation and had dispensed with this requirement.[15] Judicial opinion remained divided longer as to whether proof of breathing was necessary, though the greatest scientific authorities, like Alfred Swaine Taylor, were definite that it was not. A heartbeat or umbilical pulse might be felt before breathing starts, and the baby could have been deliberately stifled at birth. A condition of almost imperceptible breathing called atelectasis might have existed in which a child could have lived for hours without visibly inflating the lungs. And many instances of apparently stillborn babies were known who would have been written off but for timely resuscitation. By 1802 Mrs Ann Newly, midwife at the City of London Lying-In Hospital, had resuscitated no fewer than 500 apparently dead new-borns in her career.[16] Signs of breathing would of course conclusively prove the child had lived, but not necessarily that it had a separate existence; it might have respired during delivery but died before, say, its legs were out. The scientific tests of breathing were crude and unreliable. The classic test of 'docimasy', or 'hydrostasy' was based on the hypothesis that unaerated lungs would sink in water; but if the child had breathed, they would float. The test, pioneered in Germany in the seventeenth century, was treated with scepticism by doctors here in the eighteenth.[17] Dr William Hunter discounted it in his essay on the 'Uncertainty of the Signs of Murder in the Case of Bastard Children' in 1783, and it was dismissed in many early nineteenth-century courts, when 'medical evidence in every case of child-murder was regarded as altogether worthless, and the hydrostatic test was honoured by one learned judge with the title of "scientific humbug" '.[18] Dr John Mackintosh in 1838, however, wrote of at least one woman to his knowledge who was executed 'merely because the lungs of the child floated in water'.[19] The weaknesses of the test were that the lungs might have been aerated by unsuccessful attempts at artificial respiration, or buoyed up by the gases of putrefaction. Dr Taylor's opinion in his *Manual* was that hydrostatis could never be a reliable proof of life by itself but might be useful in conjunction with other evidence.[20]

The other lung-test, formulated by Wilhelm Gottfried Ploucquet in 1782, predicated that the ratio of lung-weight to body-weight doubled once the child respired, but was found to have even less reliability than hydrostatis by the 1820s.[21] An autopsy might reveal other clues to live birth – such as the state of the skin and umbilical scar, the texture of mucous matter in the intestine, the development of epiphyses, changes in the baby's circulation system as it made the transition from pre- to post-natal oxygenation, and the development of hair and toenails. But as the eminent Dr Taylor conceded in 1886 'there are at present no satisfactory medical data to enable a witness to express a positive opinion in the majority of cases'.

A truly proficient medical witness could, however, be invaluable in disproving the defence's excuses about the way a new-born child met its death. For example, in genuine intra-uterine entanglement by the umbilical cord, the cord would leave diagonal marks across the body; where it was used deliberately to strangle the baby to fake the entanglement, one would find a circular mark around the neck.[22] The 'dropped out suddenly and cracked its head on the floor' explanation was unconvincing to an expert, as the baby's propulsion would not be that fast, and even if it dropped vertically, the umbilical cord would tend to restrain its fall. And the hoary old 'fell into the privy' excuse was equally suspect. Even if a girl expecting her first child genuinely mistook labour pains for bowel movement, primiparous childbirth is rarely precipitate, and she should have had time to stop the baby falling away.[23] The vagina of a seated woman slants towards the wall of the privy, so the baby would not just have dropped down, and in any case the umbilical cord should have restrained it long enough for the mother to react; and if the mother insisted that the cord snapped, but inspection revealed a clean cut as by a sharp instrument, then on the face of it she was lying.

The 'privy' defence was so traditional and successful, however, that it was extended to the new-fangled water-closet; and bodies of babies stuffed down WC pipes were readily accepted by doctors and lawyers as victims of precipitate birth. In the case of a servant girl, Rebecca Wells, at the Central Criminal Court in 1858,[24] the surgeon testified that her baby, so discovered in her employer's house, fell in as a result of a premature and unexpected delivery; and the judge ruled that this being so, she had done nothing positive to dispose of the child and there was legally no 'concealment'!

The sympathy for mothers in infanticide cases prevailed among the public, lawyers, judges and doctors alike. As Sir James Fitzjames Stephen, the Recorder of Newark and a very distinguished jurist, explained to the Capital Punishment Commission in 1866,[25] the crime was popularly seen as less serious than other kinds of murder because the baby has no self-awareness, and the public at large did not feel a threat to themselves. The criteria applied conventionally to murderers could not, he said, be applied to a recently delivered woman who 'is so upset and in such an hysterical state altogether, that . . . you cannot deal with her in the same manner as if she was in a regular and proper state of health'; post-natal depression and 'the strangest symptoms of what amounts to temporary madness' were well understood by the lawyers, if not by the law.

There was also widespread compassion for the miserable condition of the woman, said Stephen, 'and there is a sort of feeling . . . as a general rule, against the father of the child who goes unpunished'. However, the compassion was also coloured by with what the NSPCC was later to regard as a misplaced gallantry towards women. The middle-class all-male jurors (the NSPCC was referring to inquests but the same must apply to the assizes) judged female instincts by the standards of their own class, and revolted against the very idea of a woman wilfully killing off her child by neglect: 'She is human, of course, and she is a mother; and she is weeping. All her inattentions were clearly of "ignorance", poor thing' and so she is exonerated!²⁶

But it was the extremity of the law that was blamed for the astonishing acquittals of so many women against the facts; infanticide, even by the mother, was murder, and the judge was obliged to sentence her to death, though it was almost certain that she would be reprieved by the Home Secretary. However, nobody wanted it on their conscience that they had been instrumental in subjecting the distraught and lonely defendant to the ordeal of the Black Cap. As Mr Justice Keating told the Capital Punishment Commission: 'Juries will not convict whilst infanticide is punished capitally' and even where judges do review the evidence and law objectively, 'juries wholly disregard them and eagerly adopt the wildest suggestions which the ingenuity of counsel can furnish.' Sir George Denman QC, MP said the same of all capital cases:

> . . . it seems as if almost everybody was in a sort of conspiracy in favour of the prisoner. That applies very strongly to medical witnesses. You find that medical witnesses are induced to give opinions which are perfectly startling to Judge and counsel in cases where you can attribute it to nothing but the existence of capital punishment.²⁷

It is no wonder that Justice Keating denounced the court process in infanticide cases a 'solemn mockery'. The separate existence rule in England was a godsend to uneasy medical witnesses and juries, but the leniency towards the women went further; juries were as reluctant to find manslaughter, which was non-capital, in cases of post-natal neglect,²⁸ and even the chance of a 'concealment' verdict was prejudiced by some perverse legal interpretation.

Condemnation of the 'solemn mockery' as an encouragement to infanticide became more vocal as infanticide increasingly emerged in the public consciousness from the 1850s. An early broadside was fired by the Reverend William Scott in the *Saturday Review* of August 1856. In a long article prompted by a dozen recent trials for infanticide resulting in anomalous verdicts he bitterly complained of the juries who 'will not convict under any circumstances' and the doctors 'who take the merciful view' and 'pretend to entertain very grave doubts', for example, as to whether the child was born alive or whether the body found really belonged to the defendant. Doctors were influenced by public opinion and feared a loss of clientele, he claimed. The courtroom atmosphere could be very charged when the spectators' gallery was filled with girls who identified with the defendant's plight. At Dorchester Assizes some years before, when one Celestine Sumner was acquitted on an infanticide charge in a courtroom packed with country girls, 'a general demonstration of applause took place in Court and the girls left town boasting that "now they might do what they liked".' Now, even allowing for the *Saturday Review*'s cynical view of the morals of country girls and their predilection for abortion and (allegedly) infanticide, there was no denying Scott's argument, illustrated as it was by the recent cases. For example in July at Aylesbury Assizes a girl who dosed her baby to death with opium received one month's prison. In the same month one Eliza Davies was tried at Hereford Assizes after her illegitimate child was found in a well, but the surgeon testified that it *might* have been dead before being dropped there, and the verdict was 'not guilty'.

Such was the utter indifference towards infant life, declared Scott, that leniency even extended to the father of the child. In a recent case at Truro, a man named Jose had killed his baby in front of his mistress: 'Jose holds his fingers down the infant's throat for five minutes, in the hope of suffocating it; and at last he fetches a jug of water, pours it into an open pan or pail, and holds the child's head in it till it is dead, just as he might have drowned a kitten.' To this the jury (though much to the disgust of the judge) returned a verdict of manslaughter.

William Burke Ryan in 1862 told how the judges were frequently implicated in the frustration of justice. In an Ipswich case, a girl was tried for concealment only, when the body of a baby she had secretly given birth to was found by her sister in a drawer with 'its throat cut from ear to ear'; their father was called, and the girl fell into a fainting spell that lasted some weeks. Although the girl became insensible *after* the discovery, the judge, Lord Campbell,

directed the jury to acquit her as 'there could be no concealment
on her part if she were unconscious'(!). The jury promptly replied
'not guilty', 'a result which was hailed with acclamation by a
crowded court. Never was there a greater perversion of justice.'
Burke cited another case where it was the surgeon who provided
the let-out. At Liverpool Assizes in August 1860, one Ann
Billington was tried for the murder of her new-born child: 'The girl
denied her pregnancy, but on delivery she placed her child under
the cellar steps, and the surgeon found "a large gaping wound in
the throat", but could not say that it had an "independent
existence or full birth from its mother at the time the wound was
inflicted" (!)'. The verdict was 'concealment of birth' and she
received eighteen months' prison.

Of course, if the corpse's condition when discovered ruled out
identification of the cause of death, a conviction for murder was
impossible; hence the practice by midwives or baby-farmers
sometimes of incinerating the body, allegedly 'to save the burial
costs'. In 1853 at Ditchling in Sussex, the new owner of a cottage,
in tearing down an old fireplace, found the skeletons of five babies.
These were traced back to the daughter of a farm labourer who
had occupied the cottage previously; she had two grown-up
illegitimate children. The inquest could not establish murder, but
she was brought before the Lewes magistrates on a concealment
charge.[29]

What are the facts and figures about convictions of mothers for
concealment and murder before 1870? Between the early 1820s and
the later 1850s the average number of convictions a year for
concealment rose from 7 to 62; this is consistent with other
statistical evidence of the so-called 'increase' in infanticide over this
period[30] (see Chapter 5). However, these were a tiny fraction of all
trials for concealment. In 1857 in the Metropolitan Police District
of 18 women arrested for concealment, 10 went for trial, and only 2
of these were convicted, 1 received one month's prison, the other
less than six months.[31]

The last woman to be executed for murdering her child under
twelve months old was Rebecca Smith of Wiltshire in 1849. She
was an impoverished depressive and wife of a drunkard, and
admitted to poisoning seven more of her children previously.[32]
Between 1849 and 1864 there had been only 39 convictions of
mothers for the wilful murder of their children, almost all of whom
were under 1 year and all but 5 illegitimate.[33] From 1849 the
Home Secretary invariably reprieved mothers who killed their own
infants under twelve months, but the ordeal of formal sentence to
death still had to be endured in court. Between 1849 and 1877 only

two more women were to be executed for child murder – Ann Lawrence in 1864 after irrationally venting her rage on her 4-year-old son when she found that her lover was unfaithful; and Ann Barry in 1873, who killed not her own child, but that of her lover's previous mistress, to save him paying continued maintenance.[34]

The chances of a mother going to trial for murder of her child were exceedingly remote, and the likelihood of a conviction for murder was negligible. On the Oxford Assize Circuit between 1832 and 1837 of 22 trials of mothers for murdering their illegitimate children there were 20 acquittals.[35] A rough idea of the tiny fraction of all infanticides leading to any kind of legal consequences for the mother may be gauged from the following: of the 464 'infanticides' *known* to the Metropolitan Police in a seventeen-month period over 1859 and 1860, only 14 led to prosecutions. The results were as follows:

   6 = acquittals
   1 = not stated
   3 = 12 months' or more imprisonment
   3 = 2 months' prison or less
   1 = 'death' sentence[36]

The Royal Commission on Capital Punishment in 1866 was the first official forum to raise the issue of infanticide, albeit in a narrow technical context.[37] However, its finding that the prosecution of infanticide had to all intents and purposes broken down had wider social implications; its recommendations on infanticide law reform were incorporated in the Harveian Society's own proposals and were taken up by William Thomas Charley MP on behalf of the Infant Life Protection Society in the 1870s (see Chapter 13). The Commission recommended that a new non-capital offence of Infanticide be created to cover the killing of a child by its mother during birth or within seven days afterwards, and that no proof of separate existence be required. This proposal appreciated the critical psychological condition of a woman immediately after delivery, and by reducing the penalty intended that the chance of a conviction would be improved. The jury should have no power to return a 'concealment' verdict on an infanticide charge as this would leave them a tempting soft option.

Now, the belief that judges and juries would be hauled into line by a more humane and rational law may have been deluded. Prussia's infanticide law was a model of rationality,[38] yet juries there were still reluctant to convict pathetic women;[39] and while French law classes infanticide as murder, death sentences were not automatic as in England, as judges were allowed discretion. Yet nearly a third of all infanticide prosecutions between 1851 and 1865 resulted in acquittals.[40]

Following the Capital Punishment Commission's recommendations there were to be numerous unsuccessful attempts in Parliament between 1866 and 1880 to reform the murder law, by creating two categories: premeditated First Degree (capital) and unpremeditated Second Degree (non-capital) murder, with Infanticide placed under the latter. In the 1870s there were to be two distinct groups of Parliamentary activists – the legal men, who wanted to rationalise and codify the criminal law as a juridical exercise, and the Infant Life Protectionists, for whom Infanticide law reform was one of a set of intended prophylactics against child murder. I leave the account of their efforts to Chapter 13.

9 Lifting the lid on midwives and baby-farmers 1868–71

We saw in Chapter 5 that Ernest Hart of the *British Medical Journal* commissioned an enquiry into abortion and baby-farming in 1868, and the undercover method employed was a classic of its kind, to be copied by others in subsequent journalistic investigations, the last of which was that undertaken by *The Sun* between October and December 1895.

Dr Alfred Wiltshire, a medical officer of the Privy Council, was recruited to do the actual fieldwork, and the results, a series of exposé articles from February to September 1868, were his work.[1] Wiltshire hunted down the baby-farmers and shadier lying-in houses by three methods: one was by obtaining information from local registrars of deaths about houses from which unusual numbers of death certificate applications for infants were emanating; the second was to place advertisements in the press offering a child for someone to 'adopt', and the third was to follow up advertisements offering to nurse or adopt the children of others, or publicising lying-in houses. The last two require explanation. The concept of adoption entailing the irreversible legal assumption of parental rights and duties over a stranger's child dates in England and Scotland from the Adoption Acts of 1926 and 1930 respectively. Till then the word 'adoption' as popularly used meant no more than fostering, and it was perfectly proper and legal to make private arrangements to hand over or sell one's child to another – though the 'adoption', so-called, had no force in law and could be revoked. With the multiplication of popular and local newspapers after 1855 (following the repeal of the Stamp Duty on the press) baby-farming must have received a considerable fillip, as the 'classified ad' type of advertisement now became the most effective way to attract business; and the expansion of the railways from the 1840s gave the operation an unprecedented geographical range. One could never be sure if the advertiser was genuinely interested in adoption, or, if she was a baby-farmer, what her standards were. This somewhat unctuous advert from 1867[2] was typical:

The care of a Child Wanted by a respectable person and her
daughter. Having had the charge of children for many years, a
mother's care and attention may be relief on. Highest references
can be given. Address A.B. Mr. Thompson's fruiterer, Church
St., Stoke Newington.

The use of tradesmen's addresses as letter-drops, as in this case,
was a common track-covering ploy, and assurances like 'a mother's
care' or a 'Christian family' were stock expressions.

Parallel with these were the classified ads for lying-in houses.
These were carefully composed to convey an impression of
respectability and confidentiality, in full knowledge that some of
the well-heeled clients would be 'up from the country' to get rid of
an embarrassment. Typically then, from the *Daily Telegraph* of
October 1st 1867:

Furnished (for ladies) drawing room with piano or other
apartments. Nurse recommended by physicians. Baby-linen and
other requisites found. Mrs B. Camberwell.

The description 'with piano' often appeared as a sort of warranty
of gentility,[3] while the phrase 'with attendance' in a discreet advert
for a lady's apartment was a coded clue to its real purpose.[4]

Wiltshire placed two adverts in the *Clerkenwell News* offering two
children 'for sale' to prospective adoptors for £5 and £10, and
received no fewer than 330 replies; this was the measure of the
pulling power of press advertisements, and the scale of mercenary
baby-farming, as two-thirds of the correspondents, he told the 1871
Infant Life Protection Committee, had bad motives. In following
up advertisements for lying-in houses, he posed as the gentleman
friend of the lady 'in difficulties', coming to negotiate terms.

The bulk of his report was concerned with lying-in houses and
abortionists, which we shall look at in the next chapter. His last
report, however, records a visit to a Marylebone baby-farmer,[5] and
revealed the more typical sort of operator, not a wilful murderess
like Charlotte Winsor, but a poor ignorant, struggling woman, not
bad at heart, who was doing what she could within her limitations.
Her husband was a navvy in irregular employment, and she had
taken up baby-farming to make ends meet, as she was not strong
enough to do charring. All the children born to her had died in
infancy. Of the 18 nurse-children she had had in the past seventeen
years, 12 had died quite young; and 3 had survived long enough to
go out and earn a living. Of the 3 infants she currently had, 2 had
scarlet fever and 1 had syphilis. They were all the illegitimate

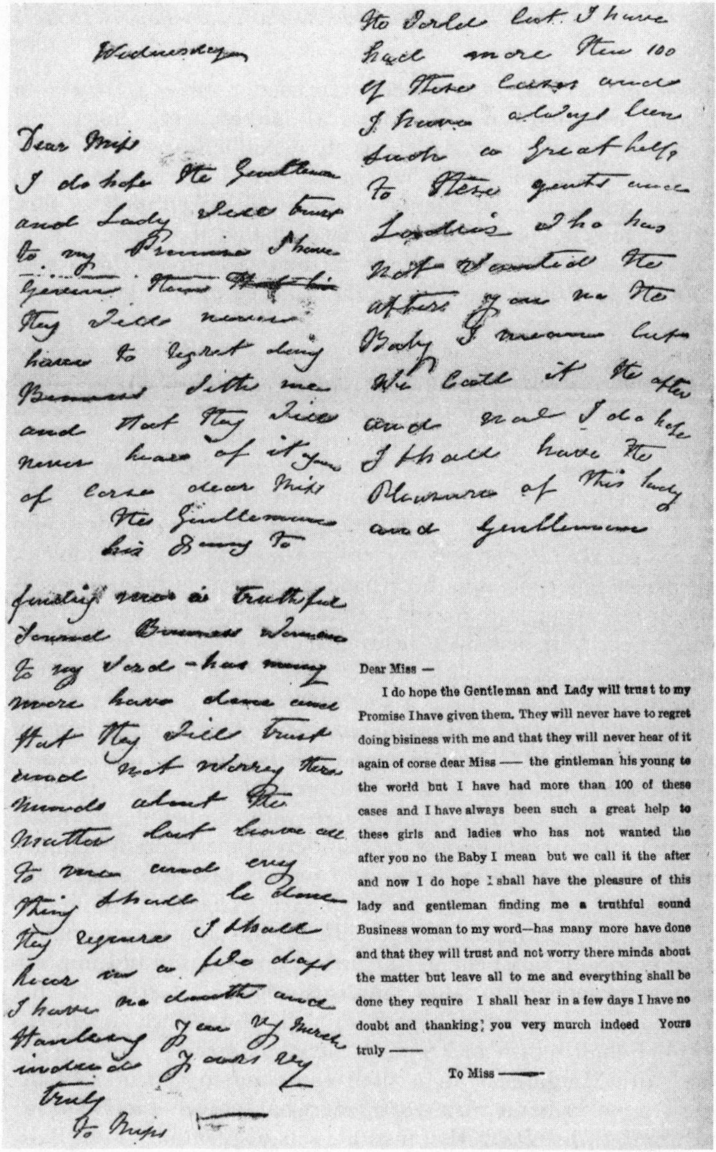

Figure 4 *Facsimile of a touting letter from a midwife received by a female 'undercover' investigator during* The Sun's *campaign exposing abortionists and baby-farmers. The investigator had approached the midwife, 'Mrs X', with a fabricated story deducible from the letter; 'Mrs X' was keen to do business, and followed up the meeting with this missive. The transcription follows the spelling and punctuation of the original; names have been deleted. (Source:* The Sun *newspaper, 2nd Nov. 1895, p.2. Courtesy:* British Library, Newspaper Collection.)

Dear Miss —

I do hope the Gentleman and Lady will trust to my Promise I have given them. They will never have to regret doing bisiness with me and that they will never hear of it again of corse dear Miss —— the gintleman his young to the world but I have had more than 100 of these cases and I have always been such a great help to these girls and ladies who has not wanted the after you no the Baby I mean but we call it the after and now I do hope I shall have the pleasure of this lady and gentleman finding me a truthful sound Business woman to my word—has many more have done and that they will trust and not worry there minds about the matter but leave all to me and everything shall be done they require I shall hear in a few days I have no doubt and thanking you very murch indeed Yours truly ——

To Miss ——

offspring of servants: the fathers were better off – a banker, a mechanic (who had run off to America), and an army officer. The women paid 4 shillings and sixpence to 6 shillings a week for their upkeep, and found payments hard going. Wiltshire concluded that in the circumstances the infants were as well looked after as they might be, but 'in spite of this, it is evident that the pressure from all circumstances surrounding baby-farming is so great, that where there is not any design to deprive the children of life, they are yet squeezed out of existence.'

The *BMJ*'s articles attracted wide publicity in the press, and for a short time advertisements for lying-in houses dropped out of newspapers[6] as accoucheuses lay low. James Greenwood, the noted journalist and chronicler of low-life, included Baby-Farming among his 'Seven Curses of London' published in 1869, in which he records a visit to the establishment of a Mr and Mrs Oxleek. Husbands were generally secondary figures in baby-farming, and in this case Mr Oxleek was evidently a layabout – 'an indolent, ease-loving, pipe-smoking, beer-soaking, wretch' who, while his wife was out, negligently nursed a child, swathed in 'a very old and woefully begrimed bedgown, bearing marks of Mr Oxleek's dirty paws and of his tobacco dust, and of physic clumsily administered and spilt'.

A fascinating independent undercover investigation into lying-in houses was undertaken by a mysterious lady signing herself 'A.B.', whose account appeared in *The Times* in July 1870.[7] She reveals a most exceptional initiative and resource, with compelling powers of description. Her thoroughness and subtlety of masquerade requires more space than I can spare to do it justice; save to say that she persuaded friends and a servant to write character replies to advertisements, in appropriate vocabulary on appropriate paper, with appropriate misspellings (in the servant's case) and appropriate tear smudges, to allay any suspicion of a trick by her correspondents (no doubt alerted to such ploys since the *BMJ*'s exposé). I shall return to her in the next chapter.

With the Margaret Waters affair rumbling to a climax in the English press in September 1870 (see Chapter 11), the Glasgow-based *North British Daily Mail* instituted its own enquiry into 'Baby Farming in Scotland'. Its 30-year-old editor, Charles Cameron, was also a qualified surgeon, and later on to become MP for a Glasgow constituency.[8] In the early 1890s he was to draw attention in Parliament to the suspicious scale of stillbirth burials, and be instrumental in the appointment of a Select Committee on Death Certification in 1893. Cameron had a strong interest in public health issues, and the investigation he commissioned in September

1870, undertaken by William Cameron, arose out of an earlier *NBDM* inquiry into public health in Scotland and its shocking revelations about infant mortality.[9] The baby-farming articles appeared between February 11th and April 7th 1871.[10] A female assistant was employed to make the undercover approach. The first three articles were devoted to a smart and cold-blooded proprietress operating from an outwardly respectable house in a seaside town near Arthur's Seat. The investigator was admitted into a decently furnished hall, but was struck by the unnatural quiet in a place that boarded children. The proprietress charged 3 to 4 shillings a week board, but was prepared to adopt a child outright for a £15 lump sum; believing the investigator to be interested, she later prepared a 'contract' for permanent adoption. (Such contracts were sometimes drawn up in 'adoptions' but had no legal force.) The baby-farmer was full of gush about her love of children, though one of the nurselings she brought out to show off seemed unhealthy and listless. She escorted the investigator out after these preliminary negotiations, and deposited the baby with furtive quickness inside a room, hastily shutting the door as she ushered the investigator through the hall, but not before the latter was able to peep inside:

> I had just time to note that the apartment was dirty and very
> scantily furnished and contained some mute little children who
> were squatted on the bare floor and were supposed to be playing,
> I presume, though I could discern no movement among them
> and could not help thinking that they looked more like miniature
> 'Aunt Sallies' stuck up at equal distances to be shot at, than
> anything else. The invalid baby was not handed over to anyone's
> care but was just set down on the bare floor in the draught of the
> door to 'fend' for itself.

Thus, behind a respectable façade, the baby-farmer was concealing a squalid stable of infants who were evidently kept drugged. Subsequent enquiry revealed from Sophia, a former servant at the house, stories which made this 'Mrs ——' appear far more wicked than the scapegoat Margaret Waters, who had gone to the gallows a few months before. Sophia told of wilful neglect and repeated beatings of the infants; how babies were left on the bare floor all night 'with only a newspaper put under them and no pillow'; of indigestible meals of skim milk and 'water sops'. When the babies cried

Mrs —— whipped them very sore. One day Mrs —— whipped

a baby in the kitchen only two months old. She gave it five heavy
slaps on the bare skin. . . . The children were whipped even
when they were ill. When little Katie was bad with bronchitis
she cried, and Mrs —— whipped her until she (the child) went
into a fit.

From time to time babies were mysteriously removed from the
premises.

The coldly sadistic 'Mrs ——' was an exceptional type. Her
scale of operations was unusually large; most Glasgow baby-farms
were found to have one to three children, and the investigators did
find many farms where there was no 'culpable negligence'.[11]
Danger to infants more commonly came from ignorance and
drunkenness among low-grade practitioners in the Glasgow slums.
The *NBDM* found in the case of one infant who died at the hands
of a notorious drunkard, a 'wild, dangerous woman'. The
neighbours were perturbed but did nothing, and such instances
rarely came to the attention of the police. The reason, said the
paper, was that in crowded slums, where mutual non-interference
was essential to live tolerably, it was better to leave well alone.

Cameron, like Wiltshire, inserted bogus adverts in the press and
received 400 replies;[12] their geographical range seemed to indicate
the wide spread of baby-farming in Scotland; however, it was
significant that no replies came from Paisley, a textile centre, for,
as in England, employment in the mills gave women an alternative
livelihood, and baby-farmers would be in less demand there as mill
girls deposited their infants with day-minders.

So much for the baby-farmer exposés both preceding and
following the Margaret Waters case; we will now turn to the
revelations about their companions in this netherworld of infant
disposal, the midwives and abortionists.

10 'Churchyard luck': midwives and murder

In Victorian Britain the midwife attended at births much more commonly than the doctor. In the industrial cities around 1870 midwives could attend as many as 90 per cent of all births. It was only the well-to-do who could afford doctors; in Wimbledon at this time only 5 per cent of deliveries were undertaken by midwives.[1] For the poor the midwife was cheap, easily available and one of their own class. The majority were untrained 'Mrs Gamps', and the typical image of the midwife was that of a boozy, ignorant slattern. For most the trade was something they had drifted into to make ends meet, sometimes combined with other part-time work, say, as washerwomen. A limited number of voluntary training places were offered by lying-in hospitals and the Obstetric Society; certificated midwives often styled themselves 'accoucheuses' to distinguish themselves from the Mrs Gamps, and appeal 'up-market'. The average general practitioner felt some threat to his livelihood from the midwives, whose trade was crowded; competition forced rates down, and many were prepared to offer shady supplementary services to draw business. Moves by doctors from the late 1860s to have midwives registered and compulsorily qualified had a strong element of self-interest; a higher calibre, and therefore scarcer breed of midwives, subordinated to doctors, would be less of an economic threat, and the criminal abuses by the Mrs Gamps were readily dilated on by doctors, who had an axe to grind; indeed, doctors had their black sheep who were just as bad. Registration finally came under the 1902 Midwives Act; all new entrants had to be qualified, but unqualified women practising regularly before the Act could continue until 1910.[2]

The stereotype at its most lurid of the Victorian midwife as a witch in her lair, ready to dispose of unwanted babies for a price, was depicted in Emma Caroline Wood's *Sorrow on the Sea* in the character of Mrs Nancy Drury.[3] It was published in 1868, the same year as Dr Wiltshire's exposé of lying-in houses. From her remote farm cottage in Essex Mrs Drury carried on every scandalous practice midwives were then suspected of: abortion, infanticide and baby-planting. I shall now examine these mal-practices in turn.

First, abortion. Under successive acts since 1803, the last being the Offences Against the Person Act 1861,[4] abortion was outlawed with the penalty rising to life imprisonment, and it was a lesser offence knowingly to supply others with instruments or medicines for the purposes of inducing abortion. Abortion, nonetheless, was very widely practised, and there was invariably strong public sympathy for any abortionist brought before the courts, even where the patient had died, for although this was technically murder, the juries usually returned manslaughter verdicts; while the few murder verdicts were almost certain to be followed by a reprieve. The law against the sale of abortifacients was almost unenforceable, since many 'innocent' items on sale, like cantharides and diachylon (lead) plasters, or purgatives like juniper oil could be abused for abortifacient purposes; and late nineteenth-century newspaper advertisement columns commonly boasted proprietary remedies for menstrual disorders, 'female ailments', 'irregularities of the system' and the like that everyone knew were thinly (but legally) disguised abortifacients. Midwives made up and sold their own preparations. Lead pills were a well-known abortifacient at the end of the century, and in 1909 Dr J.H. Taylor, a Manchester doctor, told how 'some old "Mother Gamp"' would buy 'a quarter pound of diachylon plaster, costing a few pence, picks off the pieces in her fingers, rolls them up into pills and sells them at 20/- a dozen'.[5] But it was the direct performance of abortion by midwives that Dr Wiltshire exposed in 1868. In his first report he described an establishment where the nurse charged 50 guineas 'for the job'. It was important for the midwife to reassure her client not only of her competence but also her discretion, for their high-class clients were conscious of their vulnerability to blackmail. The nurse assured him 'The lady's face need not be seen and she could keep it veiled, if she liked, and has only to lie on her side.' She told him she had been in the business for twenty-seven years and some of her patients had come back six or seven times:

'I'm a jokelar person, I am; and I says funny things and cheers 'em up. She needn't mind and musn't fret, and I'll see her right. I'm the old original, I am, and I have had hundreds.' This nurse left it to a doctor whose method, with a catheter, 'is easily done, no more than kissing your hand'. She disposed of the foetuses, which were passed off as premature births, through an undertaker.

From his investigations Dr Wiltshire concluded that abortions were 'extremely numerous', but could give no figures.[6] He thought that any legal restriction on baby-farms would tend to increase abortion, but Dr Charles Cameron told the 1871 Infant Life Protection Committee that the situation was already so bad it could not get any worse.[7] In France, as in Britain, abortion around 1900 was said to be 'a veritable industry' at the hands of some midwives,[8] who employed touts to canvass business. These might masquerade as travelling toiletries saleswomen whose sales pitch was angled to elicit useful information about a customer's 'health'; and Charles Cameron in 1871 told of professional fortune-tellers or 'spaewives' and washerwomen (whose work brought them to overhear kitchen-gossip) serving as abortionists' touts in Glasgow.[9]

There was a close link between midwives and bent doctors. The doctor might perform the operation, or supply mendacious death certificates to midwives whose patients died at their hands. The connection was graphically brought out in *The Sun*'s rather relishful exposé of 1895. Using the same methods of infiltration as Wiltshire and Cameron a quarter-century before, it tracked down a midwife, 'Mrs X', who used the 'assistance of a doctor broken down with drink'[10] to do her operations, and was ready to fabricate a death certificate to conceal the patient's true identity in the event of her death! But its most dramatic revelation involved an Anglicised Burmese doctor, James Ady, then of Brixton, who shared a house with his 'foster-daughter', Minnie Graham. *The Sun*'s reporter, Mr Cadett, had been told by Mrs Graham, a midwife, that she could get abortions done for £40 by a qualified doctor who was on the premises.[11] *The Sun* embarked on a deliberately provocative vendetta against Ady, and on November 14th under a triumphant headline, 'At Last', announced that Dr Ady had taken out a Summons for criminal libel against the paper. The hearing was Ady's undoing,[12] for it transpired that he had been evicted from a succession of premises by landlords for putting notices in the window proclaiming that he treated women's diseases, and that a bogus charity he ran, the 'Lambeth Self-Supporting Dispensary', was a disguised abortion clinic. His Summons was dismissed and Ady was subsequently struck off the Medical Register. Some two years later Mrs Graham and he were separately convicted for procuring abortions, and he received seven years' imprisonment.[13]

The second malpractice was the murder of new-borns. Dr Wiltshire's investigations turned up at least one accoucheuse who refused to abort owing to the physical dangers but was prepared instead to neglect the infant at birth and make it appear stillborn. 'Mrs X' in *The Sun*'s investigation was prepared to 'arrange' a stillbirth for £30 plus £1 for the box and undertaker, or alternatively to bury it in her own backyard: 'I've buried hundreds

in the years I've been working.' There is no doubt that this
practice was widespread and more will be said of it in Chapter 14.

In 1870 Dr Andrew Wynter, a former editor of the *BMJ*, wrote:
'Midwives wickedly inclined know well what it is to produce a
stillbirth, or in the horrible language of their craft, a "quiet 'un".'[14]
Indeed, in Yorkshire midwives with a happy knack of bringing
stillborns into the world were valued for their 'Churchyard Luck',
as the local expression had it.[15]

Dr Edmund Syson told the 1871 Select Committee how,
formerly, as a doctor at Wath, a mining village near Rotherham,
he had found that the people had no regard for the survival of
illegitimate babies:

'I have been asked myself to kill a child as it was being born,
and by a good-natured nurse, too, and I am sure she had no idea it
was murder. . . .' In the case of illegitimates, 'They think a baby
"going home", as they call it, is nothing; they look upon it, too, in
the light of a trouble to the mother from which she would be well
relieved.'[16]

The fictional Nancy Drury was too lairy even to fake a stillbirth.
She explained to her client: 'I find I don't get paid for my job if the
kids are stillborn. They say 'twas the hand of God and not my
hand, and they shirk my dues – no, no, if things are to be done, I
must see my money down first, as you've seen the babe alive and
likely to live.' Once killed, the babies' bodies were thrown down a
dry well on her farm.

Moralists branded such midwives with epithets like 'ogress',
'hag' or 'beldam' but in reality, as Syson indicated, they saw
themselves as ordinary people performing a needed service. When
'A.B.'[17] visited her first accoucheuse, she was surprised that she
did not fit the witch-like stereotype at all:

She was a buxom, merry-looking woman of middle height. Good
temper, good living and a good digestion had evidently agreed
with her, and her 40 or 45 summers sat very lightly on her. . . .
Altogether, her sparkling black eyes and jolly appearance made
up an ensemble so totally unlike what I had fancied she would
be like, that I was quite startled.

How were new-borns killed off? The methods I list cannot, of
course, be ascribed exclusively to midwives, but even where carried
out by the mother, the midwife may well have advised her on the
techniques least likely to attract suspicion. The most popular was
suffocation,[18] as this could be attributed to overlying, but babies'
bodies were sometimes found with their breathing passages

plugged up with mud, paper, cloth, wood, dough and so forth. Accidental suffocation might be simulated by pushing its head into a pillow or placing a wet cloth over its head.

Strangulation with ligatures was very common, and not infrequently the umbilical cord was used, as death could be blamed on accidental entwining of the neck during birth.

Puncturing vital organs with needles, so that they leave no trace except on the closest examination, was probably more exclusive to midwives, as it entailed a knowledge of anatomy: piercing the fontanelle, the heart, the temple, the inner canthus of the eye, or driving a needle up the nose into the brain, or into the spinal column to damage the spinal marrow – these were the grisly techniques.

Injuries to the head or neck could always be blamed by the midwife on the extra pressure exerted during a difficult delivery; indeed if the head was deliberately twisted, a doctor's casual inspection might not spot it at all, as new-born babies' neck support is loose anyway. A fractured skull could be blamed on the baby's sudden drop during an unexpected delivery, and 'surprise delivery' was the excuse for the not infrequent discovery of babies' bodies in privies: mothers claimed that they mistook labour pains for bowel movement and the baby 'shot out' fatally into the ordure; however, one could not be sure if such immersions were a method of killing or of concealment afterwards.

A midwife might sit her parturient client over a bucket of water; the baby drowned before it cried and took breath, and the lungs, if examined in an autopsy, would show no sign of inflation, and suggest stillbirth. Alternatively, even if the presence of water in the lungs pointed to suspicious circumstances, the mother and midwife had still committed no crime (in England) as the baby had had no 'separate existence' when it died.[19]

'Accidental' drowning of a baby on washdays was not infrequent, it seems. Dr Wynter remarked in 1870:[20] 'The late Mr Wakley used to observe that the number of infants who left this world on washing days was remarkable.'

One way of destroying evidence of the causes of the child's death was to burn the body afterwards. The worst that could happen to a midwife was prosecution for unlawful disposal under the Cremation Act after 1884. In December 1906 the *Daily Telegraph* ran a story of the trial of the proprietress of a 'maternity home'. A witness testified to having seen her burn nine or ten infants' bodies; the woman twitted the witness's squeamishness with the boast, 'I have burned dozens.' And a month later a Tottenham baby-farmer on trial for failing to register the deaths of infants on her premises (under current law), was revealed in court to have burned infants' bodies in her kitchen stove.[21]

Sometimes the midwife would deceive her patient by offering to find it a home, on payment of a premium for the child's welfare, which, it was claimed, would be passed on to the adopter, less the midwife's 'expenses'. The midwife would then either 'sell' the baby outright to some low-grade baby-farmer (even, perhaps, posing as its mother) for a much lesser sum, and pocket a handsome profit (this chain of sales for reducing sums was later dubbed 'baby-sweating'): or else she would have the child board-nursed for a weekly sum, and (taking care to cover her tracks) default on the payments after a few weeks. Since many of these transactions took place at railway stations – 'railway station adoptions', as they were to be called – involving babies brought from long distances, it was very difficult indeed to trace the other party. But the midwife might have another fate in store for the child, and when one of 'A.B.'s' interviewees (believing 'A.B.' to be a prospective client) was trying to reassure her that she could find a good home for the child, she blabbed too much and nearly gave the game away. 'A.B.' asked her what would happen if no one wanted the child:

> 'Oh, with money,' said the woman, 'it is easy to get someone to
> adopt them. I have often passed under the noses of the
> policemen, with my big cloak on and basket on my arm, as if
> going marketing. Few women would like to go out at night where
> I do. I have a private key of the gate through a passage not far
> from here – it's a short cut, you know, near – but that's nothing
> to the point. . . .'

and at this point she clammed up sharply, but to 'A.B.' it was obvious what the 'adopted' infant's real fate was.

On a few occasions midwives did blackmail their clients by passing the baby to a baby-farmer for safe keeping in a conspiracy to extort money from the mother later.[22] Mrs Drury also alludes to the blackmail of women whose embarrassments she has relieved:

> . . . 'when I want a few pounds, I know where to go for them,
> and if *they* forget what I've done for them, I jog their memories';
> and she laughed again a wild demoniacal laugh. 'And if the
> husbands are troublesome we give them "a seasoned pie".'

However, she is an overdrawn and melodramatic figure, and the frequency of blackmail in real life should not be exaggerated.

Baby-planting (this is my own term), which involved the

arrangement of fake confinements, was a quite bizarre but not uncommon side-racket in midwifery. As with abortion, doctors were sometimes implicated, too. According to George Edward Male in 1816[23] this 'has sometimes been practised to impose unlawful heirs on families, to displace the lawful ones, or to gratify the desires of a husband who wishes for children'. It had a long tradition – the Old Pretender James Stuart was rumoured to have been 'planted' in a warming pan – and one classic eighteenth-century *cause célèbre* was the Douglas Peerage Case 1767–9: a rival claimant to the family title held in the courts that the actual inheritor had been a planted baby, but his case failed.[24] From time to time legal actions cropped up in the courts where inheritances were at stake and both Dr Wiltshire's and 'A.B.'s' investigations revealed how the midwife went about the carefully planned charade – remember that the absence of legal adoption before 1926 made it essential that the child's delivery should appear authentic to the world. 'A.B.'s' midwife-informant told her of one client, the wife of a naval man, whose marriage was barren. She desperately wanted a child, but her husband refused to 'adopt' one. She decided to deceive him by pretending to give birth while he was away at sea. She approached the midwife who had another client who was expecting an unwanted child about Christmas. In the following months the naval man's wife progressively padded herself out until the baby became due. The baby-plant had to be orchestrated with perfect timing. The woman took a room in a hotel near the midwife's establishment, when the genuinely expectant client became confined there. The delivery of a parcel to the former in her room was to be the sign that the baby had been born, and then she was to start putting on the agony to create as memorable an impression as possible among witnesses. 'She was to have "flying pains" and give a great deal of trouble, but not to send for a doctor.' A cab was sent from the hotel to the midwife, who was ready with her gear; the baby, dosed 'with a few drops', was hidden under her cloak. On her arrival she closeted herself with the woman, who to all intents and purposes – and much to the delight of her husband – 'gave birth'.

As well as the drugged and concealed baby, a baby-planter's smuggled-in accoutrements would have included suitably stained bed-linen and the afterbirth; a midwife told Dr Wiltshire how she carried in bottles of bullock's blood acquired from the butcher's, 'and then she can make as much mess as she likes', charging £50 for the service.[25]

The year 1870 was a vintage one for court cases involving fake deliveries. The south London midwife, Mary Hall, was prosecuted that year, but as she had connections with Margaret Waters I shall leave the case over to Chapter 11. There was *Regina* v. *Skepelhorne* and wife; they had planted a baby on behalf of a Mrs Ironside, and had used 'sheep's pluck' to represent the afterbirth. Then there was the Wicklow Peerage case. The Earl of Wicklow had married Ellen Richardson, a coachman's daughter, who held to having given birth to a son shortly before the Earl's death in 1864. But was it genuine? If so, this adventuress would have secured her future through the boy's inheritance of the family title and estate; if not, the fortune would pass elsewhere. She was challenged in the courts, and it transpired that she had been bogusly confined in the lodging house of a Mr and Mrs Bloor, who were implicated in the conspiracy, and who were identified as having obtained a new-born baby from a girl in a Liverpool workhouse just before Ellen's 'delivery'.

The last British legal case was *Salisbury* v. *Rawson* in 1895, and it is pretty certain that baby-planting was becoming just an historical curiosity by the turn of the century.[26]

11 The South London Baby-Farmers 1870

Even after the publication of the *British Medical Journal*'s revelations, the government saw no occasion to act. The exposé had focussed more on abortionists than baby-farmers and when queried by Lord Shaftesbury in the Lords, the government's response was that it was a police matter and did not require new legislation.[1]

The Metropolitan Police files indeed show an awakening of interest in suspect lying-in houses after 1868, and during 1869 and 1870 there was to be a spate of police surveillances.[2] Why, however, was it the lying-in houses and not baby-farms that were kept under watch? The fact is that the police had no real interest in infant life protection; they were blasé towards abandoned corpses. As Mary Ann Baines commented in the 1860s: '. . . they think no more of finding the dead body of a child in the street than of picking up a dead cat or dog.'[3] Their move against midwife-abortionists was motivated much more by concern to protect the lives of women from the hazards of abortion (which were immense), than to safeguard the lives of unborn babies. In this they were probably reflecting the attitude of the legislature, which never revealed any clear-cut philosophy underlying its anti-abortion law.[4] Thus, if its abhorrence of abortionists was inspired in any way by reverence for the life of the foetus, why did it miss the opportunity, during the passage of the 1861 Offences Against the Person Act, to close the 'separate existence' loophole, which left the emerging baby unprotected by the law? Appropriate conclusions can be drawn. Edwin Lankester's interpretation of the Act in 1867 was quite categoric. The severe penalties against abortionists existed *only* 'in view of the danger that threatens the life of the mother'.[5]

The police were legally shackled in the matter of surveillance. As neither midwifery nor baby-farming were in themselves illegal activities, the police could not enter the premises on mere suspicion; they needed a magistrate's warrant, which would only be forthcoming upon presentation of some direct evidence of criminal activity; and as no client of an abortionist would be ready to admit involvement in a criminal act, this evidence was exceedingly difficult to obtain.[6] Even if the police had taken a risk, and burst in, in the belief that an abortion was in progress, what would they have found? A midwife could explain away the foetus in a bucket as a miscarriage or premature delivery, and the prosecution would have to prove otherwise.

Ernest Hart had a low opinion of police will to pursue baby-farmers. He was to tell the 1871 Infant Life Protection Committee:

> I believe they had never in any instance entered a house on the
> ground of negligence, unless they have received information that
> something very nearly approaching to murder has been
> committed. . . . They only interfered in the Waters' case owing
> to the number of dead bodies found in Brixton.[7]

His attitude was: if the *BMJ* could penetrate their premises, what could the police with their greater resources achieve, if they put their minds to it? Hart seemed to forget that uncorroborated indiscretions communicated to an undercover agent would not have stood up as hard evidence in court, but nonetheless it remains true that the police had no more real interest in baby-farmers than society at large for they were too much of a social necessity. As we shall see, the netting of Margaret Waters was a fortuitous side-result of a fruitless and not particularly efficient look-out for midwives suspected of baby-dumping.

Surveillance activity against midwives started with the watch on the house of a Mrs C. Martin of 33a Dean Street, Soho, who advertised herself as a certified accoucheuse. Both the Home Office and the police had received anonymous letters about her during June and July 1869; the informant alleged she had 'destroyed no less than 555 babies during the last 18 months', charging £10 to £50 a time. Whatever the accuracy of this statement, the fact remains that she was wealthy enough to employ a coachman. The police mounted a watch on her establishment in July, but her business had also come in for unwelcome press attention from late July, arising out of a reported affiliation case in which the girl testified how her lover had given her Mrs Martin's advertising handbill, obviously with a view to her obtaining an abortion.[8] The police were frustrated; no clients were willing to give evidence, and a police report notes: 'a foreign prostitute whom the sergeant saw admitted she had gone through the operation at the house but declined to come forward if she was paid a thousand pounds.' The press attention, however, was drying up Mrs Martin's custom and she moved to Woking in late 1869, dying there of 'apoplexy' in November.

By this time the police must have been aware for some months of a lying-in establishment run by a Mrs Mary Hall of 6 Chapel-place, Coldharbour Lane, Camberwell, in south London, with definite evidence that she was at the centre of a baby-trafficking and 'sweating' network. In September 1869 a woman called Anne Cummings was convicted at the Clerkenwell Sessions with exposing a baby girl to the danger of its life.[9] Cummings had been living in lodgings in Fulham, where in April she suddenly produced a baby to her sceptical landlady, claiming she had given birth to it! After moving lodgings, she took the baby out one night in early July, returning without it and telling her landlady that she had sent it away to the countryside. However, the same night a baby girl was found lying in a doorway in Brompton, and the police 'from information received' traced it back to Cummings, who was arrested. Some of her correspondence was adduced at her trial to show that she was a baby-trafficker – taking babies for money, and then abandoning them. Since January 1869 five children had been found in the streets of Fulham, and the press and police innuendo was very strong that Cummings was the suspect, for no more babies had been found there since her arrest in July.[10] A police officer at the trial stated that they had learned from Cummings of her connection with a person 'who keeps a house in Camberwell and regularly advises that she provides lodging and accommodation for ladies during their confinement'.[11] Now, two Camberwell accoucheuses are to appear in the following account, a Mrs Castle of 164 Camberwell Road, and the aforementioned Mrs Hall. There was no evidence of any link between Mrs Castle and Cummings, but there is evidence of her link with Mrs Hall in police files, so it is the latter that the police witness must have been referring to. Cummings told the police how she had become Mrs Hall's go-between and errand-runner: Hall advertised extensively in the press, as far afield as Norwich and Yarmouth, for babies to 'adopt' for £30 to £50 lump sums a time, and then re-farm them for lesser sums. Over one six-month period she had spent £100 in advertising (these were the annual earnings of a skilled artisan then). Cummings acted as Hall's agent, for a three or four guinea-a-time commission, and it was her job to collect the babies from clients and deliver them to the sub-farmers, one of whom was Margaret Waters. Hall had the services of a doctor ready to supply her with certificates attesting to stillbirth, and a local druggist to whom she was a privileged customer for the laudanum and Syrup of Poppies requisite to her trade.[12] There is no doubt that Mary Hall was a crafty and highly organised baby-disposer, yet it was not until June 1870 that the police were to begin watching her premises!

Between the time of Cummings's arrest in July 1869 and May 1870 there were no police surveillances on lying-in houses south of the Thames, but a crop of infants' bodies, 16 in all, were found in the Brixton-Peckham area by early May, and this forced the police of P-Division to Act. Yet curiously it was not the notorious Mrs Hall's establishment they turned their attention to initially, but Mrs Castle's. Sergeant Relf[13] had been assigned the task of tracing the sources of those bodies, and his preliminary investigations (the source gives no clue as to his lead) led him to Mrs Castle, whose premises he began watching from a hired room opposite sometime in May.[14] On the 14th May a 17-year-old girl, Jeanette Cowen, who had apparently been raped by the husband of a friend she was staying with, gave birth to a boy at Mrs Castle's. On the 17th May Jeanette's father and Mrs Guerra, his landlady, arrived to take the baby away, but Jeanette, no doubt still recovering from the ordeal, stayed on till the 28th May. It was her departure, minus a baby, that Relf spotted, and he followed her cab to Mrs Guerra's lodging house at Loughborough Road, Brixton. He saw Jeanette's father and learned what had happened to the baby. Mr Cowen had replied to an advertisement in the *Lloyd's Weekly Paper* of the 1st May offering to adopt a child for £4, and through it met a woman calling herself 'Mrs Willis' at a rendezvous at Brixton Railway Station.[15] 'Mrs Willis' held herself out to be the childless wife of a shipbuilder's representative, who desperately wanted an infant of her own. In fact she was a 35-year-old widow, Margaret Waters; she had received a Baptist upbringing and an education, but her comfortable life had decayed since the death of her husband in 1864. Her subsequent business venture as a collar-manufacturer in Camberwell failed, and she took to letting rooms. One of her tenants was the mistress of a City solicitor; she gave birth in the house and paid Margaret to farm the baby out. Margaret thus drifted into baby-farming, assisted by her younger sister, Sarah Ellis.

Her biography illustrates the economic pressures on unsupported Victorian women that could drive them into sordid means of livelihood; for somebody like Margaret the only respectable alternative would have been going into service or becoming a sweatshop employee, but she had more entrepreneurial inclinations. Although she had several brothers, at least two of whom were to strain every nerve to save her from the gallows later, there is no hint as to any family intervention while her circumstances were deteriorating, though her mother disapproved of her activities. Sarah Ellis is a more obscure figure and was perhaps a fundamentally nastier piece of work than her sister, as will emerge later. Although Waters claimed many professional people among her clientele, she did not prosper, and on several occasions did a flit from her lodgings to escape creditors. Her operations were low and squalid. She advertised extensively in the press as an adopter for a lump sum, and then re-farmed the babies for weekly payments, defaulting and disappearing after a fortnight. On several occasions she had rid herself of infants by pretending to be tired and asking children in the street to hold them for sixpence and to go and buy sweets. By the time they had come out of the shop, she had disappeared.

While at Brixton in 1870 five of the infants in her care died of infections, and it was almost certainly their bodies, deposited about the streets to save the cost of a burial, from late March, that were among those that had alerted P-Division.

Mr Cowen told Relf that he agreed to let 'Mrs Willis' adopt the baby. She refused to give him her address as 'they would not wish a child they had adopted to be taken from them', a plausible enough excuse as an adoption had no legal force, and after taking the baby from Mrs Castle's house on the 17th May he handed it over to 'Mrs Willis' at the agreed rendezvous, this time at Walworth Railway Station. Now, a vital factor in the affair was that Mr Cowen really did care about the fate of his grandson, and 'Mrs Willis' promised to come to his lodgings and report on his progress a few days later, which she did. Strangely, no money had passed as yet to 'Mrs Willis', who told Cowen that the £4 stipulation in the advertisement was 'to prevent numbers of applicants', and appeared most reluctant to accept even the £2 he pressed on her for expenses; the accounts offer no suggested reason for this mystifyingly self-denying conduct by Waters. Perhaps she was playing up to him as a possible long-term easy touch(?).

Relf obviously smelled a rat about this 'Mrs Willis' and took to scanning the *Lloyd's Weekly Paper* for adoption advertisements, to try and trace her. It is curious that only now was a policeman following up an 'adoptor' as a possible origin of the dumped babies. Perhaps they gave the lying-in houses priority as the putative source of baby-trafficking. But why pick on Mrs Castle, to watch first, when Mrs Hall, who lived in the same police division, was already known to be an accomplished operator? Mrs Castle, it transpired, had a somewhat ambiguous reputation. At Waters's trial later she acknowledged approaching Waters six years before to take a client's baby off her hands, but never did business as

Waters's asking price was too high. The *Medical Times and Gazette*[16] described her as 'receiving females under peculiar circumstances', yet the fact that Mr Cowen used his own initiative to find an adoptor suggests that she was not a baby-trafficker herself, and a police report on her in 1873 stated that 'she does not fear inspection at any time'[17] and no suspicion attached to her. (So what had brought Relf to watch her in the first place?)

Relf saw the following advert on the 5th June:

ADOPTION: A good home, with a mother's love and care, is offered to a respectable person, wishing her child to be entirely adopted. Premium £5 which includes everything. Apply, by letter only, to Mrs Oliver, post office, Goar-place, Brixton.

Relf wrote an interested reply under the pseudonym 'Mr Martin' and agreed to meet 'Mrs Oliver' at Camberwell Railway Station on the 10th June. Mr Cowen came too, and watched the meeting from an unobserved position. Cowen did not recognise 'Mrs Oliver', for it was really Sarah Ellis, but he did recognise her dress as the same as that worn by 'Mrs Willis'. With the link established, Relf tailed Ellis to her lodgings at 4 Frederick Terrace, Gordon Grove, Camberwell, and the following morning, the 11th June, returned with Mr Cowen and Mrs Guerra. He pressed an entry on the doubtless startled sisters, and insisted on seeing the infant Cowen. The legality or otherwise of Relf's entry was not raised at all at the subsequent trial, and does not appear in the police files. Relf was to be hailed as a public hero subsequently by the infant life protectionists, and his exceptionally vigorous, albeit impetuous, initiative lends substance to Ernest Hart's charge of lethargy as characterising the police approach in general.[18] Perhaps, in view of the embarrassing number of babies' bodies found in P-Division, Relf was under pressure from his superiors to get results soon.

The house was sparsely furnished and malodorous. Mrs Guerra later described the condition of the baby Cowen when it was produced:

There was scarcely a bit of flesh on the bones of Miss Cowen's child, and I could recognise it only by the hair. It did not cry at all, being much too weak for that, and was evidently dying. It was scarcely human; I mean that it looked more like a monkey than a child. It was a shadow.

Mrs Waters protested that she had done her best: she had called in a doctor to attend it (later confirmed in evidence) and the

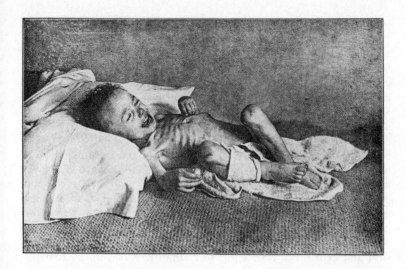

Figure 5   *From a baby-farm (c. 1891): An emaciated infant recovered by the NSPCC. It did not survive.* (Courtesy: NSPCC)

previous day had arranged for a wet-nurse to come. No evidence of a wet-nurse was produced by the defence at Waters's trial, though this would have been a decisive fact in her favour, given that breast-milk was the only effective nutriment, and it was only after she had been sentenced that one of Waters's brothers was able to obtain evidence of a wet-nurse, but it proved too late.

Relf found 5 other infants on a sofa in the kitchen, 4 of whom were badly malnourished, filthy, stinking and stupefied with opiates (as was the baby Cowen). One of the languishing 4 was Ellis's own child. In the back yard 5 more infants were found in better condition.

Waters and Ellis were taken to Lambeth Police Station; Cowen's baby was consigned to a wet-nurse, but he failed to rally and died on the 24th June. The other 9 strangers' children were taken to Lambeth Workhouse, where the 4 youngest, aged between 3 and 5 months, died unidentified and unclaimed between the 23rd June and the 11th July. The others survived, and 3 were to be reclaimed by their mothers.

The sisters were charged with conspiracy to obtain money by fraud and the murder of the baby Cowen; their trial was held at the Old Bailey between the 21st and 23rd September 1870, and drew extensive press coverage (although overshadowed by Franco-Prussian war news) as 'The Brixton Baby Farming Case'. It is interesting that of the 5 babies that died, Cowen's was the only death made the subject of a murder charge. Conceivably it was because unlike the other 4 he was not anonymous and unclaimed, but more likely it is due to the fact that the failure of even breast-milk to revive him made a murder charge more eligible than in the case of the other mites whose subsequent workhouse care might arguably have contributed to their demise.[19]

The defence counsel admitted the fraud and pressed for a manslaughter verdict instead of murder. They denied wilful intent to kill, and the burden of their case was that hand-rearing of babies was necessarily attended by malnutrition and enteric disorders under even the most well-intended régime, and the sisters had purchased a goodly amount of cow's milk, and had summoned medical advice. Prosecution medical witnesses conceded the natural dangers of hand-rearing, but against the sisters was argued their financial interest in disposing as quickly as possible of lump-sum adoptees taken for £2 to £40 a time. Relf had found that the best-nourished child on the premises was a weekly payment case, creating for the sisters an incentive to sustain it. The scale of their operations must have told against them: over the previous four years they admitted that at least 40 children had passed through their hands, and Relf found 96 pawnbrokers' tickets among Waters's effects, pledging 'a vast amount of clothing, I should say nearly a cartload'.[20] Their servant girl Ellen Connors testified how Ellis and Waters sometimes left the house at night with infants under their capes, and returned later without them, but bringing back the baby clothes; and how they hid the children when visitors arrived, for fear of putting off potential customers.

The jury's verdicts were to provoke grumbles of controversy and doubt over the next few weeks. Waters was found guilty of murder and sentenced to death; whilst Ellis was not even found guilty of manslaughter, but only of the fraud, and sentenced to eighteen months' hard labour. How do we explain this contrast? Waters, it seems, went out of her way to protect her sister and this must be the main reason. When the charge had been read at Lambeth police station she had cried out, 'Believe me, whatever my sister has done has been under my direction; I am the sinner and I must suffer.' But in fact Ellis was at least as culpable as Waters. Waters's solicitor, who fought energetically for a reprieve, maintained that it was Ellis not Waters who was the child hater, and that it was Ellis who habitually administered narcotics to the infants from a supply she kept to wean herself off alcohol; while Waters had shown her humanity in her efforts to protect her sister.[21] This was not just specious lawyer's pleading. Ellis had admitted in private to being the baby-doper: Ellis's own baby was malnourished and sedated along with the others, and she was a bad character. In May 1873, after her release from prison, she was to be convicted of stealing valuables from her employer while in service and received seven years' penal servitude.[22]

While Waters sat in the condemned cell at Horsemonger Lane Gaol a campaign for her reprieve was mounted by her brothers, her solicitor and three MPs.[23] Further evidence that Waters had indeed arranged for a wet-nurse before Cowen's death was claimed; some of the jurymen urged a reprieve, and most definitive of all were letters from two jurors indicating that the murder verdict was not unanimous; a minority had opted for manslaughter but mistakenly thought they were bound by the majority vote. This legal dynamite was presented to the Home Secretary, Henry Bruce, before Waters was hanged on October 11th, but was not reported in the press until October 29th.[24] Bruce had set his face against reprieve for Waters, and was determined to have a victim. The press had troubled thoughts about the propriety of her execution. While *The Times* of the 12th October sententiously opined that 'the law has conspicuously fulfilled its appointed office of being a terror to evil-doers', the *Daily Telegraph* of the same date described Bruce's refusal to intervene as 'more expedient than logical' and designed to create 'an example of terror'. It went on:

> It is extremely hard to be satisfied by the evidence that this woman actually 'went to work' to kill off her charges, and, failing this, while her sin might be ever so heinous, ever so serious to society, it was not 'murder' and technically she ought not to have been hanged.

But even the *Daily Telegraph* eased its conscience with the observation that however unfair Waters's fate was, similar operators must now know 'that for the future they farm these unfortunate children at the risk of their own necks'. The *South London Press* of the 8th October had already expressed its disgust with the verdict:

> We shall witness in our midst the edifying spectacle of a woman strangled as a concession to one of those outbursts of public virtue which used to excite the derision of Macaulay and Thackeray, the latter of whom designated them 'the safety valves of public vice'.

The baby Cowen had not died till a fortnight after his removal from Waters's house, and it might have been disease and not narcotic-poisoning that killed him, it is suggested. But there were to be no Parliamentary repercussions, and even the *South London Press*'s 'Startling Revelations' on October 29th that the Home Secretary had known before the 11th October that the jury's verdict was not genuinely unanimous caused not the slightest political tremor under Bruce's feet.

Why was Waters made a scapegoat? She had good reason to complain in her death cell 'confession' that people like her existed in response to a demand, and that she was being made to pay for society's sins. Her exposure had come as a climax to the public ferment over infanticide that had been building up during the 1860s; the government had been relying on the police to pull the chestnuts from the fire, and presumably now felt bound to apply the criminal sanction with a vengeance. No doubt the unusual scale of Waters's operations, plus her social origins, also helped to militate against any merciful view. Police moves against lying-in houses were proving singularly unsuccessful; perhaps the Home Secretary, baulked of any success against abortionists, decided to take it out on a captive baby-farmer instead. The government's bigger distractions, like the current Franco-Prussian war, proved prejudicial to Waters, too. As the *Illustrated Police News*, a crime rag, suggested with troubled conscience: 'appeals for mercy which, in a time when Europe was not convulsed might have been more scrupulously weighed, have been hastily thrust aside'.[25] Any hope that Waters's example would clean up the streets was immediately shattered. South of the Thames stories of discovered bodies continued to crop up. On the very day of Waters's execution an inquest was held at Camberwell on the body of a baby girl found wrapped in a paper parcel in Windsor Lane,[26] and the coroner alluded to the discovery of three other bodies in Peckham. On the 26th October he held an inquest on a baby found in a garden of a house at Dulwich,[27] and on the 3rd November the *Morning Advertiser* announced the discovery of three more tragic scraps of flotsam in south London: a boy in St Paul's churchyard, Walworth; a girl floating in the Mill Pond, Rotherhithe, and a boy floating in the Thames at Lambeth.

The *South London Press* of October 29th bitterly mocked: 'Baby farming is as lively as ever, and the only effect of what has been done has been to deal a blow at public confidence in our judicial system and those entrusted with its administration.'

Although newspapers were eagerly jumping on the baby-farm bandwagon with wild speculations, police investigations in fact failed to establish any connection between these deaths and baby-farms; but this was only part of their current frustrations. Their prime target, even since the arrest of Waters, was not the 'adoption' advertisers, against whom they had scored their one success, but, as before, the lying-in houses. Some time before July 1870 the police had become aware of a dubious midwife, a Mrs Stephens of 5 College St, Islington, who advertised in the *Daily Telegraph*.[28] In July the Home Office passed on an anonymous letter about her, alleging connections with baby-farmers, and a police watch was mounted by Sergeant Relf and Constable Tyer,[29] from a room opposite. Relf had already been involved in a watch on Mary Hall's establishment from June 1870[30] – about eleven months after the police had first become aware of her business! In the case of Mrs Stephens no inside informant could be found, only a former servant with a grudge against Mrs Stephens, whose story about a baby's body intended for the kitchen fire was discounted. Mrs Stephens was aware of the surveillance and guarded her conduct. In January 1871 the watch was called off; a second watch started later in the year also proved fruitless.

The Mary Hall affair was to end in fiasco, and must have caused Sergeant Relf, the hero of the infant life protectionists, much mortification. It is evident from Hall's comings and goings that the police surveillance was cloddish and slack, even though bodies were still being discovered around the streets of south London. Relf was involved in two simultaneous surveillances, north and south of the Thames, and perhaps was assigned specially out of his P-Division to watch Mrs Stephens as his reputation was riding high at that moment. Police liaison was conspicuously absent, for suddenly on Sunday 23rd October Mrs Hall was arrested in Peckham by a constable, acting independently of the supposed watchers, and charged at Lambeth Police Court with attempting to plant a baby on one George James Lowe[31] of Manor Lodge, Queen's Road, Peckham. This intriguing and bizarre story can only be related here in outline.

Hall had a history of arranging fake confinements,[32] and in 1868 had successfully conspired with one Annie Augusta, Lowe's mistress, to make it appear that she had given birth by him. Her motive was doubtless to secure her bond with him, since he was recently widowed. The baby died in April 1869, however, and Lowe subsequently received an anonymous letter exposing the 'plant'; this Annie vehemently denied, but Mrs Hall became *persona non grata* to the doubting Lowe. In spring 1870 Annie claimed to be pregnant again. On October 22nd, when he left for Brighton on business, Hall arrived after 4 p.m. with a concealed baby girl and, closeting herself in Annie's bedroom, 'delivered' the child. The baby in fact had been obtained from a Mrs Charlotte Farrant of Peckham who was expecting a baby she did not want. Hall had undertaken to deliver it and arrange to find it a good home for adoption. As we saw from 'A.B.'s' account in the last chapter, the synchronisation was all-important: Hall delivered Farrant's child around 4 p.m. on the 22nd, drugged it, took it by cab to Annie's address, planted it and faked up the room's appearances before the monthly nurse was due to arrive after 5 p.m. – and all coincident with the day when Lowe planned to be away from home. However, the deception came unstuck. The monthly nurse noticed the baby's sedated state, and Mrs Hall was probably already suspected by the family doctor who came later, for he insisted on examining Annie and found no signs that she had given birth. In the meantime Lowe had received a telegram at Brighton announcing the arrival and was on his way home post-haste. Hall, who had left the house, did not know she had been found out, and returned to Annie's residence next morning (the reason is not stated – but she was carrying napkins). To her surprise she was met by the furious Lowe, who now knew the whole plot, and proceeded to pursue her in a bizarre cab-chase, until he found a policeman and procured her arrest for attempted fraud. Annie was equally implicated, of course, but this adventuress ran off before the police could arrest her.

The police who were supposed to have been watching Hall's activities were now jolted into action by this surprise arrest. Sergeant Relf and Inspector Mackay searched the house and garden of Mr and Mrs Hall in late October, collecting over two hundred napkins with a large quantity of baby linen, and many letters from ladies in different parts of London. In a hat they found bonds and securities worth over £800, 'indicating the profitability of the trade'.[33] There were no babies, but the police found two illegitimate boys aged 6 and 7 that the Halls were minding for weekly sums. There was no hard evidence that babies had been murdered on the premises, and Relf's face-saving account before the 1871 Infant Life Protection Committee was larded with innuendo and hearsay to cover the police's bafflement. One of the Halls' neighbours deposed that she 'heard groanings at night through the wall' and periodically 'experienced the most sickening odour of something being burnt or boiled of a fleshy kind'. Another told variously of seeing Mrs Hall 'carry an infant from the garden into the house head downwards', of small coffins being taken away at night, a little hunchback woman carrying parcels from the house after each delivery, and Mr Hall 'throw lumps out of the clothes to two cats that he kept. . . .' No doubt a personal unsavouriness

about the Halls combined with the current baby-farm fever to
churn this bubbling witches' brew of rumour, and the police – now
only too anxious to pin a murder charge since they had been
caught napping – were only too ready to swallow it. At least six
servants in the Halls' employ had put up with them and then left
between 1866 and 1870, and from them the police totted up 46
known confinements in that period, only 8 of whose births had
been registered. All the servants told stories of babies being 'taken
away' soon after birth either by Mrs Hall or Anne Cummings. The
police traced the mothers of some of the 46 vanished babies and
learned how she charged up to £20 for a confinement and up to a
like sum to arrange the infant's adoption. The police had
information from Cummings, as we have seen, about Hall's baby-
sweating, and the scale of her advertising expenses: she advertised
in several papers including the *Daily Telegraph*, *Sunday Times*, *Lloyd's
Weekly News*, *Clerkenwell News* and the *Hereford Times*, the last
indicating the geographical scope of her operations. She had
contacts with an unknown number of sub-farmers, and Relf's
searches discovered a list of infants' clothes in Sarah Ellis's
handwriting; this established her link with Margaret Waters.

Now, one of Mrs Hall's two little boarders told the police of
babies' bodies being buried in the garden, and a more detailed
account of the same was given by Matilda Barrett, a teenage
servant employed by the Halls for a short time either in 1869 or
1870,[34] at 2 shillings a week. The police found several pits in the
garden filled with rubbish and mould, containing, said Relf, 'a
fatty sort of earth mixed with lime and cinders; there was also a
quantity of small maggots'.[35] Despite all this innuendo, of babies'
identifiable remains there were none. It should be stated here that
the burial of babies' bodies in back gardens was neither unknown
nor illegal then; it was most commonly done in the case of
stillborns to save burial fees, and even if the police had found
bones, they would have needed additional proof of murder.
Matilda told the police of being woken up one night, when there
were several expectant women in the house,[36] by the sound of a
baby crying and attendant bustle. She got out of bed and saw Mr
Hall bring a baby downstairs and bury it by candlelight in the
garden next to the fowl's house. The following morning she found
the hole filled in, and spots of blood leading to it. She also told of
another baby that disappeared soon after its birth, and of the
subsequent arrival of a 'Mrs Walters' (Waters, presumably) who
took tea in the parlour with Mrs Hall, the pair of them then
leaving the house together, with 'Mrs Walters' carrying a
mysterious brown paper parcel under her cloak.

The police in fact found no bodies in the garden, but solely on the basis of Matilda's account of Mr Hall's nocturnal movements, added a charge of murder against the Halls to charges already preferred against Mrs Hall: namely, conspiracy to defraud Mr Lowe, and exposure of the Farrant infant (by removing it to the street air immediately after its birth). At the Lambeth Police Court preliminary hearing on November 15th Matilda Barrett retailed her lurid story in the witness box. Barrett had a grudge against the Halls over her dismissal, and her story came over as a gothic farrago which the *South London Press*, still flushed with indignation over the scapegoating of Waters, ridiculed as 'very like a page from Eugene Sue or Wilkie Collins'.[37]

The subsequent withdrawal of the murder charge by the bumbling police only drew a further broadside from the paper on the 26th November against their 'frightfully mismanaged' handling of the Hall affair: 'we have something worse than a fault: we have a blunder, the effect of which is to shake still further public confidence in the intelligence, sagacity and power of the police.'

In the event, when she appeared at the Old Bailey on the 13th December, only the conspiracy charge was proceeded with; and she received two years' hard labour and £100 fine.

The South London Baby Farmers episode reflected little credit on the police. Even when they were hunting the baby-droppers as opposed to the abortionists, their instinct was still to stake out a lying-in house, like Mrs Castle's. Even if midwives were suspected as a prime source of abandoned babies, the fact that the police's one coup had been achieved by following up an *adoption* advertisement, plus the fact that Relf's dubious entry tactics had not provoked any legal repercussions, should have suggested the wisdom of a change of strategy. After all, a baby-farmer caught with a brood of neglected infants would be more vulnerable to a charge than a midwife with a 'stillborn' baby on her premises. The whole muddle of police strategy was due to a lack of any real interest in baby-farmers at all; their target was abortionists.

The Waters affair led to the creation of an Infant Life Protection Society in 1870 (see next chapter). One of its founder members, the well-meaning but do-gooding Reverend Oscar Thorpe of Christ Church, Camberwell – Waters's and Hall's neck of the woods – was plying the police with newspaper clippings of advertisements for lying-in houses up to late 1873,[38] and the police felt duty bound to follow them up. In no case did the police make a prosecution: either the midwives appeared respectable, or, in the few suspicious cases, there was no hard evidence, and the police were losing heart. They were getting quietly exasperated with the indiscriminate flow

Figure 6 *An artist's impression of incidents from Margaret Waters's career. The first picture is self-explanatory. The second picture shows an episode where she got some children to hold a baby, claiming she felt tired, and then disappeared (see p. 97). (Source:* Illustrated Police News 15 Oct. 1870. *Courtesy:* British Library Newspaper Collection.)

of offerings from the Rev. Mr Thorpe,[39] but even he was running out of steam as the Waters affair receded in time.

The police file on baby-farming thins down very abruptly after 1873, and closes in 1877, as police apathy resumed its sway. But the Waters affair did at last jolt Parliament into action, thanks to pressure from the newly-formed Infant Life Protection Society.

12 Infant life protection legislation 1870–90

In the summer of 1870, under stimulus from the build-up of the Margaret Waters affair, an Infant Life Protection Society was formed, combining leading lights of the Harveian Society, such as Hart and Curgenven, with non-medical activists like the Rev. Oscar Thorpe, and the invaluable William Thomas Charley, a barrister and MP for Salford since 1868, who was to spearhead the campaign for legislation in the House of Commons. Their prospectus listed the Society's objectives under four heads:

1 the registration of foster-nurses;
2 the formation of local committees to select and supervise these nurses;
3 the boarding-out of children from workhouses;
4 amendments to the laws of bastardy, registration of births and deaths and the law of evidence in the case of infanticide.

Article 3 was in fact to be fulfilled by the government's own initiative in the Boarding-Out Order of November 1870 (see Chapter 6). Article 4 does not mention another objective that Charley was to pursue, namely a law against 'seduction'. The background to, and activity over, the items in 4 will be looked at in subsequent chapters. The Society's first objective was the registration and supervision of child-minders. The Liberal government had higher priorities, such as Ireland and education, but the ILPS was told that the government would not obstruct any private member's initiative.[1] The Bill which Charley introduced in February 1871 was Curgenven's brainchild, for he had previewed it before the NAPSS in 1869.[2] The Bill proposed that all child-minders, board and day alike, be licensed by justices of the peace; they would be regularly inspected by the local Poor Law medical officer, and a limit was to be set on the numbers of infants a nurse could care for at any one time. As Curgenven was to point out, this only served to extend to helpless infants the same kind of protection that the Lunacy Act already accorded the insane.[3]

The Bill entailed an extension of Poor Law administration and expenditure that the government could not countenance, and its licensing provisions – particularly the inclusion of day-nurses – provoked howls of protest from the emergent female suffrage and emancipationist movement, the National Society for Women's Suffrage, which formed a 'Committee for Amending the Law in Points where it is Injurious to Women' to fight the Bill. They claimed that child-minding, especially day-minding, was an indispensable source of income to poor women, who thus provided a vital service for unsupported mothers. Compulsory licensing would reduce the supply of minders, put up charges, and so lead to more maternal infanticide. The Bill's promoters were accused of singling out women for regulation, and ignoring the obligations of male sexual exploiters who created the problem (an argument that paralleled their grievance against the anti-prostitution Contagious Diseases Acts), but this was unfair, as the ILPS had affiliation law reform among its objectives too.

Charley backed down in the face of this outcry, and shelved his bill when the government agreed to set up a Parliamentary Select Committee on Infant Life Protection to review the whole social problem and make recommendations. Its members included Charley himself and Dr Lyon Playfair, the distinguished scientist, MP and veteran public health reformer. The proceedings and report of this Committee[4] form a comprehensive and seminal source of information, and references to evidence given before it have already been scattered about the book. The Committee believed that while criminal baby-farming, with the intention of making away with the children, was known to occur in London and the larger Scottish towns, it was much rarer in Lancashire and Yorkshire, where mill girls handed their infants over to day- and week-nurses, and where 'carelessness and not crime is the principal cause of mortality among children put out to nurse'. However, this comparison should be treated with some reserve. 'Criminal' baby-farming happened to be a splash in London because of the Waters affair, and in Scotland because of the exposé by the *North British Daily Mail*. The recent Manchester case of Frances Rogers, a board-minder sentenced to 20 years' penal servitude in 1871 for the attempted murder by wilful neglect of infants in her care,[5] was dismissed before the Committee by coroner Edward Herford as unique in his 30-year experience as a public official in the city. And Dr Syson, the medical officer of health for Salford (Charley's own constituency, interestingly), also affirmed that criminal baby-farming was unknown to him there. But all that the two witnesses were saying was that they were not *aware* of it; the Barnes case of

1879 (see later this chapter), and the Pearson case of 1890 (see Chapter 15) indicate that there was more criminality in the north-west than the authorities recognised.

The Committee was not alarmist about the extent of criminal infanticide, for it acknowledged that negligence, poverty and ignorance caused 'by far the larger number' of deaths among nurse-children, but it gave frightful estimates of their death rates from 40 per cent in the best-run homes to 90 per cent in the worst, the victims being overwhelmingly illegitimate. However, this distinction between 'criminal' and 'non-criminal' baby-farming is somewhat blurred by the Committee's recognition that single mothers' indifference to the survival of their infants, and the babies' consignment through the shame and poverty to 'some inferior house', were responsible for the horrific death rate.

In its conclusions the Committee expressed a broad aspiration for improved public health measures to protect infant life, but its specific proposals against abuses included compulsory registration of births and deaths, the licensing and police inspection of all lying-in establishments, and the registration of board-nurses (but *not* day-minders, who, the Committee felt, performed a necessary neighbourly service in mill areas and should not be encumbered). Beyond its terms of reference, it suggested for consideration an anti-seduction precaution of raising the age of consent for girls (then 12); the liberalisation of the affiliation law; the banning of child life insurance (see Chapters 15 and 16); and compulsory qualifications for midwives.

Girded by such recommendations, Charley reintroduced an Infant Life Protection Bill as the first of a battery of laws the ILPS was planning, but the 1872 Bill was a heavily diluted measure and repeesented the lowest common denominator its sponsors knew to be acceptable to the House. The Act as passed[6] provided that all persons receiving for hire *more than* one infant under the age of 1 for a period longer than 24 hours must register with their local authority. The authorities were empowered to refuse to register unsuitable premises and could fix the maximum number of permitted nurselings. The nurses had to keep a record of the baby-traffic: whom the infants were received from, when they were removed, and by whom. Deaths of infants in their houses had to be reported directly to the coroner. The penalties for contravention were up to six months' prison or a £5 fine.

However, there were no express provisions for inspection, and another serious loophole was the exemption of one-baby foster-homes from the registration. So long as a nurse had only one infant under 12 months, she could cram in as many more as she saw fit above that age without having to register; and she could allow a rapid succession of lone infants to die off without having to register. Section 13 contained other exemptions: relatives and guardians (even though paid), charitable institutions, and recipients of boarded-out children under the Poor Law.

The *Saturday Review* dismissed it as 'a poor little Bill . . . feebly introduced'[7] and the ILPS were the first to concede that it was an unsatisfactory compromise. Indeed it turned out an utter failure, as Benjamin Waugh, Director of the NSPCC, branded it in 1890, a 'pompous introduction to nothing' whose 'main effect is to teach farmers how to escape its provisions and to conduct their business as they like'.[8]

The Metropolitan Board of Works (the forerunner of the London County Council) turned out to be the only authority in the country to take the Act seriously[9] and right from the start was complaining of its weaknesses in its annual reports and in correspondence with the Home Office.[10] Very few persons were coming forward to register, and in June 1873 the Board suggested to the Home Office that the Act be extended to 'one-child' cases and the protected age raised to 7, and that local authority and police powers of entry be clarified and extended. The Home Secretary at that time, Robert Lowe, was adamantly opposed to a strengthened Act, especially in regard to entry powers, as it would constitute 'an intolerable interference with the non-criminal majority of the population', and in 1877 the Home Secretary R.A. Cross suggested to the Board that instead of just complaining about its deficiencies, they should try to enforce it more effectively, before any amendments were considered. Accordingly in February 1878 the Sanitary and Special Purposes Committee of the Board (later the Public Control Committee of the LCC) appointed Samuel Babey as an Inspector of baby-farms, the only one for a city of some 3½ million people – but the only one as yet appointed by any authority anywhere!

The 1872 Act was constantly sniped at by the *British Medical Journal* which in the late 1870s was regularly reporting inquests on infants from unregistered baby-farms, and 1879 in particular was a vintage year for baby-farm scandals. In August the name of Amelia Dyer surfaced for the first time.[11] She ran a foster-home at Bristol where nine children had died in the previous two years; a doctor's refusal to grant a death certificate in one case resulted in an inquest. Her exposure led to a prosecution for failing to register her house and she received six months' prison. This was but a prelude to more lurid notoriety seventeen years later.

Also in August, Annie Took of Exeter was executed for infanticide, the first baby-minder since Margaret Waters.[12] Took was only known ever to have taken this one child, an illegitimate baby boy, which she received for £12 to cover the first year of its keep. She killed and dismembered it when the money ran out, but newspaper accounts of the grisly discovery of its remains led the trail back to her.

The John and Catherine Barnes affair in September and October[13] exposed an extensive, professional operation and the utter failure of the local authority to apply the 1872 Act. From their home in Birkenhead, on the Cheshire side of the Mersey estuary facing Liverpool, they advertised extensively and in the ten years before their trial at least eighteen babies had passed through their hands. Neighbours' suspicions had been aroused by the sounds of children and a police inspector who happened to be a friend of Mr Barnes called under pretence of a social visit. Three of the four infants found were in a shockingly emaciated state. Two of these died subsequently; the Barnes were indicted for the murder of the infant Alice Rodenhurst and received life sentences for manslaughter. The case has an aftermath pointing to more concealed baby-farming in the north-west than the 1871 Select Committee was led to believe. Following the trial, the board of guardians at Toxteth, Liverpool, received a spate of applications from foster-mothers to take infants off their hands;[14] they knew their incomes were insufficient to support the children, and were obviously worried by the Barnes example.

March 1880 must have shone like a false dawn for the Metropolitan Board of Works, when they received a letter from Mr Cross, Home Secretary, inviting their opinions on reform of the 1872 Act. Among its recommendations the Board urged extension to 'one-child' cases up to 5 years old, pointing out that of 1,096 foster homes it had investigated only 64 came within the Act. 'Lump sum' adoptions, where the farmer had a presumed interest in allowing the child to die off quickly, should be banned. The exemption of charities should be reconsidered, as some of them were dubious and cases of serious neglect of infants had come to light.

However, a general election at this time brought a change of government. The new Liberal Home Secretary, Sir William Harcourt, received approaches from the Infant Life Protection Society and the Metropolitan Board of Works, now that their hopes of action had been raised by his predecessor's initiative; but the Home Office did nothing, and we can only conclude that this departmental fitfulness was due to the fact that infant life protection 'did not excite much public interest and was not one which was widely known';[15] only scandals were likely to stir the government, and the next clutch of shockers did not come till 1888.

How was Samuel Babey coping on his own in London in the meantime? Babey relied on the police, registrars, Poor Law relieving officers, and charity officers, for information about the existence of baby-farms, and he regularly scanned the newspapers for advertisements. He had to travel the length and breadth of the Metropolis to check if they ought to be registered, a task made no easier by the undefined position of his right of entry. The results were very disappointing. In 1886, for example, only 25 houses were registered in the whole of London with 132 infants under 1 year old, 30 of whom died in the course of the year.[16] Hunting out baby-farms was like looking for a needle in a haystack, and he was on a hiding to nothing.

In 1888 three notorious cases attracted press attention: in Mr and Mrs Hayes's Swindon baby-farm case, infant life insurance figures prominently, and it will be looked at again in Chapter 16. They were linked as sub-farmers to the notorious 'baby-sweater' (the term was now coming into common usage), Mrs Jane Arnold of Wolverton.[17] Mrs Arnold made an industry out of passing on her lump-sum adoptees to third parties for lesser sums, and then defaulting on the payments. Twenty-four infants had been involved in her career. She made the mistake of trying the trick on Mrs Saunders of Richmond, whose house she had arranged to use as a letter-drop for replies to her advertisements. Mrs Saunders wrote warning letters to her, and called in a policeman. Mrs Arnold decided to return to Saunders to pay off the arrears and reclaim the child, but was met by the policeman at the house: her history now came to light as background to an inquest held under Coroner Athelstan Braxton Hicks on a baby boy she had deposited with a registered baby-farmer, Mrs Jessie Chapman. Arnold had left food for the boy and he died subsequently. As a registered minder Mrs Chapman had to notify the coroner. The inquest ruled out foul play; but Mrs Arnold's operations came in for strong censure from Hicks, and occasioned the jury's call for registration of all lump-sum payments.

The Jessie King case was the most grisly.[18] In late October 1888 some boys playing in an Edinburgh street lighted on a bundle which was found to contain the decomposed remains of a baby boy. A landlady in the street had become suspicious of her tenant (Jessie) who, when she had moved in that June, had brought a baby, which had since disappeared. Jessie told the landlady that she had adopted it for £25 and had now resold it for a lesser sum. With the discovery of the body in the street, the landlady called in the police. Jessie produced the infant's vaccination certificate, which referred to a *girl*, but the police were not satisfied and insisted on searching the house. In the cellar they found the corpse of a baby girl; Jessie broke down and confessed to its murder, and also revealed that she had murdered the boy some months before, smuggling its remains from lodging to lodging before casting it carelessly in the street where she was currently residing. Both infants were the illegitimate offspring of servants, and had been 'adopted' through advertisements she had placed in the press. Jessie was hanged in March 1889, the second baby-farmer since Margaret Waters.

It appears to have been more the Arnold case that convinced the current Home Secretary, Henry Matthews, of the need to close loopholes in the 1872 Act,[19] as she had been able to evade registration quite legally by 'sweating' infants singly in rapid succession.[20] Matthews circularised all local authorities for reform suggestions,[21] and introduced a government bill in 1890; its subsequent history will be taken up in Chapter 17.

13 Bastardy, seduction and infanticide law reform 1870–1900

With the Infant Life Protection Act safely passed, Charley now introduced his 'Bill to Amend the Bastardy Laws and for the Better Protection of Girls'[1] in furtherance of the 1871 Select Committee's recommendations. The first part broadened the affiliation process and removed some legal anomalies; the second, and unrelated, part provided for raising the age of sexual consent to 14, but this was dropped from the final Bastardy Act which passed without controversy in 1872.[2] Under its terms a woman retained her independent right to initiate affiliation proceedings, but the Boards of Guardians were also now empowered to do so on her behalf. The maximum maintenance was raised to 5 shillings a week until the child was 16, instead of 13 as before, and it now remained payable even if the woman married another man; this removed, as Charley saw it, a blight to a 'fallen woman's' marriage chances and a motive for abandoning her infant. The thirteen-week maximum arrears payment under the 1844 Act was abolished, but the 'corroborative evidence' rule, felt to be essential to protect men from blackmail, remained unaltered.

It was difficult to know where to pitch the right balance in affiliation law to maximise the protection to child life. Over-generosity to women, it was felt, would encourage female looseness, and increase illegitimacy, from which most child destruction sprang; and an over-stringent law could be self-defeating in another way, as Curgenven cautioned the 1871 Committee: the more responsible the father was made, the greater his incentive to prevail on the woman to dispose of the infant by a lump-sum adoption,[3] so baby-farming would continue to flourish.

The 1872 Act does not seem to have had any dramatic effect on the proportion of single mothers going to court (see Chapter 4). In the 1890s the official number of illegitimate births each year was 37,000 to 38,000 in England and Wales; roughly 8,500 women a year were making applications, of whom 6,000 to 6,500 were successful – that is, under a sixth of all new single mothers.[4]

The corroborative evidence rule, and the intimidating prospect for modest girls in applying in open court, remained great deterrents[5] and it is doubtful if the supportive power now given to the Poor Law helped much. In the 1880s Kensington Union was only securing orders for 3 per cent of the applications they made, and this was ascribed largely to the nature of the pauper girls they were acting for, 'either of notoriously loose character' or 'silly country girls' who had been led astray, so that corroborative evidence was impossible.[6] Between 1906 and 1908 Bethnal Green Union obtained only nine orders on 81 cases referred for action.[7] A major handicap to action was the rapid passage of single mothers who wanted to leave the lying-in wards and get out of the system as soon as possible.

It should not be overlooked, too, that while it had taken twenty-eight years to double the maintenance in 1872, it was to be another forty-six years before the 5 shillings a week maximum was to be raised again, and it is likely that with the inflation after 1900 the struggle for maintenance must have seemed less and less worthwhile.

It is appropriate here to mention another enactment arising from a recommendation of the 1871 Select Committee – the Birth and Death Registration Act of 1874. Dr Lyon Playfair was the prime mover for the Act. In 1871 he had introduced a private member's bill but withdrew it when the government promised a bill of its own, which, after some foot-dragging, it finally introduced in 1874. The workings of the Act will be examined in Chapter 14.

Charley's efforts on behalf of the ILPS to secure a Seduction Act had only the most limited success. The object was to obtain a civil process for 'breach of promise' accessible to poor girls (analogous to Mr Miles's bill of 1840[8]), and to criminalise the grosser forms of male sexual exploitation by raising the age of consent. His bills of 1873 and 1874[9] proposed that representatives for the girl could bring an action for breach of promise without having to establish a direct legal interest, but the House rejected them. The bills were (exaggeratedly) feared as a licence for foolish (working-class) virgins or blackmailing bounty-hunters. His Offences Against the Person Amendment Bill of 1875 tried a different approach: the Offences Against the Person Act of 1861 by s.49 had made it a criminal offence for any person to entice a girl under 16 by 'false pretences' and 'false representations' to have sexual intercourse with a third party. This was aimed against procurement into prostitution, and Charley's bill proposed extending it to enticement into intercourse with oneself. His hope was to raise the protected age to 21, and thereby create a completer criminal alternative to 'breach of promise',[10] which would be readily accessible to poor girls. This was rejected by the House, but a residue of his bill, a measure for raising the age of consent to 13, did pass.

Charley passed from the political scene when he lost his seat at the 1880 general election, but the 'seduction' question continued to crop up from time to time. In 1881 Benjamin Scott, the Chamberlain of London, told the Lords Select Committee on the Protection of Young Girls that juries should be empowered to return a criminal seduction verdict where proof of rape fails in a prosecution brought by a servant against her master, 'as the influence possessed by a master over a young girl prevents the vigorous resistance which would be offered to a stranger, and enables the defendant to escape any punishment'.[11]

In 1885 the age of consent was raised to 16;[12] in 1892 the last attempt at a Seduction Bill by a group of MPs failed to get beyond first reading.[13]

Were there in fact many 'seductions' of teenage girls leading to illegitimate births and infanticide? Reported trials indicate that the commonest age-bracket for defendants in infanticide cases was the twenties, and as ovulation started at 15 or 16 in Victorian times, Charley's efforts to raise the age of consent must be seen merely as a tilt against male depravity, and only most indirectly a strike at infanticide; however, comprehensive statistics from France in the late nineteenth century showed that 12–16-year-olds formed 23 per cent of all defendants, the 21–30-year-olds forming 45 per cent.[14]

I noted in Chapter 8 how the Infant Life Protection Society was to take up the fight for an Infanticide Act. Between 1873 and 1876 Charley was to introduce four bills inspired by the 1866 Capital Punishment Commission's recommendations, and although he was to receive powerful support from some influential MPs like Sir John Holker, a leading Conservative lawyer, obstructionism in the House succeeded in sinking them all.[15]

His second bill in 1874 in fact coincided with separate moves by the 'jurists' (see Chapter 8) to introduce a Homicide Law Amendment Bill.[16] This was the brainchild of Sir James Stephen, and its infanticide provisions included a penalty for wilful pre-natal neglect (by failing to arrange for assistance at the birth) thereby causing the baby's death. The two bills overlapped and were referred to a Select Committee, but failed to pass into law.

After the failure of Charley's fourth bill, the ILPS, the British Medical Association and the Obstetric Society sent a deputation to Sir John Holker, now Attorney-General, who assured them of his interest, for he was preparing to take in hand a comprehensive codification of the Criminal Law, based on a draft prepared by

Sir James Stephen in 1878. This was referred to a Royal Commission in 1879, but Holker's bill came too late in the 1879 session and was abandoned.

The 'jurists' were too disheartened to try again for twenty years, and with Charley's loss of his seat at the 1880 general election, the infant life protectionists lost their Parliamentary champion and their Society faded away.

In the courts the 'solemn mockery' of acquittal or absurdly light punishment of infanticidal mothers persisted into the early twentieth century. For example, in 1904 at the Central Criminal Court, a 20-year-old servant, Louisa Lunn, was tried for strangling her new-born baby and stuffing its body up the chimney of the house in Wandsworth where she worked. The jury's verdict was manslaughter, with a recommendation for mercy. The judge discharged her conditionally on a £10 recognisance, and the spectators burst into applause.[17]

However, there is evidence of an increasing frequency of murder verdicts against child-killers from the 1860s. Among women convicted but reprieved there was only Charlotte Winsor in the 1860s; but there were 11 in the 1870s and 15 between 1880 and 1886 alone;[18] but some were killers of other people's children and the figures perhaps reflect improved policing, for broader evidence indicates a decline in infanticide over this period (see Chapter 19). Juries were more inclined under judges' prompting to return a manslaughter verdict, but occasionally a really tragic but incontrovertible murder verdict jolted the public conscience over ordeal by trial. In 1895 Amy Gregory was convicted of murdering her baby which was found strangled on Richmond towing path. She had given birth in the local workhouse after separating from her husband, and put the child out to nurse until she could no longer keep up payments, and had to retrieve it. Her father turned her out of the house in bitter weather with the baby and, lacking a job and shelter, she had finally killed it in desperation. After solemnly pronouncing the death sentence, the judge assured her he would pass on a recommendation for mercy to the Home Secretary.[19]

There appears to have been a humanisation in prison treatment of such reprieved women between 1896 and 1908. In 1896 one commentator complained of the excessive 10–12-year prison sentences they usually had to serve,[20] but in 1908, following the tragic case of Daisy Lord, the Home Office assured the NSPCC that the women were placed under the eye of voluntary ladies committees in jail to assist their rehabilitation; if they responded, they were conditionally released and a watch was kept on their progress.[21]

   This was not enough for organisations like the Penal Reform League and the Society for the Abolition of Capital Punishment, which was now just becoming active against the 'cruel farce' of death sentencing in infanticide cases.[22] The revived Parliamentary interest in infanticide law reform after a lapse of over twenty years led to a series of bills between 1908 and 1914,[23] but success was not to come till after the First World War (see Chapter 20).

14   Cradle and grave: birth and death registration and infanticide

Prior to 1836, parish churches' baptismal and burial registers provide the nearest approximation to a national record of the mortal passage. The Registration Act of 1836[1] (applying to England and Wales only) established a system of civil registration under a Registrar General, with a national network of super-intendent and local registrars. The object of the Act was primarily to collect statistics, a fundamental tool for the emerging lobby in public health matters; it was not intended as an aid to the detection of foul play. Birth registration was not even compulsory under the Act; while the obligation to register deaths, in a curious roundabout way, only applied at the point of burial, not at the time of death itself; and this was to be crucial in assisting the concealment of deaths under suspicious circumstances. Under s.27 a burial could only take place if the person in charge of the funeral received a registrar's burial certificate from the bereaved. However, the burial could legally take place without the certificate so long as the person conducting the funeral notified the registrar within seven days.

Applicants for registrars' certificates were not obliged to supply a medical certificate of causes of death; the Act does not mention medical certificates at all. Only those persons who happened to be present at the death or attended the deceased during the last illness (which might or might not include a 'doctor') were required to give the registrar details of what they *thought* were the causes of death, and this formed the official entry. Before the Medical Register Act of 1858 there was no standard qualification for a doctor, and any quack could style himself as such, so a 'medical certificate' in 1836 carried no singular authority. If the registrar was only notified of the death after the burial under s.27, his task was to summon informed parties to ascertain the cause of death in the same way, but even if he was suspicious enough to think of notifying the coroner, decomposition of the interred corpse was likely to be fairly advanced: working-class practice, in the early Victorian period, especially in Irish immigrant areas, was to keep the corpse in the house sometimes up to a fortnight before burial[2] so the time-lag before the registrar was finally notified could be considerable. Stillborns were not registrable as they had come into the world already dead, so no official statistics of stillbirths were compiled; and if the graveyard officers were satisfied by assurances that the infant was stillborn, there was no requirement to notify the registrar. All they usually asked for was some unofficial written attestation from any woman calling herself a 'midwife' that she had been in attendance at the delivery and the child was born dead.

The Scottish Registration Act of 1854[3] was on paper more advanced than the English: registration of births was compulsory; and it expressly allowed for application to registrars for burial certificates to be accompanied by a death certificate signed by a 'medical person' who was in attendance upon the deceased during his last illness. However, this was not compulsory; obviously it was impossible if no doctor ever attended the deceased, and it was up to the registrar to decide what action to take (if any) should a medical certificate be absent. The law did make it obligatory for the doctor last in attendance to supply a certificate on demand, but doctors occasionally refused certificates as a way of alerting registrars to their suspicions. The English Registration Act of 1874,[4] passed in the wake of the recommendations of the 1871 Infant Life Protection Committee, followed similar lines: births now had to be registered, but there was a 42-day period of grace (in Scotland it was 21 days); this created a loophole, as it gave mothers so inclined time to conceal the baby's existence from officialdom before she came within the purview of registration law. The provision for death certificates and the practice surrounding it followed the Scottish model, except that the English law specified signature by a 'registered medical practitioner' – now that qualifications were definable since the 1858 Medical Registration Act. There was nothing in the 1854 and 1874 Acts to stop registrars accepting certificates from midwives, herbalists and the like in lieu, especially where there was no qualified doctor who had last attended the deceased.

Registration of stillbirths was still omitted under the 1874 Act (as in Scotland) and the only precaution in the 1874 Act (but not in the Scottish law) against the fraudulent burial of live-borns as stillborns was to require their delivery to a cemetery to be accompanied by a written declaration of stillbirth from either a doctor or a 'midwife' – in other words, to make the cemeteries' customary requirement before 1874 now statutory. In addition, where infants were buried in coffins along with adults (not an uncommon practice, as we shall see) the person conducting the funeral must be notified of their identity and whether stillborn or live-born. As with the 1836 Act, the application for registrars' certificates was linked to the timing of burials, not the instant of death, and burials could still take place before the registrar was notified. The reader should be clear of the distinction between the registrar's burial certificate and the 'insurance' certificate he was empowered to issue for a fee to be presented in an insurance claim on the deceased's life. This was governed by separate legislation.

The 1874 Act remained unaltered until the Registration Act of 1926. Victorian registration processes were riddled with loopholes and widely abused; the secret or falsified disposal of babies in cemeteries around the country was an everyday occurrence, and the revelations of the 1893 Select Committee on Death Certification were to show how common such malpractices remained even at the end of the nineteenth century; it was not the law on paper, but changes in social conditions from the early twentieth century, that were to suppress them eventually. I shall now examine the workings of the Victorian registration and burial system in regard to the facility it afforded to the concealment of infanticide.

First, registration of birth. Although not compulsory before 1874 voluntary registration was prevalent before then because of the advantages to a parent of having a birth certificate, to prove, for example, the child's eligibility for a burial insurance policy, or to start work. The registrar was not infrequently given false information, however, as we have seen in Chapter 4; estimates of non-registrations before 1874 varied. In 1867 Edwin Lankester reckoned that 15 to 25 per cent of all births in some parts of London were not registered;[5] the government's estimate in 1871 was 20,000 to 30,000 live births out of 800,000 a year[6] in England and Wales. In the case of illegitimates, non-appearance in the official returns has two elements: non-registration, and false representation as legitimate to the registrar.[7] We can be sure that the non-registration rate among illegitimates was significantly higher than among legitimates, as unmarried mothers' motives for secrecy were all the greater, and it is for this reason that the 1871 Select Committee strongly recommended compulsory birth registration – but kept silent over the more contentious question of registration of stillbirths. Even Lyon Playfair's Registration Bill of 1871 (Chapter 13) dared not include this, and we shall be looking at the reasons later in this chapter.

How efficient were the registrars as functionaries? Under the 1836 Act the local Poor Law unions became responsible for appointing registrars, and they generally gave first refusal as superintendent registrars to the clerks of the unions, while local registrars' jobs went commonly to subordinate Poor Law officials. The job was a sideline and part-time;[8] medical appointments were rare – Dr Bachoffner, Superintendent Registrar of St Marylebone in the 1860s, was an able exception. In 1843 Henry Coppock, solicitor and town clerk of Stockport, and himself a registrar, commented to Edwin Chadwick, who was investigating national burial as a supplement to his great official public health inquiry: 'None of our registrars . . . are medical men and no case of infanticide has been discovered through the instrumentality of the Registration Act.'[9]

The next fifty years saw very little change. In 1893 over half the 1,500 registrars in England and Wales were Poor Law relieving officers; 145 were solicitors and solicitors' clerks; 124 were farmers; 69 were grocers. Only 72 were medical men, and the remainder was an assortment of schoolteachers, tradesmen and artisans.[10] Earnings were based on the number of entries in their books, and they were not above adding fictitious names.[11] Since, as part-timers, they were not always available, mourners had a plausible excuse for not presenting the officiating clergyman with a burial certificate at the time of the service.

The 1836 Act gave registrars discretion to refer doubtful cases to the coroner, and the 1874 Act made this obligatory where death was due to violence or attended by suspicious circumstances, whether or not there was an accompanying medical certificate; and in 1885 the Registrar General instructed local registrars to refer cases automatically where the cause of death was stated to be 'unknown' (whether certified or not) or 'sudden' and was not certified.[12] This anticipated the 1887 Coroners Act which obliged coroners to conduct inquests in such cases, and accounts for the rising proportion of inquests to deaths from 1885 (see Chapter 7).

In 1858 11 per cent of *all* deaths were unaccompanied by any kind of medical certificate, but in the last quarter of the century the proportion fell sharply; this was partly due to registration practices from 1874 which made it increasingly likely for registrars to refer uncertified deaths to the coroners. But the rapid expansion of life insurance among the working classes in the late nineteenth century must have also strongly reinforced the trend, as a medical certificate was a legal requisite in applying for a registrar's 'insurance' certificate under the Friendly Societies Act of 1875 (see Chapter 16).

By 1882 3.9 per cent of all deaths in England and Wales were uncertified, and a decade later this was down to 2.7 per cent; in Scotland, however, the figure was 5.8 per cent in 1893.[13] These averages concealed a wide local variation, however, and the figures were lowest where the local coroner's known penchant for inquests was greatest.[14] They also concealed huge differences according to the deceased's age. In Glasgow (where a record of dead infants' legitimacy status was kept) between 1886–90 23 per cent of all legitimate infants and 29 per cent of all illegitimate infants who died under 1 month old were medically uncertified, compared with 5.8 and 18.8 per cent respectively for 1- to 12-month-olds, and 3.2 and 11.6 per cent respectively for 1- to 5-year-olds.[15] The attitude probably was that the younger you were, the more expected the death, so the less 'necessity' there was felt for the support of a doctor's certificate; and the prodigious figure below one month is swollen by the fact that most burial insurances did not pay out on deaths so young, so reducing further the motive for a doctor's certificate. The disparity between the levels for legitimates and illegitimates must also have an insurance link, as insurance on illegitimates' lives was less frequent (see Chapter 16). However, the scale of Glasgow's non-certifications remains surprising in view of the city's policy since 1873 of sending its sanitary officers to follow up every case of an uncertified infant death.

How reliable was the medical information supplied to the registrars? The more one looks into the answers, the more apparent it becomes that the whole construction of the Registrar General's annual return is a house of cards. As early as 1867 the Manchester and Salford Sanitary Association dismissed them as 'to a great extent useless as scientific records and comparatively useless as a basis for legislation for sanitary purposes'.

Where there was no medical certificate, the registrar might accept the opinions of the untutored working people who happened to be in the same lodgings as the deceased and the registrar might even concoct a technical 'cause of death' from their descriptions. As the Medical Officer of Health for Bradford remarked in the 1880s:

> Gastritis and meningitis [for example] are not diseases either
> known to the laity, or such as they could diagnose. I entertain no
> doubt that in many cases the registrar, who never saw the cases,
> suggested the names on hearing some the symptoms alleged to
> have been present in some of the cases.[16]

Doctors' certificates themselves had long come in for strong criticism. Dr George Greaves of Manchester in 1863 had complained of doctors' readiness to sign certificates without having seen the body, and this was repeated by the veteran Manchester coroner Edward Herford in 1871.[17] The 1874 Registration Act under s.20 laid down that where the deceased 'has been attended during his last illness by a registered medical practitioner' the latter must fill in a certificate upon request, but it did not specify the maximum time limit since the last attendance; weeks may have passed since the doctor saw the patient, and it was notorious that they could be easily induced by relatives to fill in certificates giving the last symptoms they could remember as the cause of death. The official blank certificates issued free to doctors by registrars under the Act did not require a doctor to specify the period of time since the last attendance; nor did the pro-formas seek to elicit the background causes of death; a statement of the immediate symptoms only was sufficient. For instance, if the doctor saw an emaciated baby, he need only write 'atrophy' on the form; if he suspected a history of wilful neglect it was entirely up to his own conscience whether to refuse a certificate and perhaps notify the coroner directly, or to write some alerting comment on it for the registrar's attention.

Doctors were not legally obliged to fill in every detail on the certificate, nor to use the official forms at all. Some unscrupulous doctors printed their own forms omitting the words 'attended in the last illness' and were ready to issue certificates to order for a fee.[18]

The expanding demand for infant life insurance in the last quarter of the nineteenth century gave the abuses and laxities associated with medical certification a worrying new dimension. The NSPCC, newly-formed in 1889, came to grips with the issue once it had safely secured the passage of the Prevention of Cruelty to Children Act in that year. It was raised before the Commons Select Committee on Friendly Societies of 1889, the Lords Select Committee on Child Life Insurance in 1890, and the Commons Select Committee on Death Certification in 1893.

What were the reasons for the laxity? First, filling in certificates was an obligatory, unpaid chore, and even where intended for presentation not to the registrar but an insurance society, a doctor was denied the right to a fee under the 1875 Friendly Societies Act.[19] It was not in a doctor's own interests to ask the next-of-kin too many questions; a suspicious doctor would lose custom.[20] Even a responsible man like Horatio Nelson Hardy, the Dulwich police surgeon, let the 1893 Select Committee know that as a family doctor he would never be so foolishly public-spirited as to inform a coroner directly in the case of a suspicious death; the most he would do was to refuse a certificate and leave it to the registrar's decision whether to pursue matters. And if a doctor's conscientious action did lead to an inquest, he would be penalising himself, for he would lose money in obligatory attendance. As Dr John Bransom, the Rotherhithe Medical Office of Health, told the Lords Committee, the chances were overwhelming that the case would come to nothing anyway:

> In most cases doctors feel themselves bound to give a certificate because, it is difficult to get legal evidence upon which to get a conviction. Besides that, there are so many other reasons; the doctor is not a prosecutor; he does not like to be in that position; that is rather the duty of the police; it is a great waste of his time; I have had many days wasted over a single case. It does not pay the doctor, in fact. . . . The loss of time in attending before the coroner, and then before the magistrate and then two or three days at the assizes is a very serious thing. And if after all, the case fails there is damage and discredit to the man and his practice. When certificates are refused the cases have to go to the coroner. As a rule these cases fail for want of sufficient evidence. . . .

The second reason was that the doctors most frequently plied for certificates, especially in the case of infants, were the least remunerated and most overworked ones in the slums, where infant mortality could reach 20 or 30 per cent. The overloaded charitable dispensaries and hospitals were notoriously easy touches for a certificate. A correspondent signing himself 'Medicus' in the *Sunday Times* in 1890 told how dispensary doctors avoid instigating inquests 'by hook or by crook' and were prepared to issue certificates even though they had last seen the infant weeks before, relying solely on the word of the parent, without examining the corpse. In one instance a child had been 'treated' for a cold three weeks before, the only occasion that the dispensary doctor had seen it. 'Medicus' saw the child after it died and was sure that its cause of death 'had not the slightest appearance of a cold'; he notified the local coroner, who told him that the dispensary doctor had already issued a certificate, for a cause of death he could not possibly have known.[21] One vigilant dispensary doctor was Dr Ernest Snape of St Marylebone General Dispensary. In July 1890 he attended a sick child obviously neglected by the mother. He warned her that if it died he would refuse her a certificate. When it deteriorated, she took it to a hospital (he withheld the name), where it died in a few hours. Snape was surprised to learn that the hospital gave her a certificate without difficulty, and he asked for details. After much difficulty he extracted from the hospital the information that the child had died of 'tubercular meningitis' but it refused to tell him whether there had been a post-mortem or not.[22]

The NSPCC's organ, the *Child's Guardian*, of the 1890s was peppered with cases of murder, cruelty and neglect (generally with insurance overtones) which figured useless and misleading doctors' certificates. Some of the most apposite cases will be touched on again in Chapter 16, but a few graphic instances here will bring the message home. In 1873 the mass murderess, Mary Ann Cotton, who is believed to have poisoned up to twenty people, was convicted at Durham Assizes. For all her victims the death certificates had recorded sundry 'natural causes'; for example her step-son, whom a subsequent autopsy revealed had died of arsenic, had been buried on a certificate stating 'gastric fever'. In 1884 the infamous 'Liverpool prisoners', Catherine Flannagan and Margaret Higgins, were convicted of murdering four relatives by arsenic – but the certificates had stated variously diarrhoea and lung infections. In 1888 at Derby, Mary Ann Whitfield was discovered to have murdered her two insured sons by laudanum poisoning; yet the death certificate for one had stated 'congestion of the lungs' and for the other, kidney disease. And at Liverpool in 1890 the baby-farmers William and Elizabeth Pearson were tried for poisoning three of their insured charges: one certificate had, however, given 'bronchitis' and another 'inflammation of the lungs' as causes of death.

Busy doctors were often in the habit of putting vague symptomological descriptions on the certificates, which gave the registrars no real idea and were a source of irritation to coroners and judges:[23] terms like 'inanition', 'debility', 'marasmus', 'atrophy' – all just meaning 'wasting', said nothing meaningful about the background to a baby's demise.

It was only a long-term process of improvement in diagnostic skills and the relief of pressures on doctors in the poor districts as the infant death rate began to fall after 1900, that were to bring a marked improvement in the integrity and quality of doctors' certificates in the early decades of the twentieth century.

Midwives' certificates of 'stillbirth' had an even longer record of untrustworthiness. The Home Office's attention had been drawn to the practice of burying live-born babies as if stillborn, with attendant suspicions of infanticide, at least as early as 1844.[24] Now, the motive for feigning stillbirths was not necessarily sinister; they were cheaper to bury. In 1893 St Pancras Burial Board charged 7 shillings and 8 pence for burying a live-born as against 2 shillings and sixpence for a stillborn,[25] and by paying an undertaker to stuff a stillborn secretly inside a coffin with an adult, the cemetery fees could be avoided altogether. Stillborns were dumped in exposed places, and not unusually, and quite legally, buried in people's own back gardens to avoid all burial costs.[26] If a baby lived for a few hours, it was still casually treated as stillborn. In 1903 a Manchester midwife, Jessie Donough, was tried for certifying six infants of one mother, who had all lived up to ten hours, as 'stillborn'. Her excuse was ignorance: she believed she was entitled to do this if the baby lived less than 24 hours, and we can guess that this was a popular old midwives' tale.

Any disposal of babies in a way that obviated an official record of their existence was bound to give rise to the worst suspicions. In 1851 the coroner for eastern Middlesex informed the Home Secretary of a case at Hackney where a midwife had written a false declaration of stillbirth. A 19-year-old single girl, Charlotte Draper, had a live-born baby girl which died soon after delivery. The midwife did not arrive until after the child had died, but she brought its body to the gravedigger with a note as follows:

'I, Mrs Wilson, midwife, do certify that I attended Mrs Smith Williams with a stillborn female child on the 22nd February 1851.' There was no signature.

It was untrue in every respect: the 'attendance' and 'stillbirth' were fabricated, and Draper had also given the midwife a false name. The sexton was paid 1 shilling and sixpence to bury the body and the vicar had been none the wiser.[27]

Sometimes the midwife was bypassed altogether. In 1844 Mr Hitchins, the Lincoln registrar, had grown suspicious when a woman, who had applied for a burial certificate for her baby, failed to return with the person who had been present at its death, as he had insisted. He was also the coroner, and in this capacity instituted an inquiry. There was no foul play, but it transpired that the baby had been buried as a stillborn by the parish sexton, who had taken the sealed box from the woman's house without asking any questions. He told the coroner:

I suppose it was a stillborn child. I was not told so. I did not ask any questions. I have been nearly twenty years sexton and have always upon application buried infants without enquiry whether they were stillborn. I may have buried thirty or more – I seldom see them – they are generally nailed up; when I go the parents pay me my fee of one shilling.[28]

In 1850 the sexton of Bromley in Middlesex was prosecuted for the same misconduct under the 1836 Registration Act, in burying a live-born without a registrar's burial certificate.[29]

Registration of Deaths.

CAUTION

To Persons burying, and omitting to give Notice thereof to

THE REGISTRAR.

WILLIAM EDWARDS, Sexton of Bromley, Middlesex, was summoned before Mr. YARDLEY, at the Thames Police Court, on 20th February, 1850, to answer a Complaint preferred against him at the instance of THE REGISTRAR GENERAL, under the authority of THE SECRETARY OF STATE, for a violation of the twenty-seventh Clause of the Registration Act, in omitting to give Notice to the District Registrar of Births and Deaths, of the fact of his having, on the 7th January last, buried, as STILL-BORN CHILDREN, the dead bodies of two Male Infants, who had been BORN ALIVE, AND DID NOT DIE UNTIL SEVERAL HOURS AFTER THEIR BIRTH.

The facts of the case, as stated by Mr. BODKIN, Counsel for the Prosecution, were fully proved in evidence, whereupon Mr. YARDLEY, after commenting severely upon the Offence of which the Defendant had been guilty, CONVICTED him in the Penalty provided by the Act, at the same time intimating to him that, for any similar infraction of the Law, he would not only incur the pecuniary Fine of TEN POUNDS, but render himself liable to a Prosecution by

Indictment for Misdemeanor.

EXTRACT FROM THE REGISTRATION ACT,
(6 & 7 Wm. IV., Cap. 86.)

By Section 27, it is enacted, "That every Registrar immediately upon registering any death, or as soon " thereafter as he shall be required so to do, shall, without Fee or Reward, deliver to the Undertaker or other " person having charge of the Funeral, a Certificate under his hand, according to the form of Schedule (E) to " this Act annexed, that such death has been duly registered, and such Certificate shall be delivered by such " Undertaker, or other Person, to the Minister or Officiating Person, who shall be required to bury or to " perform any religious Service for the burial of the dead body, and if any dead body shall be buried for which " no such Certificate shall have been so delivered, the person who shall bury, or perform any Funeral, or any " religious Service for the burial, shall forthwith give notice thereof to the Registrar * * * * * ; and " *every person who shall bury,* or perform any Funeral, or any religious Service for the burial of *any dead* " *body,* for which no Certificate shall have been duly made and delivered as aforesaid, *and who shall not within* " *Seven Days give notice thereof to the Registrar,* SHALL FORFEIT AND PAY ANY SUM NOT EXCEEDING TEN " POUNDS *for every such offence.*"

GENERAL REGISTER OFFICE,

February, 1850.

Figure 7 *Notice from the General Register Office 1850 publicising a recent prosecution of a sexton for burying two live-born babies as if still-born, and reminding those whom it concerned of the relevant statutory provision. (Source: PRO HO45/3600. Courtesy:* Public Record Office.*)*

However, it was the undertakers who were probably much more widely experienced in this kind of concealment. They received infant corpses from the mothers or midwives on assurances that they were stillborn, and for a fee stuffed them into adults' coffins 'like so many blind puppies'.[30] This was still common in the 1890s, and was quite legal under the 1874 Act so long as their presence was disclosed at the burial. The coroner Athelstan Braxton Hicks told the 1893 Death Certification Committee how strategically placed undertakers were, by keeping their ears open in their customers' parlours, to judge whether the 'stillbirth' was genuine or not. But it was bad for business to inform coroners. Said Hicks, '. . . I have only had two informations from undertakers during the whole of my time.'[31] Undertakers' shops became veritable depositories for 'stillborns' awaiting suitable adult coffins. In 1870 a Kilburn undertaker was found to have the bodies of a dozen decomposing infants on his premises, but was committing no offence unless their burial was ordered by the sanitary authority.[32] And in 1895 *The Sun* reported an inquest involving a Peckham undertaker, the smell from whose premises had attracted the local sanitary inspector. A collection of decomposing babies was found dumped unceremoniously around the place, but the jury was satisfied that they were all stillborn.

From the mid-nineteenth century came calls for the registration of stillbirths. It was mooted at the International Statistical Congress in 1860, for example,[33] and the calls rose to a clamour in 1867: the Manchester Statistical Society and Manchester and Salford Sanitary Association urged it on the Home Secretary;[34] the NAPSS, following Dr Arthur Ransome's address on improvements in the Registration system, espoused it; while the Harveian Society placed it at number two in their twenty proposals for tackling infanticide. The argument was that without stillbirth figures, the true scale of infant mortality was incomplete. Speculative estimates of the numbers of stillbirths were bandied about. For example, in 1858 Lord Shaftesbury compassed at least 60,000 a year[35] (when official figures of live births were about 650,000); and in 1892 Dr Robert Reid Rentoul (of whom more soon) offered a figure of 60,000 to 70,000 a year (against 750,000 live births), and cited the French authority Bertillon whose studies indicated that the rate of stillbirths among illegitimates was double that for legitimates.[36] The scope for concealed infanticide appeared staggering, but registration of stillbirths, it was claimed, would at least put an end to the fraudulent burial of live-borns as stillborns.

Yet the 1871 Infant Life Protection Committee did not expressly call for registration of stillborns; and it was omitted from Dr Lyon

Playfair's Registration Bill of 1871 and the Act of 1874. Why was the nettle not grasped?

The answer lay in the staunch and perennial opposition of the long-incumbent Registrar General of Births, Marriages and Deaths, Sir James Graham. He told the Home Office in 1851 and again in 1867[37] that there would be grave practical problems in determining the age of the expelled foetus for classification as a stillbirth as opposed to a miscarriage. This would entail the most offensively intrusive questioning of women:

> To investigate every miscarriage and every abortion and the
> exact time of conception and the precise period of gestation
> appears to me an indelicate, indecent and nasty enquiry; and I
> have yet to learn what real practical good is attained in those
> countries where such births are recorded.

The calls for stillbirth registration were coupled with proposals for a system of sanitary or poor law authority 'verifying doctors' on the French model, to examine every corpse prior to burial where it was unattested to by a medical certificate. Graham was equally opposed to this, claiming that in the many instances where no doctor had attended the deceased before his death, the delays involved in such an examination would cause the bereaved much distress; and his warning of the additional costs to the Poor Law of these extra duties no doubt sank home within the government, too. The ineffectual precautions against fraudulent and surreptitious burial of stillborns contained in the 1874 Act were Graham's doing, and were as far as he was prepared to go.[38]

Even limited surveys of the numbers of *known* burials of alleged stillborns made disturbing reading. In four Liverpool cemeteries a total of 664 stillborns were known to have been buried in 1868, and only in one had anyone been bothering to double check the veracity of the midwives' certificates before allowing the burial; this precaution, employing the coroner's beadle, had in fact exposed many deceitful certificates;[39] the Liverpool Northern Medical Society which conducted the investigation even sent the Home Secretary examples of the tatty bits of often semi-literate scrawl accepted as 'certificates' by the cemeteries. It was the suspicions of such malpractice by midwives that partly underlay the movement from the late 1860s to have them qualified and registered.[40] The Scottish physician, Robert Reid Rentoul, was an active campaigner. When a midwives registration bill was sponsored in 1890 he set about equipping himself with evidence of unqualified midwives' incompetence, and an important aspect, he reckoned, was their

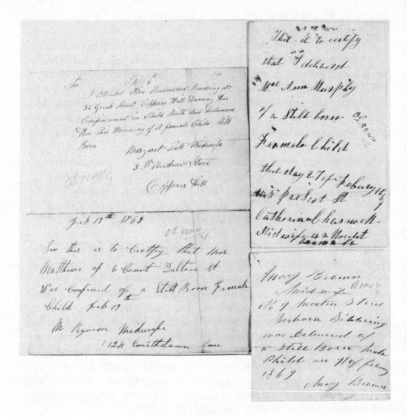

Figure 8   *A selection of midwives' stillbirth attestations showing varying degrees of literacy, received by the Necropolis Cemetery, Liverpool, in 1869. (Source: PRO HO45/8044. Courtesy:* Public Record Office.*)*

responsibility for large numbers of preventable stillbirths. He collected statistics of known stillbirth burials from a hundred parish burial boards, and sent the results to a colleague, Sir Charles Cameron MP[41] (who had been editor at the time of the *North British Daily Mail*'s investigation into Scottish baby-farming twenty years before). At his prompting in Parliament, the government published a return from 1,333 burial boards. These were a kind of municipal sanitary authority, distinct from church graveyards and private cemetery companies, and it was supposed that stillbirth burials there were fewer and their procedures more careful. In 1890 they recorded 17,335 burials of stillborns, over three-quarters of whom were attested by doctors', not midwives' certificates.[42] However, this was the best sample: in the early 1890s the declarations of midwives and other 'unskilled persons' accounted for 45 per cent of all stillbirth certifications in Manchester cemeteries.[43]

Rentoul expressed his views on midwives and stillbirths before the 1892–3 Select Committee on Midwives Registration,[44] and the time was ripe for a comprehensive review of death certification and burial procedures. On Cameron's motion in the Commons in March 1893, the Select Committee on Death Certification was appointed.[45]

Its recommendations, so far as they relate to this study, were as follows:

Midwives' certificates of stillbirth should be abolished as there was 'reason from the evidence to think that a great number of cases of crime are concealed under statements that children are stillborn'.

Stillbirths – defined as the issue of a foetus of at least seven months' gestation – should be registered; back-garden burials should be outlawed, and cemeteries should cease placing them in mass graves as this prevented subsequent identification.

'Medical certifiers' should be appointed in every sanitary district to inspect all bodies unaccompanied by a doctor's death certificate, before they were buried.

Medical certificates should be made more stringent; for example they should require a doctor to state the time since he last attended the patient, and whether or not they actually saw the dead body.

The loophole in the 1874 Act that allowed burial before the issue of the registrar's certificate should be closed.

No action, however, was taken on these by the Home Office, and prior to the First World War medical and public health bodies, and various Parliamentary Committees, like the Physical Deterioration Committee of 1904, vainly called for a ban on uncertified death registration; but in 1914 the Registrar General took the administrative initiative and instructed registrars to refer all uncertified applications automatically to the coroner.[46]

In the meantime there were successive private members' bills between 1908 and 1914 to make stillbirths registrable but all were squashed by the government on the excuse 'that they would involve considerable public expenditure or were badly drafted or contained objectionable incidental matter'.[47]

However, other pre-1914 public health legislation was to contribute collaterally to an improved public recording of infant births and deaths. The steady improvement in the calibre of midwives, once unqualified women were debarred from 1910, was to effect the disappearance of improper stilbirth certification before the mid-1920s. The (permissive) Notification of Births Act of 1907 empowered local authorities to require those in attendance at a birth, *including a stillbirth*, to notify the local health authority within 36 hours. The development of local health visiting services to advise new-delivered mothers from the 1890s was handicapped by the 42-day period of grace before registration of birth allowed under the 1874 Act. Health visitors combed the registrars' birth lists to know where to go, and this interval was sometimes fatal to an infant's survival; but now they could be notified independently in under two days.

A growing body of statistics on stillbirths became available as the Act's adoption spread, for it did not become mandatory until 1915.[48] These emerging local data served to confirm a belief that had been growing since the 1890s that stillbirths were linked to another phenomenon, namely the rising proportion of infant deaths from premature birth. In the period 1875–84 13.7 out of every 1,000 live births resulted in death from prematurity; between 1895 and 1904 it averaged 19.8 per 1,000 and was still rising; this was a real trend, not a distortion caused by improved statistical profiling.[49] Why, with long-term advances in public health and nutrition, were women producing more defective new-borns? The answer lay in the rampant use of pernicious abortifacient medicines, whose popularity was increasing with the urge towards smaller families from the late nineteenth century. A Yorkshire medical officer, Dr James Robertson Kaye, told the Infantile Mortality Conference in 1906 of experts' 'alarm at the general spread of Malthusian principles [birth control] among the masses' and of 'evidence that the use of abortifacients in our industrial centres is rapidly growing'. In 1914 Dr Amand Routh, a noted authority on pre-natal pathology, used data available through the 1907 Notification of Births Act to estimate that the proportion of aborted and stillbirths to live births was *at least* 11 per cent, and probably much higher.[50]

It was not until 1926 in fact, when infanticide was fading as a social problem, that a Registration Act was passed which fulfilled some of the recommendations of the 1893 Select Committee.[51] Stillbirths – as defined by that Committee – now had to be registered, but it was a measure of the transformation of the quality of midwives since 1893 that midwives' certificates were not abolished; on the contrary, the standard certificate of stillbirth to be presented to the registrar under the Act was either a qualified midwife's or a doctor's where they had attended at the delivery. Another overdue provision was the prohibition on all burials before the issue of a registrar's certificate.

15 Burial insurance and child murder (I)

Since the Friendly Societies Act of 1793, the insurance habit among the working classes had grown by leaps and bounds. The Act allowed friendly societies whose rules were approved by the county quarter sessions to register with them, and this gave them important legal advantages over non-registered societies: they acquired quasi-corporate status and could, for example, sue and prosecute as a legal entity. After 1828 local registration was superseded by a centralised national system of registration under an official later to evolve as the Chief Registrar of Friendly Societies.

'Friendly Societies' in their most rounded form offered a range of benefits – sickness, widow's, emigration, and funeral, for example; their subscriptions were relatively high – perhaps sixpence a week – and were designed for the thrifty artisan class. Some, however, offered only funeral benefits, and because their subscriptions were much lower, reached down among the lower strata of the working classes and went for quantity of membership rather than quality.

Side by side with these were the unregistered funeral clubs – 'funeral briefs' or 'death briefs' as they were known in the north of England. They were commonly got up by the local publican in association with the undertaker; their rules were non-approved and their administration was amateurish, lax and often corrupt. Meetings were held on pub premises, and accompanied by much heavy imbibing encouraged by 'mine host'; and rules sometimes even allowed for benefits to be part-paid in drink. The publican acted as banker, and the funeral clubs were conducted with no regard to actuarial or accounting principles; embezzlements and collapses were quite common. Yet they had a wide following because they were cheap (subscriptions were ½d or 1d a week), offered a spurious aura of conviviality, and did not ask too many questions when an insured life was claimed upon.

Some idea of the popularity of working-class insurance may be gauged by the fact that by 1858 there were over 20,000 *registered* societies in England and Wales with over 2,000,000 members; so that, if we include members' beneficial dependants, some 40 per cent or more of the population were covered; to this we must add the unknown membership of unregistered clubs; but multiple memberships, perhaps combining registered and unregistered societies, were common. Although the resulting accumulation of benefits accruable in the case of life policies on members' children was to arouse the worst suspicions, we must also remember that multiple-insurance was a way of spreading the risk at a time when burial societies were so unstable.

Societies sprang up all over the land, in town and country alike, but they were especially thick on the ground in the industrial north-west, and it is from the Lancashire-Cheshire marches that the earliest criminal cases involving the alleged murder of children for the burial money were to emanate from 1840.

Some of the more successful funeral societies expanded beyond their own locality to a regional or even national network, and came to be popularly termed 'collecting societies'; their impersonality precluded informal subscription meetings at the local tavern; instead an army of doorstep agents went round collecting weekly premiums and touting for new members. The largest of these was the Liverpool-based Royal Liver with 550,000 members in 1872. The collectors depended entirely on commissions for an income, and had to be a hard-boiled, pushy and not over-scrupulous breed to hustle successfully for a living. Many of their malpractices were to have a direct bearing on the link alleged between insurance abuses and family murders, particularly infanticides.

To clarify our terminology, we have the 'death briefs' or 'funeral clubs' – these were the local, tavern-based unregistered associations; and the 'Collecting Societies', which offered death benefit only, but were technically and legally 'Friendly Societies' if they were registered as such. The term Friendly Society in *popular* parlance meant those registered societies that offered other benefits besides funeral payments.

From 1854 the commercial insurance company (a joint-stock enterprise whose profits went to the shareholders, not, as with Friendly Societies, to the insuring subscribers) entered the field and was destined to dwarf the other forms of burial insurance. This commercial business was called 'industrial life assurance' because the companies were venturing from their traditional market, the middle classes, into the industrial classes. Their benefits were lower than those offered by the meretricious 'funeral briefs' but they offered actuarial soundness and proven success. The pioneer was the Prudential, which in 1856 was to start recruiting collectors – the

'men from the "Pru"' – to make it viable and, after some hesitation
in 1860, extended its portfolio to infant life insurance. It was very
conscious of the cloud of suspicion hanging over this area, but
found that it really made the market for industrial life assurance;
its tables pitched the benefits low, particularly because it was the
actuarially sound thing to do in view of the high infant mortality
rate among the working classes, and partly to guard itself against
any accusation that it was tempting people into infanticide.

Burial clubs would not admit child lives from birth, as the
neonatal death rate was so prodigious, but admission ages might
vary from a fortnight upwards, and the less sophisticated the
society, the less regard it had for the principle of graduating
benefits (and this could be fatal to its solvency). The Preston
Original Legal Friendly Society, founded in 1831, admitted
children after 2 months old, and in 1853 was paying out a flat rate
of £2 15 shillings on the death of any child member under 4,
provided there had been at least sixteen weekly contributions of
½d.[2] The Prudential would not admit infants before 3 months old,
and they had to be in contribution at 1d a week over three months
for a benefit of only 10 shillings in its 1860 table. This rose to £1
after a year's contribution, and £2 after two years. The scales were
designed to keep the benefits low for the younger infants, and then
accelerate them if a child was enrolled after 4 years old; thus a
child entered at 4 received 15 shillings after three months, but a
child entered at 5 received £2 10 shillings after the same period.

Lodges of 'true' Friendly Societies offered even lower rates; in
1891 the Order of the Sons of Temperance offered only £1 on
deaths under 3, for example.[3]

What was the actual cost of a child's burial? Propagandists
against infant life insurance played down the sum, to 'prove' that
the benefits were a profitable bounty and an incitement to
infanticide; the Reverend John Clay in 1854 gave it as 25 shillings
and Benjamin Waugh in 1890 put it as low as 15 to 18 shillings.
Defenders of insurance emphasised the cost of the extras,
considered so important in Victorian funerals, such as bell-tolling,
the pall and bearers, and the hire of mourning clothes; and a
variety of sources indicates that the real expense was two or three
times the figures just cited.[4]

Now any claims to purity by any single society, like the
Prudential or a Friendly Society, in respect of the modesty of their
benefits, must ring hollow in view of beneficiaries' practice of
topping up benefits by multiple insurances; and though laws were
to be passed to regulate this, they were to prove ineffectual, as we
shall see.

One thing must be emphasised here. The whole field of child-life insurance was non-legal. The law deemed that normally parents and guardians had no legal 'interest' in the continued survival of the child and such insurance contracts were void in the civil courts. The whole industry grew up on good faith alone; societies paid out readily because it attracted further custom, and they frequently made additional *ex gratia* payments – for instance, if the child died before eligibility – to promote goodwill in the neighbourhood. Life insurance was a cut-throat business – rival collectors were known to come to blows on doorsteps – and a society could not afford a reputation for fussiness over pay-outs.

The Prudential, which prided itself on careful management and selectivity over its collectors, became the giant in infant life insurance. Growth was rapid; in 1871 it had about 309,000 children up to 10 on its 'industrial' books, and by 1891 this had risen to 2,400,000 in a working-class child population up to 10 of some 6,500,000. The total numbers of insured children in the population around 1891 were a matter of dispute; estimates ranged from 2,750,000 to 4,000,000, and accurate figures were impossible, as companies and societies counted *policies*; and many – 30 per cent was one estimate – were duplicated among different societies on the same child. But even on the lowest figure, the fact stands out that infant life insurance had grown immensely popular among the working classes and was big business at the end of the nineteenth century. Of the £13,000,000 total value of child life insurance among the commercial companies alone at the end of the 1880s, £9,500,000 were held by the 'Pru'; the Pearl Life Assurance Company came a poor second with £1,400,000.[5]

The two earliest official exposures of infant life insurance in its worst light came in Edwin Chadwick's Report on Interment in Towns in 1843, part of his pioneering public health study, followed by the Reverend John Clay's special report for Preston for the Commission on 'The State of Large Towns and Populous Places' in 1844.[6] Clay was chaplain to Preston jail and an active social reformer, and was associated with Mary Carpenter and Matthew Davenport Hill in the campaign for reformatories for juvenile offenders; he became perhaps the most authoritative single voice against infant life insurance from his base right in the heart of burial-club country in the north-west.

Chadwick's attention had been drawn to the death clubs by a poisoning case – the first of its kind to come into the courts – from Stockport, in the same part of the country, in 1840, and before his report was completed, another case at Chester Assizes in 1843 was brought to his attention.

The 1840 case involved two poor, related couples Robert and Anne Sandys, and George and Honor Sandys, who lived in adjoining cellar rooms in Stockport.[7] Robert and Anne had four children, all enrolled in a local (unregistered) burial club, the 'Philanthropic', which had over 2,000 members, and paid (after administrative deductions) £3-8s.-6d plus 2 shillings-worth of drink on a child's death. In September 1840 a daughter, Elizabeth, died, and Robert obtained the burial dues from the club the next day, giving 'inflammation' as the cause of her death. The club was very lax, and evidently no doctor's certificate was required. Henry Coppock, Stockport's town clerk, described how the club's officers disposed of claims: 'The officers met at a public house at 12 o'clock at noon; they got the men there at their dinner hour, and the sooner they got quit of the payments the better.' In the Sandys case, typically, they made no check.

On October 12th two of the three surviving children developed severe stomach pains after eating bread and butter, and were taken to two local doctors in succession. Both prescribed emetics, and one of them indeed diagnosed arsenic. (This did not necessarily suggest foul play, as arsenic could be commonly purchased then, for example to kill bed bugs or as a rat poison in the slums, and would be left lying about.) However, both doctors testified later that the mother had failed to give the children the emetics. (This illustrates a suspected crafty ploy that became more widely adverted to later in the century: late in the children's illness parents would make a show of resorting to a busy doctor, to deflect criminal accusations and ensure a subsequent medical certificate of death. For example Dr C.S. Redmond, a Gateshead dispensary doctor, was to comment in 1890: 'Over and over have I been called to cases too late to do any good but where it was only too apparent that the doctor was sent for, not in the hope of rescuing the child from death but of saving the parents from punishment. . . . In many of such cases I find the infants' lives insured.'[8])

One of the two sick Sandys children, Marianne, died. The Sandys accused another woman of poisoning her, but Anne Sandys's odd behaviour at the inquest aroused suspicion. Elizabeth's and Marianne's bodies were exhumed and found to contain arsenic. The police were now alerted to the fact that George and Honor Sandys's daughter Catherine had died in July and the cause of death was registered as 'measles'; she, too, had been insured.

Robert and Anne Sandys were tried for murdering the two girls; Robert was found guilty but Anne was acquitted, as the jury, misunderstanding the law, believed that a wife was presumed to be acting under her husband's influence and could not be guilty. Much suspicion surrounded Honor Sandys and she was charged with Catherine's murder; but the evidence against her was less conclusive than that against Anne, and in view of the unsatisfactory verdict against the latter, Honor's case was dropped.

The prosecution also faced disappointment in the trial of Robert Standring at Chester Assizes in 1843, accused of poisoning his mentally defective daughter for the £8 burial money. The jury acquitted him, against overwhelming evidence, owing, it was suggested, to their qualms over capital punishment.

John Clay's description of the burial clubs in Preston in 1844 was a classic, if statistically defective, study unrepeated anywhere else in the nineteenth century. He followed it up with a long and detailed letter in *The Times* in January 1849,[9] which in turn formed the basis of a noted pamphlet on 'Burial Clubs and Infanticide' in 1853, a copy of which was read by the then Home Secretary, Lord Palmerston, who asked for its circulation in the Cabinet.[10]

Preston was a rapidly growing town; in 1841 its population was 50,000; in 1851 nearly 70,000. The 1849 letter does not mention Preston by name but it must be the anonymous town of 61,000 he is referring to. It had then 52,000 enrolments in its eleven burial clubs (three-quarters of which were children), compared with only an estimated 2,000 in the town's dozen or so sickness clubs which offered sickness as well as burial benefit; the enrolments, remember, must exaggerate the numbers of actual persons, owing to multiple memberships. In 1844 he had estimated that two-thirds of the town's working-class 0–5-year-olds were enrolled in the 'Preston Original Legal Friendly Benefit Society' alone. Clay was struck by the contrasting infant death rates among the town's social classes: among the 'gentry', 'tradesmen' and 'operative' classes in 1844 the death rate of 0–5-year-olds was 17.6, 38.2 and 55.4 per cent respectively. Now he saw that ignorance, poverty and filth were the basic factors, but when he became aware of the near-universality of child life insurance among the working class, the suspicion was kindled that this had something to do with the excessively high infant death rate among that class. He pointed out in 1849 that despite the prevalence of sickness among working-class infants, Preston doctors who practised in the poor districts had told him that only 13 per cent of their patients were below 5. Clay acknowledged that wilful murder was exceptional, but was certain that insurance fostered parental indifference. As he told the 1854 Select Committee on the Friendly Societies Bill:

I must do the parent justice to say, that the parent herself is not conscious of the influence which is actually taking place in her mind; she might be startled if it were put to her directly, 'You are letting this child die for the sake of the burial fees.'

Clay purported to prove that infant deaths in the 'Preston Original Legal' were higher than they ought to be compared with the rate of infant death in the town at large, but his statistical approach was fallacious. He did not compare the proportion of infant members to all members in the Society with the age-structure of the town's population, to draw any sound conclusions. Moreover, since he gives the impression that working-class children were overwhelmingly insured in *some* society, how can he distinguish between 'insured' children and 'town' children?

Before the 1854 Select Committee on the Friendly Societies Bill, Clay presented another statistical case: the death rate among the poor working-class 0–5-year-olds in Preston was 55–60 per cent; yet a sample survey from the burial clubs indicated a death rate of 62 to 64 per cent; the first set of figures included all infants from birth, while the latter excluded the first 2 months of life, the most vulnerable period, so the comparison was even more adverse to the societies, he claimed. Yet again, we know nothing about the sample, and the same objection – how can you distinguish 'society' deaths from 'town' deaths? – still applies.

The year 1846 saw two 'infant burial insurance' trials: Joseph and Mary Pimlett of Runcorn, Cheshire, were tried for murdering two of their infants and poisoning a third. The two dead children were insured with the 'Victoria Legal Burial Society', and their corpses showed traces of arsenic when exhumed. Murder was not proven, however, and the couple were acquitted.[11] However, John Rodda was convicted at York Assizes of murdering his 1-year-old child – insured for £2 10 shillings – by pouring acid down its throat. His three surviving children were all insured.

The Friendly Societies Act of 1846 made the first crude and totally ineffective attack on infant life insurance by banning it altogether on children under 6 in registered societies. The unregistered clubs, where one would imagine that scope for abuse would be greater, were ignored; and the ban only applied to registered societies coming into existence *after* the Act was passed![12]

In 1848 the connection between murder and burial insurance shifted its focus away from the Mersey region to rural Essex from where news broke in September of a series of suspected poisonings in and around the villages of Thorpe, Kirby, Ramsay, Wix, Mistley, Bradfield and Great Oakley, in those days secluded backwaters.[13]

In July 1848 one Mary May of Wix had been convicted at Chelmsford Assizes of murdering her half-brother with arsenic; unbeknown to him she had insured him in a Harwich burial society for £9 or £10. Some of her children, it transpired, had died quite suddenly, and tongues started wagging. In March 1849 her sister Hannah Southgate was tried for poisoning her first husband, to be free to marry her lover, but was acquitted. Mary May and her sister were rumoured to have been at the centre of a whole web of poisoning conspiracies; for the inquiries conducted by the north Essex coroner into the 'Essex Poisonings' in the aforementioned villages had been instigated by the exposure of Mary; and the suspected perpetrators (nothing more seems to have been proved) all knew Mary and her sister. The newspaper accounts are somewhat obscure, but suggest a burial club connection.

The 'Essex Poisonings' episode shows that the same motivations were at work in the more remote rural areas as were imputed to Merseyside. Infants were not uniquely vulnerable as insurance victims. The pattern of exposed crimes, which almost invariably featured the use of poison, suggests that the perpetrators were psychopaths and unusual types. They usually had a succession of victims, child and adult alike; indeed the financial motive was even greater against adults for there was to be no legal limit set on the amount of their life insurance. The infamous Mary Ann Cotton of County Durham in 1873 and the Liverpool poisoners of 1884, Catherine Flannagan and Margaret Higgins, were murderesses of this type (see Chapter 14). Margaret's murdered husband, Thomas, for example, had been insured in a number of societies by his wife for a total of £108/19 shillings.

In fact it was not the poisoning cases that worried the critics of infant burial insurance so much as the suspicion that the far more typical and elusive kind of infanticide was murder by neglect, for the defence could so easily raise the plea of 'ignorance' to get their client off the hook. As the Surrey coroner, Athelstan Braxton Hicks, was to observe later in the century it was not possible to convict for manslaughter 'unless a medical man can state positively that the child's life might have been prolonged by medical aid or other necessaries or that its death had been accelerated by the want of such aid or necessaries'; no doctor could do more than state an opinion in court, and this was insufficient for a conviction.[14] John Bransom, the Medical Officer for Rotherham, told in 1890 of a case he had once attended where a child was on the point of death while the two women of the house were 'singing and laughing away' at the washtub. When he upbraided them for plying the child with sops it could not take from a filthy container, and warned them that he would refer the matter to the coroner if it died, they blithely replied, 'Oh master, we are ignorant and young.'[15]

For the most part, then, the evidence was tantalisingly suspicious and laced with hearsay, but legal proof was another matter. Chadwick's report mentions a Manchester family in which six infants had died; one of these was worth £20 from multiple insurances; another, enrolled in ten clubs, yielded £34/3 shillings. A rent collector told him:

> The poor people have often told me that they were unable to pay at that time; but when a certain member of the family –
> generally a child – died, they would be able to pay. Most of the children at the houses which I visit are in the burial clubs.

And John Clay told of a lady friend who offered to send medical help to the ailing child of the woman she was employing as a wet-nurse. The woman replied, 'Oh! never ma'am; it's in two burial clubs.'

Against blanket class innuendo of this sort representatives of working men waxed indignant. The Select Committee on the Friendly Societies Bill of 1849[16] heard protesting evidence from two burial society spokesmen, embarrassed by the recent poisoning cases. William Jenkins, Secretary of the United Legal Friendly Benefit Society of Liverpool, with 47,000 members, said: 'I have made it my business to watch very closely and I have never yet found a case where there was the least suspicion of anything of that kind. I generally find the poor people are very strongly attached to their children.' The same protestation of working-class affection for their children was to be offered cogently before the House of Lords Committee on Child Life Insurance in 1890 by Will Crooks, the dockers' leader and Poplar resident and councillor.

Parliamentarians were only too aware that legal curbs on infant life insurance were politically fraught even long before the working classes got the vote, and so were loath to do anything really effective; apart from the implied class slander, they would be undermining the cherished Victorian totem of 'self-help' – for without private insurance, the working classes would be burying more children at the Poor Law's expense. The new approach tried in the Friendly Societies Act of 1850[17] was to allow a maximum insurance of £3 in registered societies for children under 10, and make the presentation of a medical certificate compulsory upon a claim. However, it also added the 'undertaker clause' which the

working classes found provocative and insulting. As a disincentive
to infanticide, the proceeds were to be kept from the claimants'
hands. Instead the money was to go directly to the undertaker
appointed to make the funeral arrangements.

The hated clause was destined to last five years, and was
repealed by the Friendly Societies Act of 1855. Yet despite
experience of the reaction it triggered off, Benjamin Waugh, whose
political touch was conspicuously maladroit, was to seriously try
and revive the idea a generation later, when working-class
resistance to class paternalism was even more highly matured.

Like the 1846 Act, the 1850 measure left unregistered clubs
totally unregulated, so its effect if anything must have been to put
the better-run societies at a disadvantage.

In 1853 two more burial club murders hit the news. In April
Honor Gibbons, aged 21, and her mother Bridget Gerraty of
Stockport were convicted at Chester Assizes of killing Honor's
infant daughter by pouring sulphuric acid down her throat.[18] As in
the Sandys case, Honor made a show of seeking medical advice
about her daughter's ailing condition from a local druggist. The
girl was insured in the Provident Society of Stockport which was
evidently more careful than the Philanthropic in the Sandys case
(perhaps all local societies had tightened up their procedures since
that scandal had broken). The Provident demanded a medical
certificate, and a Doctor Gibbons approached refused her one, as he
was suspicious of the burn marks in the girl's throat. The Society
official's suspicions were aroused by this lack of a certificate and he
made inquiries of his own. At this point, Gibbons rashly
approached another officer, and offered a bribe if he would
sanction the burial payment – and this proved her undoing.

In December 1853 Thomas Moore, an unemployed factory
worker from Stockport, was charged at Liverpool Assizes with
murdering his two step-sons, 8 and 4½ years old, who were
insured for amounts totalling £19/4 shillings. Their bodies were
found floating in a canal at Reddish, but there was insufficient
evidence to convict Moore.

The two cases prompted the Grand Jury at Liverpool Assizes
(this was a citizen's panel whose task *inter alia* was to present a
general statement to the assize judge on the state of law and order
locally) to declare to the judge their concern that burial clubs
'operate as a direct incentive to murder',[19] and the judge passed on
their Presentment to the Home Office. The foreman of the jury was
William Brown, Liberal MP for South Lancashire, and this
Presentment was the circumstance that prompted John Clay to
publish his pamphlet on Burial Clubs and Infanticide under the

heading 'A Letter to William Brown M.P.'. He called for the
'undertaker clause' principle to be extended to unregistered burial
clubs, and mooted an idealistic scheme requiring the clubs to pay a
bonus to parents upon the child's survival to a certain age –
replacing 'death lists' with 'life lists' as he called it.[20] The latter
idea was not taken seriously by the Home Office, as it would put
up premiums beyond what the working class was able or willing to
pay. Palmerston, as Home Secretary, was as convinced that burial
club murders were a social epidemic as he was frustrated by lack of
hard evidence to prove it; for the sporadic poisoning cases that
came to light could be claimed by working-class representatives
and sympathetic Radical MPs to be atypical.

He ordered a bill to be prepared along the lines of Clay's first
suggestion, but withdrew it when he learned that John Bright, the
Manchester MP and famous Free Trader, was introducing an
amendment along these lines in a private member's bill (then going
through the House) to consolidate the laws relating to Friendly
Societies. It reveals the highly individualised and non-partisan
attitudes of MPs towards infant burial insurance that his great
Free Trade associate, Richard Cobden, should have been
vehemently opposed to the amendment, calling it a 'slur on the
character of the working classes'.

The bill in fact was referred to a Select Committee, which heard
various witnesses speak of the deep resentment caused by the
'undertaker clause', and this was acknowledged by Clay himself in
evidence. Evidently the working-class lobby had become sufficiently
organised to make an impact, and Clay's own statistics were less
than convincing, for the Committee concluded that burial
insurance murders were 'so few as by no means to impose upon
Parliament an obligation for the sake of public morality to legislate
specifically with a view to the prevention of that crime', and it
recommended the abolition of the undertaker clause so heartily
'disliked by the mass of the people, who desire to have absolute
disposal of the arrangements of the burial of their children'.

The 1855 Friendly Societies Act abolished the undertaker clause
and liberalised the insurance maxima of the 1850 Act to £6 for a
child up to 5, and £10 for a child from 5 to 10; above that age there
was no limit. The claimant must present the (obligatory) doctor's
certificate not to the society now, but to the local registrar of births
and deaths upon which he would issue an 'insurance' certificate for
a shilling fee. This procedure was quite distinct from the standard
application for a burial certificate, though the doctor's certificate,
of course, did double duty. The interposition of a public official to
scrutinise the medical certificate was intended as an extra

safeguard. To stop applicants going the rounds of the societies and raking in over-the-limit sums, each society the certificate was presented to had to endorse it with the sum awarded.

Again, the fatal weakness of the Act was its restriction to registered societies; an advantage was not only perpetuated for the unregistered clubs, but the advent of industrial assurance from 1860 gave subscribers an even safer opportunity to invest outside the scope of the Act. The only practical limit was the amount of money they could afford to spread around.

The registrar's certificate was unpopular (and no doubt widely ignored) because the claimant had to pay fees for two certificates – the doctor's and the registrar's; under an amending act of 1858 the registrar was dropped from the procedure, but was destined to be reintroduced under the Friendly Societies Act of 1875.

16   Burial insurance and child murder (II)

As no insurance murder scandal appeared during the 1860s, burial club infanticide took a back seat to 'mainstream' infanticide at this period. Burial insurance infanticide, in fact, was distinct, as it was legitimate children who were the more likely victims. Later statistics for Glasgow illustrate this: of all babies under 1 who died there in 1876, 20.7 per cent of the legitimates and 3.9 per cent of the illegitimates were insured. In 1892 the figures were 41.5 and 10.3 per cent respectively. The figures for the 1–5-year-olds in 1876 were 46.8 and 22.2 per cent respectively; in 1892 71.2 and 35 per cent.[1] The figures show clearly the rapidly increasing insurance habit among the working classes, and the lower level of insurance among illegitimates. This was due to the societies' practice of refusing to insure very young illegitimates, as their lives were such a bad risk. The Prudential refused to insure on illegitimates below three years;[2] nevertheless, unscrupulous collectors *were* taking on illegitimates regardless, for the sake of the commissions, and deceiving their head offices by falsifying the information on the enrolment forms. Insurance was, moreover, known to be taken out by baby-farmers on their illegitimate charges, as we shall see.

The duplicity and button-holing methods of doorstep collectors were widely condemned as the root-source of many of the evils of life insurance: collectors were accused of enrolling sickly babies, babies they had not even seen, babies they knew (but the parents did not appreciate) were already insured to the legal limit in other societies, and babies below the enrolment age. They did not bother to check out the relationship of the insurer to the child, and that is how baby-farmers, calling themselves 'parents' or 'guardians', slipped through the net. They connived with claimants to get their money through promptly, as a reputation for quick pay-outs brought them more custom. Head offices were none the wiser, though they had a lot to answer for in failing to make adequate checks. From the companies' point of view, the losses caused by collectors' deceptions had to be balanced against the extra overall business their methods brought in. However, as the doctors' certificates the offices relied on were so often inaccurate, they have some excuse. The Prudential itself described its own collectors as 'the veriest scum of England' before beginning a purge in the 1870s but the same abuses were being imputed to collectors in the 1890s. The Liverpool Poisoners case of 1884 (though involving adult victims) revealed a scandalous state of affairs. The most lucrative victim, Thomas Higgins, had been insured by his wife in five companies, and in only two of them had the collector actually spoken to Higgins; the Prudential collector was one of the defaulters.[3] The collector, however, was indispensable to the viability of 'industrial' life assurance. When William Gladstone as Chancellor of the Exchequer in 1864 introduced a Post Office Savings Bank Scheme of life assurance that cut out the doorstep collector, it failed.

In 1868 Lord Lichfield introduced a bill that marginally tightened up Friendly Society law in regard to infant insurance, but became the victim of a smear campaign got up by the insurance interests that he was seeking to ban all such insurance, and he had to withdraw it. Parliament's consciousness of working-class touchiness on the subject must have increased since the extension of the franchise in 1867. (Indeed, as the NSPCC's journal the *Child's Guardian* was to observe in March 1892, the country's army of doorstep collectors might now be feared as potential electoral canvassers against any party that attacked the insurance interests.) The government promised Lichfield a new public inquiry, but this did not come until the Royal Commission on Friendly Societies was appointed in 1872; its Fourth Report of 1874 dealt with child life insurance, and the Mary Ann Cotton case of 1873 was most timely. The murder she was actually convicted for out of her multiplicity of victims was that of her 7-year-old stepson who was insured for £4 10 shillings. A suspicious doctor had refused a medical certificate, and this led to an inquest. This was a hurried job and the medical witness initially diagnosed 'gastric fever'; it was only his unease after the burial that led to a second autopsy and the discovery of poison.[4]

The Commission heard various witnesses testifying to the dangers of infant burial insurance. Many of the themes repeat what has already been written, and more dubious statistics were presented, and I will not devote the limited space of this book to elaborating them. One 'chicken-and-egg' issue argued inconclusively before the Commission is worth noting: was the inordinately high infant mortality rate in Lancashire *caused* in part by the popularity of burial insurance there, or was insurance

popular *because* so many children were expected to die through
environmental factors, as the insurance interests insisted? In the
1860s among 0–1-year-olds, 30 per cent died in Liverpool and 25
per cent in Manchester; for 1–2-year-olds it was 18.5 and 13.6 per
cent respectively. It was this juxtaposition of the prevalence of
death clubs and excessive infant mortality that made the Mersey
region such a crucible for the whole controversy.

It was less confident than the 1854 Select Committee that burial
insurance caused no significant mischief but came to no firm
conclusion; as ever in this story it was a question of suspicion
versus proof. In the ensuing Friendly Societies Act of 1875[5] infant
life insurance was governed by section 28. It left the insurable
limits as they were under the 1855 Act, and, as we saw, restored
the registrar's certificate, which was to be issued only upon the
production of a doctor's or coroner's certificate or 'other satisfactory
evidence . . .'; the Chief Registrar of Friendly Societies was most
dissatisfied with the latitude this last phrase allowed registrars.

Industrial insurance companies like the 'Pru' were now brought
within the same limits as the registered friendly societies; however,
trade unions which offered their members friendly society services
were not included until the Trade Union Amendment Act of 1876.
The Act was unclear whether it applied to unregistered societies,
but a subsequent judicial decision ruled that this was so. Thus the
basic effect of the acts of 1875 and 1876 was to bring all types of
insurance societies under the same rule as regards claim procedures
and insurable limits.

Section 28 had another critical drafting defect. Lawful claimants
were 'parents or personal representatives'; the less scrupulous
operators were free to identify 'personal representatives' as more
distant relatives, step-parents and baby-farmers claiming to have
'adopted' the child.

The Act was flouted, more often by the unregistered societies,
who paid out sums in excess of the statutory limit to draw more
custom; and registrars' certificates were often by-passed to avoid
imposing extra fees on the claimants. Societies were prosecuted
from time to time at the Chief Registrar's instigation, but a
successful and quite legal evasion was to pay the excess sum in the
form of a 'gift' or gratuity.

Two scandalous cases were to come to light in 1878 and 1884
that showed how flimsy the safeguard of a doctor's certificate was.
In 1878 Ellen Heesom of Lower Walton near Warrington in
Lancashire was convicted of murdering by poison her two young
daughters and her mother, all of whom had been insured in a
burial club. The doctor's certificates on the two girls gave

unsuspicious causes of death, and doubts arose only through the close sequence of their grandmother's death.[6] The other case was the even more lurid and already cited Liverpool Poisoners affair of 1884. Both sets of murders involved the use of arsenic, then in common domestic use, and one would have thought that doctors would have been familiar enough with the symptoms of arsenic poisoning – stomach pains and retching – for it figured in so many Victorian murder trials; probably in an age when enteric disorders were commonplace, unsuspecting doctors were easily misled.

The shocking insurance company laxities exposed by the 1884 case in respect of the adult victims carried even more dire implications for the helpless infants and at the Diocesan Conference in 1884 the Bishop of Truro branded infant life insurance as 'a growing danger' and petitioned the Home Office. The Attorney General, Sir William Harcourt, agreed with this view privately but told the Home Office that there was 'great difficulty in dealing with the subject' owing to a strong and indignant working-class lobby.[7]

The same year saw the formation of the London Society for the Prevention of Cruelty to Children by the Reverend Benjamin Waugh, and in 1888 the National Society was formed. This was one manifestation of the child welfare movement that was developing from the 1880s, and the NSPCC was to spearhead the campaign against child life insurance from 1889, once its first objective, the passage of the Prevention of Cruelty to Children Act, had been achieved.[8] The Act made it an offence for parents to ill-treat, neglect, abandon or expose their child in a manner 'likely to cause such child unnecessary suffering or injury to its health', and where a parent was tried at the assizes (the less serious cases were dealt with by magistrates), the Act allowed for a doubling of the £100 fine if the parent was found to have an insurance interest in the child's death. The Act enabled the NSPCC to swing into action, and its work expanded rapidly. In the administrative year 1889–90 it instituted 496 prosecutions; in 1899–1900 it undertook 2,729. The increasing exposure by its inspectors of cases of neglect, cruelty and death made the *Child's Guardian* a veritable cabinet of horrors in the 1890s, and the custom grew up both in the *Child's Guardian* and press reports, of ritually appending the rider, 'The child was insured', to such accounts, where appropriate.

The trial of George and Mary Hayes of Swindon in 1888 coincided with the formation of the NSPCC. They were baby-farmers with seven children they had 'adopted' into their care, herded in a room twelve feet square and all in a shocking state of filth and neglect; they were convicted of neglecting two of the children, an infant girl too weak to walk and a boy who had been found tied to a chair. Mrs Hayes received two years' prison and her husband nine months. All the children were insured in the Victoria Legal Friendly Society for ½d a week each. Its agent had exploited the 'personal representatives' phrase in s.28 of the 1875 Act to qualify these 'adoptors' as insurers, and the Chief Registrar called for a tightening up of the law expressly to restrict payments to parents.[9]

Mr Justice Day, in sentencing the Hayes, branded the burial societies as 'those pests of society which insured the lives of children but which seemed to be instituted for their own destruction' and called for their suppression; these were to become Benjamin Waugh's watchwords.

The next three years were to be the most intensely embattled period in the history of infant life insurance. On one side were ranged Waugh, and an array of Poor Law medical officers, Medical Officers of Health, coroners and a sprinkling of judges; Waugh's cohorts could all tell first-hand stories of cruelty and neglect in which an insurance connection *appeared* to be more than coincidental. Waugh could only retail second-hand accounts, drawn from his inspectors' reports, letters and statements of opinion by others. His conviction was as strong as Palmerston's a generation before that insurance spelled murder, but his rhetorical emotiveness combined with a reliance on hearsay as evidence, and a certain weakness for conjuring up statistics from pure supposition, made him a rather poor spokesman for his cause before a panel of hard-headed MPs.

On the other side were ranged the representatives of the insurance societies, whose chief protagonist was Thomas Dewey, manager of the Prudential. If Waugh's allies could sow suspicions with a catalogue of individual case histories, Dewey relied on general statistics to counter them and had the advantage that Waugh must make an impossibly overwhelming case to overcome any government's reluctance to take measures so provocative to working-class voters.

Argument and counter-argument were fired off and repeated before the Common Select Committee on Friendly Societies of 1888–9,[10] the House of Lords Committee on Child Life Insurance of 1890–91,[11] and in a side exchange between Waugh and Pembroke Marshall, representing the Prudential, in a series of articles in the *Contemporary Review* and *Fortnightly Review* during 1890 and 1891.[12]

The Committee of 1888–9 was set up under Sir Herbert Maxwell MP to review Friendly Society law in general. Its members wanted hard facts and figures, and some of them, notably Charles

Braudlaugh MP, gave Waugh a rough ride for retailing hearsay. However, even this Committee was not totally convinced of Dewey's statistics, and conceded on Waugh's behalf that 'from the nature of the cases it is almost impossible to obtain direct and inculpating evidence of criminality. . . .' I will just run over some of the basic statistical arguments and point out their flaws.

Dewey (and Marshall) claimed that insurance industry figures showed that 80 per cent of working-class children under 10 were insured, and with such a mass appeal it must be a force for good; otherwise Waugh was implying that the working classes *en masse* were bent on destroying their own offspring. Waugh claimed that the figure was much lower – less than 50 per cent – and that Dewey was citing *policy* statistics, which exaggerated the numbers of insured subjects because of multiple insurances, and also that he under-stated the total number of working-class children in the population (a point later conceded by Pembroke Marshall). Out of these disputed figures arose the unresolved argument whether it was the thrifty types who insured, or, as Waugh's allies claimed, a shiftless and opportunistic element of the working class, who spent much of the burial money on drink.

Dewey claimed that with such a high proportion of insured children, it was inevitable that insurance would figure in many cruelty and death cases, but the link was coincidental, not causal. When Dr Roderick Macdonald, coroner for north-east London, produced his inquest statistics for June–December 1888 before the Commons Committee, he showed that, for example, of 39 dead infants aged 3–6 months, 21 were insured; and of the 36 aged 6–12 months, 26 were insured. To Macdonald there appeared on the face of it a causal connection, but Dewey argued that such figures proved nothing since insured infants predominated in the population.

Marshall made an unfair observation in 1891 that the fledgling NSPCC's own figures showed that of all the cases it had so far intervened in, only 10 per cent of the children were insured. Now the NSPCC's tables[13] show the numbers of children *known* to be insured; in many cases the parents concealed this fact. By the turn of the century the known proportion had risen to nearly a quarter, and by the late 1920s to 45 per cent; but since infant life insurance had by then long ceased to be a 'danger' as far as the NSPCC was concerned, the figures really contribute nothing to 'proofs' one way or the other.

Dewey put it for the companies that if life insurance did promote child mortality, it would *ipso facto* cease to be commercially viable; the insurance industry had an interest in seeing children survive and he produced figures to show that the child death rate in the Prudential was less than in the population at large. Now since he was claiming that 80 per cent of working-class children were insured anyway, a comparison between 'insured' and 'national' figures must, in his own terms, be meaningless – as with Clay's arguments over forty years earlier. Waugh claimed that the companies really made their profits out of lapsed policies – that is, contributions that ran to waste because subscribers could not keep up payments (a consequence, he claimed, of the importunate selling methods of doorstep agents). He gave an undoubtedly exaggerated figure for the proportion of lapsed policies, and claimed that the 'Pru' included the death rate among the child subjects of its lapsed policies (where the insurance motive for their disposal no longer existed), to arrive at a bogusly depressed average death rate for *all* its insured children. But he did not prove this allegation (hotly denied by Dewey), and in any case how would the 'Pru' keep track of the deaths of children no longer actively on its books?

The Prudential's strongest case statistically was that since the 1840s child mortality had been declining, at a time when the child life insurance business had grown by leaps and bounds, so there was no statistical correlation between the two. Now, as observed in Chapter 2, until 1900 infant mortality below 1 year of age was stubbornly holding steady – yet insurance on the first 2 or 3 months of life, the most vulnerable period, was debarred by societies' rules anyway; and after 1900 this infant mortality rate began steadily declining when insurance was never more popular, as the Prudential actuary, Mr F. Schooling, cogently challenged the delegates at the 1906 National Conference on Infantile Mortality.[14]

While the Maxwell Committee was sitting, the respected Surrey coroner, Athelstan Braxton Hicks, wrote a letter to *The Times* published on the 14th February 1889, listing eleven proposals for combating the dangers of child life insurance, as he saw them. They included a lower ceiling on insurance benefits, so that they covered burial costs only; a restriction of payments to parents only; an 'undertaker clause'; a reference of the deaths of all insured children to coroners, and where inquests returned a 'neglect' verdict (that is, short of the almost impossible-to-establish manslaughter verdict) a forfeiture of payments.

A few months later a case broke in the press that put the insurance companies in the worst possible light and must have helped compensate for Waugh's lame performance before the Committee. A Mrs Ethel Winters of Deptford and her daughter Elizabeth Frost were indicted for the murder by poison of three people: 11-year-old Sidney Bolton (a niece's child she was caring for), William Dutton (the aged father of another relative by marriage), and an older namesake of Elizabeth Frost (whose relationship is not made clear in the accounts). Sidney's life had been insured by Winters, and when he died suddenly of stomach pains in February 1889, the doctor's certificate merely gave 'gastrodynia, diarrhoea and convulsions' as the cause. Winters was only exposed as his murderess when the boy's father grew suspicious on finding out that she had misinformed him of the scale of her insurance interest on the boy's life; police inquiries and other exhumations of persons connected with Winters and Frost followed, resulting in their commitment for trial.[15]

It transpired that Mrs Winters had insured the lives of no fewer than 22 persons for a total of £240 with the Liverpool Victoria Friendly Society alone, and their agent claimed that 'he believed' they were members of her family. Since June 1886 five of these had died, and the Society had paid out on them without any prickles of doubt! She also had fourteen policies with the Prudential, which likewise serenely paid out on the five lives. There had been no checks on her relationship with the subjects and no suspicions aroused at the offices over this cycle of deaths. Moreover, Winters had just written an 'X' by the written-in name of Sidney's mother (who knew nothing of this) on the Liverpool Victoria's acceptance form, and they had taken her word for it. Remissness at headquarters was at least as much to blame as the agents' free-dealing and the implications were clear for the potential dangers to infants' lives.

The Commons committee recommended a tightening up of s.28 of the 1875 Friendly Societies Act: insurance policies in excess of the statutory limits should be made punishable at the time of contracting, and not just when benefits were actually paid: the phrase 'personal representatives' should be more closely defined, medical and registrar's certification procedures made more stringent, and maximum payments should be scaled down (combined with an extension of the protected age range), for example to a maximum of £4 for children under 5, and £8 for 10–16-year-olds. But it was sceptical about an 'undertaker clause', as undertakers could cut corners but inflate the bills to make undue profit; and if insurers were allowed to nominate the undertakers to the societies, this could lead to connivance between parents and undertakers, the latter not being an overly-scrupulous fraternity, as we have seen.

With the Cruelty to Children Act now passed, and the Select Committee's recommendations published, Waugh concentrated on preparing a child life insurance bill; this was presented by a sympathiser, Dr Magee, the Bishop of Peterborough, in the House of Lords in May 1890. The bill adopted the Select Committee's scale of maximum payments, but otherwise differed in two fundamental respects: instead of narrowing down the permitted categories of insurers, it sought to open them up further, to allow beneficent insurance by strangers (the NSPCC had itself in mind) on infants' lives – an indication of the paternalistic 'do gooding' spirit in which the bill was conceived. But the really provocative proposal was the revival of a stringent undertaker clause. Working-class reaction was immediate. On July 16th at the Memorial Hall, Farringdon Street, representatives of trade unions met and passed an indignant resolution 'against the sweeping and slanderous statements made in the House of Lords and elsewhere that working class parents insured their children's lives with improper motives'.[16]

Against such strength of feeling the bill was referred to a Lords Select Committee under Dr Magee. The Committee sat during June and July of the 1890 Session and was reappointed in the next session, meeting between January and July 1891. Even in presenting himself before this more sympathetic Committee, Waugh appeared to be his own worst enemy; he was oblivious to the sensitivities of the class of people his inspectors worked among, and failed to consider opinion among the provincial branches of the newly federated NSPCC. These *were* attuned to popular feeling in northern burial club country, and their spokesmen before the Committee rejected the undertaker clause, as did the Scottish SPCC. Accordingly, at the close of the 1890 Session, the Committee resolved on its deletion from the Bill. Dr Magee was elevated to the Bishopric of York early in 1891, but was ailing and died shortly after. As he was the prime mover behind the Bill, it was pointless continuing the Select Committee, and the Bill was dropped.

Over the next four years several abortive bills were prepared and presented from several quarters,[17] but the NSPCC pinned its main hopes on Sir Richard Webster, a Conservative lawyer MP, and an active proponent of child welfare law. In 1894 he introduced a bill that was to become the Prevention of Cruelty to Children Act 1894, and had intended to introduce child life insurance clauses, but withdrew them as they were controversial and could prejudice the whole bill. In 1895 he tried again with the Funeral Expenses of Children Bill.[18] This went beyond the recommendations of the Maxwell Committee and introduced a new principle: that the insurable limits in Friendly Societies (which offered child sickness insurance as well as funeral benefit) should be favoured as against those for the Collecting Societies, which offered no sickness insurance. Orchestrated opposition from the Collecting Societies forced its withdrawal, too.[19]

Governments of both complexions were very loath to touch the subject. Even when fundamental and comprehensive rationalising acts for Friendly Societies, Collecting Societies and Industrial Assurance Companies were passed in 1896, 'section 28' was reincorporated unamended. In a climate of opinion that was left uncertain if touchy since the polemical duels of 1888–91 no government felt compelled to act, but the residual unease was expressed by the Chief Registrar of Friendly Societies, who wanted to see the Maxwell Committee's recommendations implemented. In his Annual Report for 1893[20] he wrote that even if widespread criminality was unproven, '. . . it cannot be doubted that to allow a parent to profit by the death of a young child is calculated to have a bad moral effect and tend to that neglect described by Clough –

"Thou shalt not kill – but needst not strive

Officiously to keep alive".'

However, some weighty opinion had swung the other way. Dr Arthur Newsholme, a noted medical statistician and destined later to become Medical Officer to the Local Government Board, wrote of child life insurance in the 1889 edition of his work *Vital Statistics* that it was 'to say the least . . . an additional hazard for children', but in his 1899 edition he was much more cautious: 'There is no proof that neglect and crime have been greater in their incidence upon insured children, and it can scarcely be held that the prospective receipt of insurance money has been the incentive to child neglect and child murder in more than a very small number of cases.' This later view was shared by Dr George Newman in his work *Infant Mortality – A Social Problem* in 1906 and in the same year the Infantile Mortality Conference's deliberations could reach no conclusion on the alleged evils.

The NSPCC kept up a sniping campaign but by the later 1890s was shifting its attention more towards alcoholism and its relation to overlaying and cruelty. By the turn of the century the child life insurance issue had gone off the boil, as there appears to have been no really sensational case of multiple poisoning since the trial of the Liverpool baby-farmers William and Elizabeth Pearson in 1890.[21] Ironically, it was the NSPCC's own expanding operations that doubtless had been increasingly forestalling fatalities since then; in 1893–4 it dealt with 15,679 cases of cruelty, etc.; by 1908–9 this had grown to 49,792. Still, nerves remained raw under the surface, and the occasional exceptionally scandalous case of cruelty after 1900 would quickly evoke some MPs to call against child life insurance in the House, with the inevitable prevaricating answer from an embarrassed minister. With the introduction of the Liberal government's comprehensive Children's Bill in 1908, the Home Office could not avoid the matter entirely, but adopted the minimal and least controversial reform. The Select Committee on Infant Life Protection in 1908 (see Chapter 17) had been told by Waugh's successor Robert Parr how baby-farmers were insuring their charges' lives, and this is all that the Act proceeded against. Under s.7 those who minded children for reward were debarred from taking out policies on their lives, and contravention became punishable by up to £25 fine or six months' prison for the minders and the insurance officials alike (where, in the case of the latter, they *knew* the insuring party was a paid minder). The offence was committed at the time the contract was issued, not just at the time of payment. This highly diluted form of the 'Maxwell' recommendations was as far as it went: illicit overpayments to parents, and certification procedures, were left covered by the 1896 Acts.

Yet fascinatingly the whole question of child life insurance fades away completely after 1908. The *Child's Guardian* shows no cases for 1908; there is one for 1909,[22] and the last reference comes in March 1910, in reporting the successful prosecution of an insurance official under the 1908 Act. Up to 1937 the NSPCC's annual tables still traditionally returned the numbers of children known to be insured among its cases, and the proportion grew steadily to 50 per cent or more in the 1930s, without attracting any concerned comment. Acts of 1923 and 1924 raised the insurable limits. A government report on Industrial Assurance in 1934[23] revealed a significant amount of illegal overinsurance by parents, but blamed the persuasive techniques of insurance salesmen and in no way imputed darker motives to the parents.

The end of child life insurance came about through the post-1945 welfare state legislation. The National Insurance Act of 1946 (operative from 1948) introduced a state burial grant which made private burial insurance on others superfluous, and the Industrial Assurance and Friendly Societies Act of 1948[24] complemented it by abolishing such insurances among *every* age group.

The experience after 1908 indicates that the opinions of Dewey and the insurance interests were right all along, for it was environmental and social improvements that proved to be the long-term infant-life conservers after 1900 and the child life insurance issue just faded away. It remains curious, however, that the controversy ceased so abruptly after the very modest reform of 1908.

17   Infant life protection 1890–1914

The long-awaited government infant life protection Bill of 1890,[1] which we left at Chapter 12, contained a number of proposals for strengthening the 1872 Act, but the real bone of contention was its intent to extend registration to 'one-child' foster-homes. Backbenchers complained that this could inconvenience 'neighbourly arrangement' cases – for example, where infection in the family demanded that a baby be boarded away temporarily with a neighbour for its own safety. The government agreed to refer the bill to a Select Committee[2] which produced an amended version. This confined the 'one-child' registration to illegitimate children, the baby-farmers' staple, with the intent of letting out the 'neighbourly arrangement' which was assumed to relate primarily to legitimates. To the same end it extended the range of exemptions under the 1872 Act to cases where the child was boarded away because the parent was seeking work, indisposed or for 'any other reasonable and temporary cause'. The looseness of the drafting – minders might be deceived about the child's legitimacy, and the phrase 'reasonable and temporary cause' could mean anything – made it a non-starter, and it was dropped in August 1890.

The case of Joseph and Annie Roodhouse, who were tried in London in 1891, kept the issue of 'baby-sweating' before the public eye. Through advertising they had acquired and passed on at least 35 infants in their career (10 of whom subsequently died) and the payments made to them had totalled £219 plus £35 in clothes and jewellery. Also in 1891 there was the conviction for manslaughter of Alice Reeves, a particularly cold-blooded baby-farmer from Lambeth; some 300 children's garments were found in her basement.[3] Another case at this time showed up the very worst abuse of the Poor Law boarding-out system (see Chapter 6). Two genteel ladies had fostered a boarded-out girl, under the supervision of the Plympton Board of Guardians. The ladies themselves fell on hard times, and no doubt out of sympathy for one of their own class, the Guardians not only allowed them to retain the girl for the income, but also actively assisted them in fostering other infants outside the Poor Law jurisdiction – to become baby-farmers, in fact, in order to save the ladies from the workhouse. Conditions at their home, previously satisfactory, were transformed. Three of the babies they had taken died from neglect within a short time; one had been 'adopted' for £18 and there was a 50 shillings burial insurance policy on it. In the event one of the ladies, a Miss Hockley, received twelve years' penal servitude for manslaughter.[4]

In 1895 Lord Onslow, chairman of the Moderate party on the LCC, introduced in the Lords on behalf of the LCC a bill similar to the government's original 1890 draft, except for a stronger provision against baby-sweating: no commercial minder could pass on a child under 5 without written permission from the local authority. This was overtaken by the dissolution of Parliament, but reintroduced by Lord Denbigh in the 1896 Session. The 'one-child' registration clause was again the sticking point – the prime minister Lord Salisbury did not like it – and the bill was referred to yet another Select Committee, chaired by Denbigh, in 1896. In the meantime Lord Herschell, acting on behalf of the NSPCC, and with apparent disregard for the hold-up of the other bill, introduced an unrealistically stringent Safety or Nurse-Children Bill covering the same ground;[5] its severity and mistiming bear all the hallmarks of Waugh's unhappy maladroitness as a lobbyist; naturally it had no hope, and was referred to the Select Committee for consideration.

While the Committee sat, the infamous Mrs Dyer (see Chapter 12) was hitting the news again after seventeen years in more sensational circumstances; her trial and execution in 1896 no doubt ensured that *this* time a Select Committee report would lead to some positive enactment.

Mrs Dyer, who had used a succession of aliases, and was currently known as Amelia Dyer, had a history of mental instability and suicidal depression.[6] In 1893 she was released from her last spell in a mental asylum and subsequently resumed her long-standing career of baby-farming with her daughter and son-in-law. Subsequently, they separated, and Mrs Dyer, after some moving about, took lodgings in Reading. The NSPCC had already had occasion to investigate her activities, when on the 30th March 1896 some bargemen fished out from the Thames at Reading a bundle containing a baby girl's body. Some writing on the wrapping paper enabled the police to trace the bundle to Mrs Dyer. In the meantime, Mrs Dyer was arranging the 'adoption' of two other infants. On the 4th April she was arrested, and while in custody six more infants' bodies, including her two recent adoptees (who were postively identified), were taken from the Thames, strangled and weighted in similar fashion. At her trial the defence pleaded insanity, but she was found guilty of murder and hanged in June 1896. The 'Ogress of Reading' made such an impact on the public imagination that she inspired a popular ballad, whose chorus carolled:

> The old baby farmer, the wretched Mrs Dyer
> At the Old Bailey her wages is paid
> In times long ago we'd 'a' made a big fy-er
> And roasted so nicely that wicked old jade.

The Infant Life Protection Act that now passed in 1897[7] still exempted the 'one-child' minder, but raised the protected age. Any commercial minder keeping more than one child up to the age of 5 was obliged to 'notify' the local authority; 'notification' was a concessionary modification of 'registration' under the 1872 Act. No record of the child's identity and parenthood need be kept (Parliament was tender towards concealing the shame of the first-time lapser); but as a gesture against baby-sweating, the minder must notify the local authority of a child's transfer, though prior permission was not required.

Local authorities were expressly empowered (but not obliged) to appoint inspectors to see that the premises and conditions of care came up to the standards defined in the Act. The settlement of precisely defined entry rights, long pressed for by the LCC, was a compromise with libertarian principles: inspectors refused entry might now apply for a magistrate's warrant. Other clauses, including the exemption clause, were similar to the 1872 Act, and one useful proposal in the NSPCC's bill was incorporated: workhouses were now formally obliged to take in children removed from unfit baby-farms; previously they had enjoyed discretion, which had made it harder to put rescued children into safe keeping. But a most ill-conceived provision was Clause Five – the '£20 rule' – whereby lump-sum adoptions of infants up to 2 years old were only to be notified to the local authority if the sum involved was less than £20. The thinking behind this was that only in cheap, low-class 'adoptions' was the child really at risk, but the scope for connivance to hoodwink the authorities was obvious.

The inadequacies of the Act were to come in for persistent criticism, to be finally thrashed out before the Select Committee on Infant Life Protection in 1908, appointed while the Children's Bill was in passage. The whole turn-of-century baby-farming scene comes out in the evidence given before the Select Committees of 1890, 1896 and 1908.

The exemption of 'one-child' establishments left the great

majority of minders outside the scope of the law. The Select Committees were told that minders were generally very poor, coming from the 'casual labouring class and even lower than that'[8] and that more typically fostering was undertaken to supplement incomes, not to provide an independent livelihood. Often the foster-infant was found to be no worse treated than the minder's own child, and the high death rate, due to ignorance and poverty, was common to both. Profit margins were low. Five shillings a week seemed the average weekly fee (in London, at least) in the 1890s, and the cost to a responsible minder of feeding a 1-month-old child was 3s. 8½d a week.[9] Nearly all baby-farms known to the LCC inspector in 1890 had fewer than five children.[10] Samuel Babey, the inspector, told the 1890 Committee that most houses had only one child, and Miss Frances Zanetti, the energetic infant protection visitor appointed for Manchester under the 1897 Act, found the same ten years later. On a house-to-house visitation between 1898 and 1901, to check the existence of baby-farms, she found that of 809 children she saw nearly 80 per cent were in single-child establishments and therefore not subject to statutory inspection.[11] Critics of the Act, like the NSPCC, Miss Zanetti and the umbrella organisation for the country's major Poor Law authorities, the Poor Law Unions Association (many of whose members, however, were remiss in implementing the 1897 Act, as it stood), called for extension to 'one-child' homes; resolutions to this effect were passed at various Poor Law Conferences, and by the 1906 Infantile Mortality Conference.

Ranged against them was a line-up of charitable organisations, like the Charity Organisation Society, the Church of England Waifs and Strays Society and the London Foundling Hospital, which made their own private arrangements for selecting and inspecting foster parents for the infants in their care, and generally allowed only one child per home. If these foster-parents became subject to local authority inspection *as well*, argued the charities, they would find this too irksome and feel 'tarred with the same brush' as the more disreputable class of baby-farmer; the supply of good homes would therefore dry up. In any case, it was claimed, in 'one-child' establishments children were more likely to be better cared-for, and inspection was less necessary than in multi-child farms. Against this, Miss Zanetti pointed out to the 1908 Committee that in France and Germany, where the law required inspection of 'one-child' foster-homes, there was no shortage of offers of good homes, and Robert Parr, the NSPCC Director who succeeded Waugh, said that between 1903 and 1907 his society had dealt with 2,101 cases of cruelty involving one-child establishments.

It was also argued that in one-child homes the child was at least as likely to be neglected, because it provided only a supplementary income and the nurse had to leave it to do other work, like charring; and that cruelty and neglect were less likely to be spotted by observant neighbours than in the case of a more conspicuous multi-child establishment.[12] Before 1896, Alfred Spencer, the Chief Officer of the LCC's Public Control Department (which operated the 1872 and 1897 Acts), had supported 'one-child' extension but changed his opinion before the 1896 Committee wound up. The Department's official line thereafter became one of sceptical neutrality, partly out of appreciation of the charities' point of view, and partly because such extension, it was felt, would do no practical good; as Spencer's successor, James Ollis, told the 1908 Committee, there were an estimated 15,000 illegitimate children under 5 in London, and as these were the ones generally put out to nurse, it would stretch his department's resources too far to include the 'one-child' cases.

The 'one-child' proponents did concede that much depended on the type of inspection. The charities claimed that their own supervision took the form of helpful advice, while local authority inspection amounted to 'brass-button' policing and suspicious probing. The Infant Protection Visitors under the Act needed to have counselling skills, and preferably be female. Even Benjamin Waugh acknowledged in 1896 that 'over half' the nurses his Society had dealt with 'were not evilly disposed' and were amenable to advice on improving child care: 'On the whole, I should say the large proportion are good, well-meaning people; the smaller proportion of them are either doubtful or very bad in their motives.'[13] The failings of local authority inspection lay partly in the Act itself and partly in the spirit in which it was implemented. The statutory enforcing authority for London was the LCC, but elsewhere it was the Poor Law Unions; the latter thus had grafted on to them functions which had strictly speaking nothing to do with pauperism, and as the ethos of so many Unions was to minimise expenditure, they exploited the permissive nature of the Act in regard to inspection, which the Minority Report of the 1909 Poor Law Commission complained 'is by most of them wholly neglected'.[14] The Manchester Unions, as we have noted, appointed a female inspector, as did Dewsbury, but in 1908 it admitted that in Glasgow the Act had been practically a 'dead letter', for the *total* number of 'notified' houses there since 1897 had been 44![15] In London, the most conscientious authority, Samuel Babey had worked on his own till 1894, when two assistants were appointed, and even in 1908 the total inspectorate for a metropolis of over

4,000,000 people amounted to five. The two men did the tracing up of non-notified establishments, and the three women concentrated on inspecting the notified ones. The average number of establishments on their books just prior to 1897 was about 50, and by 1907 this had quadrupled, but was still a drop in the ocean.[16]

Outside London, inspection, so far as it was undertaken, was loaded on to the (mainly male) Poor Law relieving officers, as they did peripatetic work in poor neighbourhoods, checking the means of applicants for poor relief. The emolument for this extra work was little or none; at Newcastle-on-Tyne in 1908, for example, the Superintendent Relieving Officer received a princely £1 a year.[17] Apart from the low incentive, there was so little time to do the work. As the chief relieving officer to the King's Norton Union told the 1909 Poor Law Commission: 'I find that I cannot, with my other duties, do that as I should do it. To find out these children I should have to make a house-to-house visitation, and that, of course, my other duties do not allow.'[18]

Both sides in the 'one-child' exemption controversy were at one in their objection to the '£20 lump sum' clause in the Act; it had always been assumed that 'lump-sum' infants were far more at risk than the weekly payment cases, since the former had a financial interest in the child's demise. Various sources indicate that lump-sum payments ranged from £5 to £50, but occasionally could reach £300 after 1900.[19] Such sums were usually beyond the resources of working girls, notably servants, and apart from the case histories already cited in this book, common sense points to settlement by financially better-off male 'seducers'. Other evidence indicates that weekly-payment infants were no better off. Waugh was certain that the foster-mother's character, not the method of payment, mainly determined the way the child was treated, and he postulated that a continuous turnover of weekly-payment infants, done to death by rapid starvation, was as economically advantageous as lump-sum adoption. Ninian Hill of the Scottish SPCC pointed out that the frequent defaulting on payments by mothers made the supposed security of weekly-payment infants illusory.[20] Indeed there was no justification for assuming an invariable risk to the lump-sum child. Hill told the 1908 Committee of a somewhat compulsive urge to adopt children among the working classes, and he hazarded the motives as 'first a desire for company; they seem to adopt children much in the same way as people in another class of society adopt cats and dogs and parrots', and secondly as an income supplement. This bonding was borne out in a Local Government Board Inspectors' Report to the Home Office in 1911. They believed that nurse-children were 'generally . . . well treated' though suffering from the nurses' ignorance in the same way as their own children, and went on: 'Where the mother is unable or fails to continue payments it seems to be usual for the foster-parent to keep the child as long as possible, making no difference to its treatment', and in many cases 'the foster-parent is unwilling to part with the child'.[21]

Interestingly, while much evidence was given to the Select Committees between 1890 and 1908 of the prevalence of 'Adoption' adverts in the press and its importance to baby-farming operations, no witness suggested a legal curb on such advertisements, though *The Lancet* in 1891, in the wake of the Reeves case, suggested that such advertisements should be subject to prior check by the local authorities.[22] Outright prohibition was presumably out of the question while there was nothing unlawful about the 'adoptions' themselves, and one could never be sure whether the offers to take a child were genuine (say, from childless couples) or mercenary. In 1868 the *British Medical Journal* reckoned that a third of those replying to its decoy adoption advertisements were genuine.[23] During 1888–9 the Chief Constable of Edinburgh did a similar decoy investigation in the city following the Jessie King scandal and found that of 181 respondents 124 *admitted* doing it only for the money.[24]

Very few newspapers could claim to be completely innocent. Such advertisements were 'a perfect source of income',[25] and too tempting for high-principled rejection. In 1867 the *Pall Mall Gazette* and the *Sunday Times* took a sanctimonious line against the *Daily Telegraph* as an irresponsible advertiser which had helped promote Mrs Jaggers's operations,[26] but *The Lancet* of the 12th October pointed out the *Gazette*'s own hypocrisy in publishing similar advertisements itself; while the *Sunday Times* was to turn out to be one of the papers that Margaret Waters used![27]

Even *The Times* was not above reproach. On October 9th 1894 it advertised 'A beautiful boy for Adoption', a 3-year-old whose father, 'a gentleman', claimed he was going abroad. The NSPCC follow-up found that the advertiser was really an 'impecunious farmer and bachelor'.[28]

'Adoption' adverts abounded round the turn of the century. Samuel Babey told the 1890 Select Committee that he had counted 39 such adverts in *The People* over a two-week period; and the NSPCC did its own survey to prepare evidence for the 1908 Select Committee. It collected the advertisements of 386 separate people around the country over a two-week period (many of these repeated their advertisements, so the actual number of inserts exceeded 386); London alone accounted for 161 of these. They

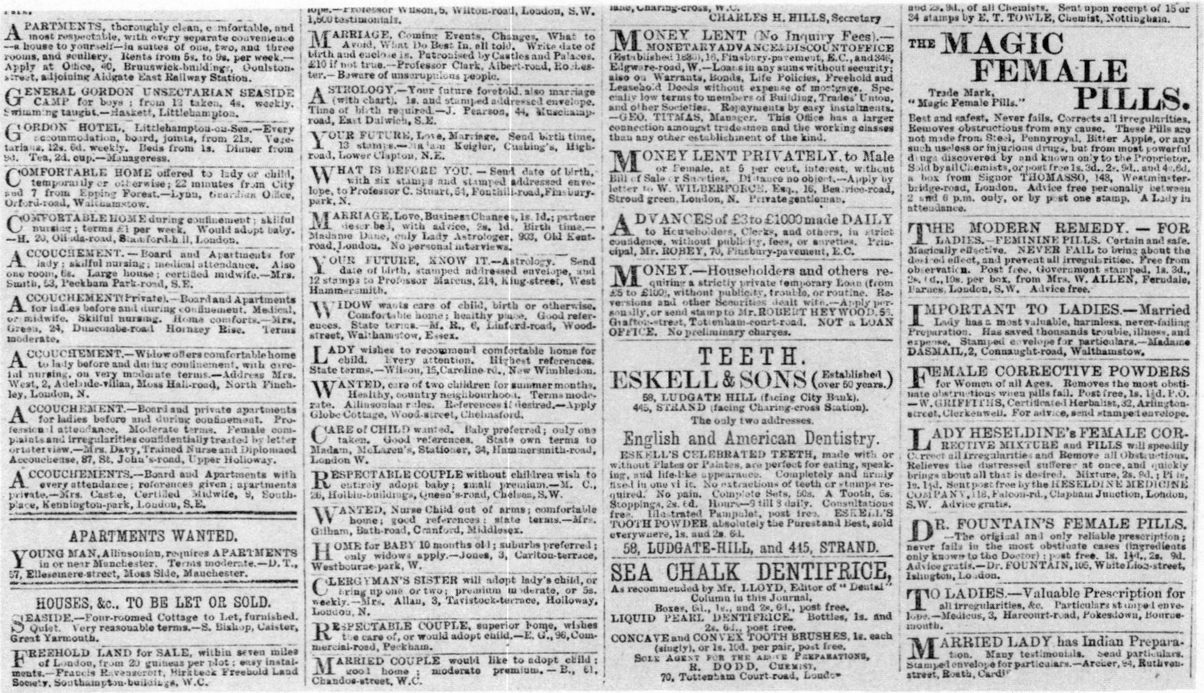

APARTMENTS, thoroughly clean, comfortable, and most respectable, with every separate convenience—a house to yourself—in suites of one, two, and three rooms, and scullery. Rents from 5s. to 9s. per week.—Apply at Office, 40, Brunswick-buildings, Goulston-street, adjoining Aldgate East Railway Station.

GENERAL GORDON UNSECTARIAN SEASIDE CAMP for boys; from 12 taken, 4s. weekly. Swimming taught.—Haskett, Littlehampton.

GORDON HOTEL, Littlehampton-on-Sea.—Every accommodation, board, joints, from 21s. Vegetarians, 12s. 6d. weekly. Beds from 1s. Dinner from 9d. Tea, 2d. cup.—Manageress.

COMFORTABLE HOME offered to lady or child, temporarily or otherwise; 22 minutes from City and 7 from Epping Forest.—Lynn, Guardian Office, Orford-road, Walthamstow.

COMFORTABLE HOME during confinement; skilful nursing; terms £1 per week. Would adopt baby.—H. 20, Oil-da-road, Stamford-hill, London.

ACCOUCHEMENT.—Board and Apartments for lady; skilful nursing; medical attendance. Also one room, 6s. Large house; certified midwife.—Mrs. Smith, 53, Peckham Park-road, S.E.

ACCOUCHEMENT (Private).—Board and Apartments for ladies before and during confinement. Medical, or midwife. Skilful nursing. Home comforts.—Mrs. Green, 24, Duncombe-road Hornsey Rise. Terms moderate.

ACCOUCHEMENT.—Widow offers comfortable home to lady before and during confinement, with careful nursing, on very moderate terms.—Address Mrs. West, 2, Adelaide-villas, Moss Hall-road, North Finchley, London, N.

ACCOUCHEMENT.—Board and private apartments for ladies before and during confinement. Professional attendance. Moderate terms. Female complaints and irregularities confidentially treated by letter or interview.—Mrs. Davy, Trained Nurse and Diplomaed Accoucheuse, 87, St. John's-road, Upper Holloway.

ACCOUCHEMENTS.—Board and Apartments with every attendance; references given; apartments private.—Mrs. Castle, Certified Midwife, 9, South-place, Kennington-park, London, S.E.

APARTMENTS WANTED.

YOUNG MAN, Allinsonian, requires APARTMENTS in or near Manchester. Terms moderate.—D. T., 57, Ellesmere-street, Moss Side, Manchester.

HOUSES, &c., TO BE LET OR SOLD.

SEASIDE.—Four-roomed Cottage to Let, furnished. Quiet. Very reasonable terms.—S. Bishop, Caister, Great Yarmouth.

FREEHOLD LAND for SALE, within seven miles of London, from 20 guineas per plot; easy instalments.—Francis Ravenscroft, Birkbeck Freehold Land Society, Southampton-buildings, W.C.

lope.—Professor Wilson, 5, Wilton-road, London, S.W. 1,500 testimonials.

MARRIAGE, Coming Events, Changes, What to Avoid, What Do Best in, all told. Write date of birth and enclose 1s. Patronised by Castles and Palaces. £10 if not true.—Professor Clark, Albert-road, Rochester.—Beware of unscrupulous people.

ASTROLOGY.—Your future foretold, also marriage (with chart). 1s. and stamped addressed envelope. Time of birth required.—J. Pearson, 44, Muschamp-road, East Dulwich, S.E.

YOUR FUTURE, Love, Marriage. Send birth time, 13 stamps.—Madam Keigler, Cushing's, High-road, Lower Clapton, N.E.

WHAT IS BEFORE YOU.—Send date of birth, with six stamps and stamped addressed envelope, to Professor C. Stuart, 54, Fonthill-road, Finsbury-park, N.

MARRIAGE, Love, Business Changes, 1s. 1d.; partner described, with advice, 2s. 1d. Birth time.—Madame Dane, only Lady Astrologer, 903, Old Kent-road, London. No personal interviews.

YOUR FUTURE, KNOW IT.—Astrology. Send date of birth, stamped addressed envelope, and 12 stamps to Professor Marcus, 214, King-street, West Hammersmith.

WIDOW wants care of child, birth or otherwise. Comfortable home; healthy place. Good references. State terms.—M. R., 6, Linford-road, Wood-street, Walthamstow, Essex.

LADY wishes to recommend comfortable home for child. Every attention. Highest references. State terms.—Wilson, 15, Caroline-rd., New Wimbledon.

WANTED, care of two children for summer months. Healthy, country neighbourhood. Terms moderate. Allinsonian rules. References if desired.—Apply Globe Cottage, Wood-street, Chelmsford.

CARE of CHILD wanted. Baby preferred; only one taken. Good references. State own terms to Madam, McLaren's, Stationer, 34, Hammersmith-road, London W.

RESPECTABLE COUPLE without children wish to entirely adopt baby; small premium.—M. C., 26, Holbin-buildings, Queen's-road, Chelsea, S.W.

WANTED, Nurse Child out of arms; comfortable home; good references; state terms.—Mrs. Gilham, Bath-road, Cranford, Middlesex.

HOME for BABY 10 months old; suburbs preferred; only widows apply.—Jones, 3, Carlton-terrace, Westbourne-park, W.

CLERGYMAN'S SISTER will adopt lady's child, or bring up one or two; premium moderate, or 5s. weekly.—Mrs. Allan, 3, Tavistock-terrace, Holloway, London, N.

RESPECTABLE COUPLE, superior home, wishes the care of, or would adopt child.—E. G., 96, Commercial-road, Peckham.

MARRIED COUPLE would like to adopt child; good home; moderate premium.—E., 61, Chandos-street, W.C.

lane, Charing-cross, W.C.
CHARLES H. HILLS, Secretary

MONEY LENT (No Inquiry Fees).—MONETARY ADVANCES DISCOUNT OFFICE (Established 1830), 16, Finsbury-pavement, E.C., and 346, Edgware-road, W.—Loans in any sums without security; also on Warrants, Bonds, Life Policies, Freehold and Leasehold Deeds without expense of mortgage. Specially low terms to members of Building, Trades' Union, and other Societies. Repayments by easy instalments.—GEO. TITMAS, Manager. This Office has a larger connection amongst tradesmen and the working classes than any other establishment of the kind.

MONEY LENT PRIVATELY, to Male or Female, at 5 per cent. interest, without Bill of Sale or Sureties. Distance no object.—Apply by letter to W. WILBERFORCE, Esq., 16, Beatrice-road, Stroud green, London, N. Private gentleman.

ADVANCES of £3 to £1000 made DAILY to Householders, Clerks, and others, in strict confidence, without publicity, fees, or sureties. Principal, Mr. ROBEY, 70, Finsbury-pavement, E.C.

MONEY.—Householders and others requiring a strictly private temporary Loan (from £5 to £100), without publicity, trouble, or routine. Reversions and other Securities dealt with.—Apply personally, or send stamp to Mr. ROBERT HEYWOOD, 53, Grafton-street, Tottenham-court-road. NOT a LOAN OFFICE. No preliminary charges.

TEETH.
ESKELL & SONS (Established over 50 years.)
58, LUDGATE HILL (facing City Bank).
445, STRAND (facing Charing-cross Station).
The only two addresses.
English and American Dentistry.
ESKELL'S CELEBRATED TEETH, made with or without Plates or Palates, are perfect for eating, speaking, and life-like appearance. Completely and firmly fixed in one visit. No extractions of teeth or stumps required. No pain. Complete Sets, 50s. A Tooth, 5s. Stoppings, 2s. 6d. Hours—9 till 8 daily. Consultations free. Illustrated Pamphlet, post free. ESKELL'S TOOTH POWDER absolutely the Purest and Best, sold everywhere, 1s. and 2s. 6d.
58, LUDGATE-HILL, and 445, STRAND.

SEA CHALK DENTIFRICE,
As recommended by Mr. LLOYD, Editor of "Dental" Column in this Journal,
Boxes, 6d., 1s., and 2s. 6d., post free.
LIQUID PEARL DENTIFRICE. Bottles, 1s. and 2s. 6d., post free.
CONCAVE and CONVEX TOOTH BRUSHES, 1s. each (singly), or 1s. 10d. per pair, post free.
SOLE AGENT FOR THE ABOVE PREPARATIONS,
R. DODD, CHEMIST,
70, Tottenham Court-road, London

and 2s. 9d., of all Chemists. Sent upon receipt of 15 or 34 stamps by E. T. TOWLE, Chemist, Nottingham.

THE MAGIC FEMALE PILLS.
Trade Mark, "Magic Female Pills."
Best and safest. Never fails. Corrects all irregularities. Removes obstructions from any cause. These Pills are not made from Steel, Pennyroyal, Bitter Apple, or any such useless or injurious drugs, but from most powerful drugs discovered by and known only to the Proprietor. Sold by all Chemists, or post free 1s. 3d., 2s. 9d., and 4s. 6d. a box from Signor THOMASSO, 143, Westminster-bridge-road, London. Advice free personally between 2 and 6 p.m. only, or by post one stamp. A Lady in attendance.

THE MODERN REMEDY.—FOR LADIES.—FEMININE PILLS. Certain and safe. Magically effective. NEVER FAIL to bring about the desired effect, and prevent all irregularities. Free from observation. Post free, Government stamped, 1s. 3d., 2s. 6d., 10s. per box, from Mrs. W. ALLEN, Ferndale, Barnes, London, S.W. Advice free.

IMPORTANT TO LADIES.—Married Lady has a most valuable, harmless, never-failing Preparation. Has saved thousands trouble, illness, and expense. Stamped envelope for particulars.—Madame DASMAIL, 2, Connaught-road, Walthamstow.

FEMALE CORRECTIVE POWDERS for Women of all Ages. Removes the most obstinate obstructions when pills fail. Post free, 1s. 1½d. P.O.—W. GRIFFITHS, Certificated Herbalist, 32, Arlington-street, Clerkenwell. For advice, send stamped envelope.

LADY HESELDINE'S FEMALE CORRECTIVE MIXTURE and PILLS will speedily Correct all Irregularities and Remove all Obstructions. Relieves the distressed sufferer at once, and quickly brings about all that is desired. Mixture, 2s. 9d.; Pills, 1s. 1½d. Sent post free by the HESELDINE MEDICINE COMPANY, 118, Falcon-rd., Clapham Junction, London, S.W. Advice gratis.

DR. FOUNTAIN'S FEMALE PILLS.—The original and only reliable prescription; never fails in the most obstinate cases (ingredients only known to the Doctor); post free, 1s. 1½d., 2s. 9d. Advice gratis.—Dr. FOUNTAIN, 105, White Lion-street, Islington, London.

TO LADIES.—Valuable Prescription for all irregularities, &c. Particulars stamped envelope.—Medicus, 3, Harcourt-road, Pokesdown, Bournemouth.

MARRIED LADY has Indian Preparation. Many testimonials. Send particulars. Stamped envelope for particulars.—Archer, 94, Ruthven-street, Roath, Cardiff

Figure 9 *These were typical of the ads found in popular papers of the period. The left-hand column carries a series of advertisements for accoucheuses. Note that the last one is a Mrs Castle. From her address in Lambeth, adjacent to Brixton and Camberwell, she is very likely to be the same Mrs Castle who figured in the Margaret Waters case twenty years before (see Chapter 11). Column two contains fostering and 'adoption' inserts, and column four the thinly disguised adverts for abortifacients then common in newspapers and magazines. (Source: small-ads of the* Weekly Times and Echo *29th June 1890, p. 15. Courtesy:* British Library, Newspaper collection.*)*

were customarily misleading, for most gave the impression that they wanted to care for a single child, while the NSPCC follow-ups revealed that many advertisers admitted their readiness to take more than one.[29]

A few newspaper editors, perhaps, around 1900 were refusing all adoption advertisements; many more squared their consciences by insisting on clergymen's testimonials from would-be advertisers. These the NSPCC in 1891 dismissed as worthless, as clergymen were notoriously naive: 'In no class of men is good feeling more easily imposed upon, and by none is the good character of apparently respectable and needy people so readily assumed.'[30] Although the 1908 Children's Act in no way touched upon advertisements, there appears to have been a voluntary tightening up by the press on adoption adverts between 1908 and 1914; as we shall see, the effect of the 1914–18 War was to stimulate the market for adoptions afterwards, and the press began relaxing its policy; however, they readily co-operated in the early 1920s when the NSPCC brought abuses to their attention.[31]

Statistical evidence indicates a long-term decline in infanticide by 1900 since the peak of the 1860s, as Chapter 18 discusses; but between 1900 and 1907 there were no fewer than three baby-farming trials to end in executions, an acceleration of murder convictions that probably indicates a greater police vigilance and a lower public tolerance of infant disposal. In 1900 Asa Chard Williams, a schoolteacher's wife, was executed following the discovery of a strangled baby girl in the Thames, and in 1903 Amelia Sach, a midwife, and her inept baby-disposer, Annie Walters, both went to the gallows.[32] In 1907 Leslie (sic) James, alias Rhoda Willis, enjoyed the dubious distinction of being the last baby-farmer in Britain to be executed. James came from a prosperous background but, after her marriage to a marine engineer failed, she went steadily downhill. By 1907 she was an alcoholic, had spent a period in jail for theft and had sunk into prostitution for a time. She now took up the 'adoption' of babies from her lodgings at Abertillery in South Wales, and subsequently from the lodgings of a Mrs Wilson in Cardiff, who was implicated, too. In June 1907 after telling Mrs Wilson she was going to Bristol on 'adoption' business, she returned home dead drunk, and carrying a parcel. In her stupefied state she fell off the bed and Mrs Wilson went to her room on hearing the thump. There she found a baby's corpse stuffed under the mattress. James was tried, convicted of murder and hanged at Cardiff Jail in August 1907. It was claimed that she had killed the child on a train journey back to Cardiff, but her lawyers fought unavailingly for a reprieve on the grounds that the baby, already neglected and vulnerable when she received it, might have been accidentally killed through James's drunken mishandling. The Women's Purity League of Cardiff campaigned on her behalf, as a feminists' 'martyr', insisting that, repellent as her occupation was, she was only responding to market demand.[33]

The case was timely for the campaigners for reform of the 1897 Act. In each of the Parliamentary Sessions between 1901 and 1908 private members' amending bills, proposing 'one-child' extension and the abolition of the '£20 lump sum' clause, were introduced, but failed because of the contentious nature of the former. Herbert Samuel, the Liberal Parliamentary Under-Secretary to the Home Office, was known to be planning a comprehensive consolidating act relating to children and in 1907 receiving deputations from supporters and opponents of 'one-child' extension. In February 1908, when the Children's Bill was introduced, the Select Committee was appointed to examine the 'one-child' issue, and its recommendations were incorporated in the Bill during its committee stage in July, to be finally enacted.[34]

The main advances on the 1897 Act were as follows:

The '£20 lump sum' rule was abolished.

The protected age was raised to 7, and 'one-child' establishments were now included, but subject to local authorities' discretion to exempt individual premises as they saw fit. Where charities boarded-out children into foster homes, the authorities were empowered to delegate the statutory inspection to the charities' own inspectorate. This was the compromise answer to their objections over local authority inspection of 'one-child' homes. It now became obligatory for authorities to appoint inspectors, but outside London those authorities still remained the Poor Law unions.

'Notification' was retained, as against 'registration' and in other respects, with drafting amendments, the principles of the 1897 Act were retained. Exemptions from inspections included hospitals, boarding schools and boarding-in charitable institutions. The exemption of the last was to come in for criticism in the 1920s as some were unsatisfactorily run,[35] and under the Children and Young Persons Act of 1932 they were brought under direct Home Office inspection, with the result that more abuses came to light in the 1930s.

The Home Office built up a bulky file of correspondence with the NSPCC, local authorities and the Local Government Board concerning the working of the new Act between 1908 and 1912.[36] Subjects included the necessity of advertising the duty to 'notify'

more extensively: the need for more female Infant Protection
Visitors; complaints (from Robert Parr of the NSPCC) that Boards
of Guardians were 'soft' on prosecuting delinquent nurses and
reluctant to remove children from unfit homes, and that magistrates'
fines were too low (sometimes as little as 1 shilling); technical legal
points and legal loopholes; and (a perennial topic of correspondence) the undesirable persistence of 'lump-sum' adoptions. In
1911 the Home Office sought a report from the Local Government
Board Inspectors (who oversaw the Boards of Guardians) on the
implementation of the Act, and their conclusion was that 'With
very few exceptions Boards of Guardians have made adequate
arrangements to meet the increased duty imposed upon them by
the Act' but acknowledged that they were too lenient in regard to
prosecution, and that the Act still did not reach 'a proportion' of
nurses. In 1912 Robert Parr sent a lengthy account of prosecutions
for non-notification and neglect instigated by the NSPCC.

But authorities *were* to stir themselves in a way that they had
failed to do under the 1897 Act. During six months in 1911, for
example, Glasgow, where we saw that the 1897 Act had been a
flop, boasted 236 notices from new 'guardians'.[37] The number of
houses on the LCC's books, about 200 in 1907, had risen to 2,164
by October 1910 and 3,168 in March 1914,[38] but I am not clear
whether the post-1908 figures now included also those foster-homes
under the aegis of charities acting as delegated inspectors under the
1908 Act. Also subject to this query is the officially estimated peak
figure of 22,000 children in notified homes in England and Wales
in 1920;[39] this was to fall markedly in the Depression years of the
1920s as fewer women could afford the charges, or were laid off and
did not need to board their children out during the working week.[40]

18 Bastardy, eugenics and affiliation law reform to 1939

We saw in Chapter 13 that the 1872 (and 1873) Bastardy Acts, which remained the principal statutes for the remaining period of this book, did not dramatically ease the single mother's lot, and further affiliation law reform was not an issue likely to commend itself to Parliament's valuable time.

From the 1890s the worth of the bastard was the subject of two intellectually opposed outlooks; a small but esteemed eugenic élite saw him as innately unfit, a view that allowed moral prejudice to distort scientific objectivity; but the increasingly prevailing opinion recognised his potential if given a fair start in life.

The faster fall in birth rate among the higher classes in the late nineteenth century had begun to stir fears among an intellectual élite that the nation was heading for racial suicide, as the lower intelligences outbred the higher. The science of eugenics was born to study the social forces that made for racial degeneration and to suggest means for improving the racial stock. It should be emphasised that eugenics was *not* proto-Fascist, but a genuinely learned movement very eager to compile objective sociological data[1] (though interpretation of those data was another matter). Its nerve centre was the Biometric Laboratory of University College London, founded in 1906 and the movement's most controversial protagonist was Professor Karl Pearson, geneticist, astronomer and biologist, a man of immense gifts. His very ivory-towered eminence, however, led him into dogmatic certainties and he was not above turning a blind eye to statistics that contradicted his case. He represented the 'negative' school of eugenics: unfit stock, like the feeble-minded, should be weeded out by sterilisation; epidemics were beneficial as they eliminated weak offspring; bastards were an aberrant strain and their survival should not be encouraged; it was not the environment that *caused* degeneration but innate degenerates who dragged their environment down. For example, he claimed that the higher death rate among back-to-back dwellers in Rochdale was not due to the circumstances of their housing; it was the low-grade, weak stock, already disposed to a shorter life-span, that gravitated to the slums because they could not hold down a decent job. Social welfare and public health programmes were 'dysgenic' as they helped the unfit to survive. Such rigid and extreme 'survival of the fittest' ideas were challenged by an opposing school of eugenists, who were much more in tune with the spirit of the times. 'Nurtural' and 'preventive' eugenists like Dr Caleb Saleeby had a sound grasp of modern medical research, which was demonstrating the effects of environment in general, and pre-natal influences in particular, on a child's mental and physical development;[2] how, for example, maternal alcoholism, TB and malnutrition critically debilitated the foetus. Social welfare programmes must be supported, he urged, to eliminate 'racial poisons' like alcoholism, VD and industrial diseases, notably lead poisoning – the cause of so many premature and stillbirths. Saleeby branded the Pearsonites in their attitude to disadvantaged babies as the 'better dead' school, and in 1914 condemned the infant mortality rate as 'simply national infanticide on a gigantic scale'.[3]

The Pearsonites were not without sympathisers in high places but their views were never translated into practical politics, and indeed the one practical venture they did inspire was a private initiative: when Dr Marie Stopes opened her first birth control clinic at Islington in 1921 as a mission to working-class women, her underlying motive was eugenic rather than emancipationist. As she wrote in 1926: 'For want of contraceptive measures the low-grade stocks are breeding in an ever-increasing ratio in comparison to the high-grade stocks, to the continuous detriment of the race.'[4]

However, the Minority Report of the 1909 Royal Commission on the Poor Law felt that the views of a luminary like Pearson were prominent enough to warrant express rebuttal. It stoutly asserted that 'there is no scientific justification for the assumption that the preventable deaths of infants either result in the survival of the fittest . . . or tend to the improvement of the race', and defended the worth of bastard children: illegitimacy was no proof of inferiority of stock, for while in some Poor Law institutions they were mostly the backward and badly-formed children, 'those in Hampstead, Kensington and Chelsea were often the most refined, well-built and promising'.[5]

The Pearsonites were going against the tide, in fact, for social attitudes towards bastardy were slowly becoming more clement from the end of the nineteenth century. In 1893 there was an attempt, albeit unsuccessful, to pass a legitimation Bill, whereby bastards would be legitimated upon the subsequent marriage of their parents (as was already the case in Scotland). In 1899 the *Westminster Review* called for more state assistance for illegitimate children as the only way to check infanticide and abortion, since unhelpful censoriousness towards the 'fallen woman' just aggravated the problem.[6] Illegitimacy had in fact slowly been declining: in the 1890s the absolute (official) numbers of illegitimate births each year now fell below 40,000 (in England and Wales). Up to the First World War they hovered around 37,000 a year, that is roughly 4.5 per cent of all births. The upheavals of 1914–18 saw a progressive rise in the illegitimacy rate to over 6 per cent by the end of the War, falling back to about 4.5 per cent, once peacetime family stability recovered, and continuing to fall well into the 1930s. (This contrasts with a 1984 rate of nearly 20 per cent, but this is partly accounted for by large numbers of couples opting to live openly in an unmarried partnership in our 'permissive' times.)

Criticism of the 1872 Bastardy Act only began surfacing forty years after it was passed. In 1913 a pamphlet called 'Filius Nullius' by Joseph King MP called for reform. In 1911 less than a quarter of all fathers of recent illegitimate births were made the subject of maintenance orders. He listed a number of proposals, for example raising the 5 shillings a week maximum payment, now grossly inadequate, and allowing for payments to be increased as the father's income rose over the years; ending open-court applications, a notorious deterrent to mothers; and appointing a court officer to receive the money, which under existing law had to be collected directly from the father by the mother.

From 1914 there was a quickening pace of reform; under two acts in 1914 magistrates were allowed to vary an original maintenance order but only up to the existing 5 shillings a week, and the courts were empowered to appoint collecting officers, though they were slow to take this power up. The Registrar General's revelation during the First World War that the gap between the legitimate and illegitimate infant death rates (then roughly 10 and 20 per cent respectively) had widened in recent years prompted the foundation of the National Council for the Unmarried Mother and her Child in 1918 as a lobbying vehicle for improved affiliation and welfare rights, and as a counselling and accommodation bureau for girls in distress. In 1918 maintenance payments were raised to 10 shillings a week, the first increase in forty-six years; five years later they were doubled (but remained at £1 a week until 1952).[7] The Maternity and Child Welfare Act of 1918 was a landmark in official policy towards unmarried mothers. It provided for an extensive range of pre- and post-natal welfare services to be set up by local authorities outside the Poor Law, for married and unmarried mothers alike. The local Government Board encouraged the Poor Law unions to abandon the Victorian practice of separating unmarried mothers and their infants as soon as possible, and to keep them together, at any rate during the infants' first year. Nevertheless, private charities persisted in discriminating against unmarried mothers. In 1922 few maternity hospitals were letting them in, and they still had to resort to the workhouse lying-in wards; and the old prejudice that illegitimates had 'bad blood' was still widespread enough for one authority on infant mortality to plead on their behalf in 1922: 'Illegitimate children are not worthless and if looked after at the start of life grow up to be the best of citizens.'[8]

After a succession of bills from 1920 a Legitimation Act was passed in 1926 – not unconnected with the passage of the Adoption Act the same year, as it would have been anomalous to vest a stranger's child with full filial rights, but not the pre-marital offspring of both parents. Affiliation reform bills in the 1920s fared less well, and triggered off traditional fears in the masculine preserve of Parliament that over-generosity towards women would open the door to blackmail of innocent men. One controversial proposal was that the father should be made financially responsible for the woman's support during pregnancy; any idea of affiliating the child before it was born was totally unacceptable to the House, even where the mother's pregnancy made her plight desperate.[9]

As I have observed, there was a wartime rise in illegitimate births to nearly 42,000 in 1919, and the pattern of anxious wives with illegitimate babies awaiting the wrath to come from their returning husbands, became a familiar part of the post-war scene.[10] The abandoned baby syndrome received a tragic boost, and the February 1920 issue of the *Child's Guardian*, under the headline 'Babies Thrown Away', recorded a selection of the cases then regularly cropping up in the press. They are as appalling as any case reported in the 1850s and 1860s: a baby dumped down a pit shaft, or hidden in a pig-sty; an infant left on a doorstep by a munitions worker; a beheaded 3-year-old boy found in a river; a child found drowned with an iron weight attached to it, and a baby left on a doorstep because the mother feared her husband's anger when he returned from the Front – to cite just a few.

However, in absolute terms illegitimacy became a sharply declining problem between the wars as the birth rate fell. In 1922 there were 34,138 illegitimates born in England and Wales; in 1935 25,105. Affiliation machinery appears to have worked no better than before the war, for the proportion of single mothers winning maintenance orders remained obstinately at a fifth or less; indeed,

in 1948 it was down to a tenth.[11] Now, although the official figures
may have been concealing a trend towards out-of-court settlements,
the 'corroborative evidence' rule remained the same bugbear as
ever. In the 1928 edition of Lushington's *Law of Affiliation and
Bastardy*, the editor remarked of its arbitrariness that it 'produces
more injustice than it prevents. The more modest the unmarried
mother, often the less likely is corroboration to be forthcoming;
while on the other hand the formal requirement is sometimes held
to be satisfied by very inadequate materials.'

Blood tests began to be used in the 1930s, but they are more a
tool for the defence, as they can prove a man's innocence, whereas
a positive match does not by itself establish paternity.[12]

The extension of public welfare facilities outside the Poor Law
probably did more for the unmarried mother than the liberalised
maintenance allowance after 1918. Still, while the illegitimate death
rate was falling in parallel with the legitimate rate, it persistently
held at twice the latter – 10.5 and 5.8 per cent respectively in 1930
– and it was not until the late 1930s that the gap began to
narrow.[13] The spreading use of contraception between the wars,
and a high incidence of abortion, as confirmed by the Inter-
Departmental Committee on Abortion in 1939, reinforced by a
disinclination to bring children into the world during the
Depression, reduced the numbers of unwanted babies being born
to unprecedentedly low levels; this made the single most important
contribution to the near disappearance of infanticide as a social
problem at this time.

19   Infant conservation
       1890–1920

With babies becoming a scarcer commodity at the end of the
century, there was a growing public emphasis on infant life
preservation (notwithstanding the 'negative' eugenists). To some
extent this was stimulated by Britain's growing sense of international political and economic vulnerability; an abundant and
healthy stock of youthful emigrants was seen as a necessity to
populate our dominions rapidly and create an Imperial ring of
confidence against any threat from without.

From the 1880s voluntary middle-class female 'missioners' like
those of the Ladies Public Health Society of Manchester (1887)
and the Ladies Sanitary Institution of Liverpool (1893) offered
domestic instruction to women in the slums; professional health
visitors appeared in the 1890s, and the Notification of Births Act
1907, as we have seen, was designed to make their work more
effective. 'Schools for Mothers' sprang up round the country, and
'mothercraft' became the in-word. From 1899 milk depots –
municipal centres for distributing subsidised or free milk of
guaranteed purity to poor mothers as baby food – began to make
their appearance, inspired by the French 'Goutte de Lait'
movement. The Dairies, Cowsheds and Milkshops Order of 1899
was the first, albeit ineffective, attempt to regulate dairy and milk
hygiene standards for the public; and the relative merits and
demerits of 'certified' and pasteurised milk were being forcefully
discussed at this period.[1] Eugenic concern about our racial stamina
was quickened by the poor physical standard of volunteers at
recruiting stations during the Boer War, and prompted the
appointment of the Departmental Committee on Physical Deterioration in 1904, which included a review of the conditions of infant
nurture.

How did this increasing value placed on infant life reflect itself in
the long-term trend in infanticide? The number of inquest verdicts
of murder on infants under one had been steadily falling from
150–200 a year in the 1860s down to 90–110 a year in the 1880s,

and 60–80 a year by the late 1890s.[2] But babies always remained grossly and disproportionately vulnerable to murder, and the decline was only relative. In the late 1870s 0–1-year-olds formed over 50 per cent of all murder victims at a time when they were less than 3 per cent of the population; the proportion steadily declined to 35 per cent by 1900, but the proportion of babies in the population by then had fallen to about 2.3 per cent.[3] This 35 per cent figure indeed held steady into the early 1920s,[4] and does not on the face of it provide really positive indication of an enhancing regard for infant life. One should remember, however, that a high proportion of such 'murders' were committed by depressed or temporarily deranged mothers in the wake of childbirth (as the legal distinction between Infanticide and Murder was to reveal from 1922) and this probably lent a degree of constancy to the figure when other social conditions were changing. Moreover, the statistics reveal only crimes *known to the police*, and we can bet that a lot more infant murders were unknown to the police in 1880 than in 1920. The criminal statistics furnish only the narrowest of indicators anyway, when we look at the absolute number of infant murders: ranging around 70–75 a year in the late nineteenth century and down to around 65 by 1920.

Interestingly, however, the number of trials for concealment – traditionally the soft prosecution option against infanticidal mothers – had declined sharply from an average of 103 a year between 1871 and 1875 to 44 a year between 1896 and 1900.[5] I am not sure what this tells us: were women cannily dumping bodies more frequently in public places to avoid a technical 'concealment' charge? Was there a real decline in baby-dumping? The 231 babies' bodies found exposed in London in 1895 do not suggest this,[6] though the trend in inquest murder verdicts I have cited suggests the opposite. Or was there an emboldened trend in prosecution policy away from 'concealment' towards manslaughter or even murder charges?

One area of 'violent death' that appeared to be increasing in the late nineteenth century was infant suffocation; overwhelmingly this was suffocation in bed, generically termed 'overlying', from the assumption that parents crushed them in the shared beds then almost universal among the poor; however, much was due to asphyxiation from over-cladding in cold weather, and we have become increasingly aware since the early 1940s of the phenomenon known as 'cot death', the as-yet scientifically elusive 'Sudden Infant Death Syndrome' in which apparently healthy babies suddenly cease to breathe in their sleep. It was the rising living standards between the world wars and the increasing practice of bedding babies apart from their parents that brought this phenomenon to light, and we may guess that this accounted for some of the alleged 'suffocations' prior to 1914.[7]

Thomas Wakley was probably the first coroner to make public issue of the flow of suffocation deaths that came before the inquests, and stated his belief in 1855 that virtually all of them were asphyxiations, not true 'overlyings',[8] for his analysis of inquest frequency patterns showed a peak in the winter months. A decade later Edwin Lankester adverted to the problem, but attached more significance to overlying.[9] Both coroners accepted that suffocations were overwhelmingly accidental and urged parents to take greater care. However, during the infanticide alarms of the 1860s thoughts were bound to fly to more sinister possibilities. Mr T. Littleton, in his address to the NAPSS in 1872 'On the Mortality of Infants', showed that the *rate* of suffocation deaths had increased by about 40 per cent between 1858 and 1865. Taking 1867 as a further case, he showed that just over half the suffocations were caused by bedclothes, less than a third by overlying, and the remainder by food.

As a contributor to total infant mortality, suffocation was negligible. For example, in 1860, of 101,000 deaths of infants under 1 in England and Wales 760 were due to suffocations. In 1904 less than 1/70th of all deaths of such infants was due to suffocation, compared with just under a fifth for diarrhoeal diseases alone.[10] Not surprisingly, the younger the infant the more vulnerable he was; in 1898 of 2,010 victims below 5, 1,941 were 0–1, and 626 of these were below 1 month old.[11] In the context of concern about child-murder, however, suffocations assumed a significance out of proportion to their murders. Nevertheless, after the 1860s it began receiving attention again in the medical journals only from the early 1880s, and became an increasing social concern later in the decade. From 1889 the judicial statistics started showing separate figures for the number of inquests on infant suffocation victims. In 1889 there were 1,331, and from then to 1907 the annual figure hovered around 1,500, occasionally rising to 1,700. Ninety-five per cent of the verdicts were 'accidental death'; there were only one or two murder and manslaughter verdicts recorded in any year.

The Registrar General's Annual Report for 1890[12] was something of a landmark, for he published an analysis of 2,020 inquests showing the weekly frequency patterns. Sunday was the worst day by far for reporting suffocation deaths; twice as many cases were reported on that day as on Saturday or Monday, and the figures stayed low during the week until the next Sunday peak. The conclusion seemed obvious: as Saturday was then pay-day, parents were smothering their infants in a drunken stupor following a Saturday night spree. The specific problem of overlying thus came to the fore, bound up with Temperance propaganda at the time, and the NSPCC took the lead in the 1890s in inveighing against alcoholism as the single most important root-cause of parental wickedness. The Medical Officer for the LCC collected statistics for 1901–7 showing that bed-suffocations and overlyings increased by 50 per cent during weeks in which there was a bank holiday.[13] London and Liverpool had particularly bad records for suffocation deaths, though the formation of the Liverpool SPCC in 1886 plus the vigilance of and public strictures by the coroner, Clarke Aspinall, seemed to reduce the Liverpool figure somewhat.

The NSPCC compared British law unfavourably with Germany's. In the latter country 'overlying' was a criminal offence, and the onus was on the parent to prove she was not negligent. As a result such deaths in Germany were very few, for the custom for parents to share the bed with infants was discouraged. In Britain we had only the more serious charge of manslaughter and the burden of proof was on the prosecution. As a result it was virtually impossible to secure a conviction, and prosecution in the negligible number of cases where inquest juries returned inculpating verdicts was scarcely worthwhile. In Dundee over a period of ten years prior to 1893, in none of the 400 reported overlying cases had the police bothered to prosecute. Juries felt an instinctive sympathy for the mother – the usual defendant. As a Scottish barrister told the 1893 Death Certification Committee, 'one could not lose an overlaying case if one was defending a woman'.[14]

Even where coroners like Aspinall in Liverpool and Athelstan Braxton Hicks of Surrey were themselves 'hot' on overlying, this perverse leniency among juries often frustrated their efforts. In one inquest at Lambeth in 1895 the subject was a suffocated baby girl. The parents had appeared before Hicks less than twelve months before over the suffocation of a previous child, when they had received a caution. Yet the jury's verdict in the current case was 'accidental death'; Hicks was astonished and moved to bitter irony:

> The Coroner: 'Accidental death, gentlemen? Nothing else?'
> The Foreman: 'No Sir.'
> The Coroner: 'You are perfectly satisfied it was a pure accident?'
> The Foreman: 'Yes, Sir.'
> The Coroner: 'Very well, Mrs Wigden, you can go on
>   smothering your children as much as you like, the jury say.
>   The foreman says it was a pure accident, and the jury says,
>   after all these warnings, it doesn't matter. Well, gentleman, if

> you think that is a proper thing to do, by all means say it was
> an accident; but we may as well hold no inquests at all – it is a
> perfect farce.'[15]

Now, in fact there were two schools of thought about suffocation
at the turn of the century. One, like the NSPCC and Hicks,
emphasised the contribution of overlying and the drink connection.
The other, represented for instance by the Battersea coroner, Dr
Troutbeck, discounted overlying and emphasised other factors.
This distinction was crucial, for it raised the hotly contended
question: Were the deaths primarily drink-related? In which case
we should have special criminal penalties for overlying, on the
German model. Or was it primarily the tragic but inescapable
consequence of overcrowding, which forced poor parents to share
their beds with their infants, making accidents inevitable? Now the
correlation between overcrowding and the suffocation rate was
undisputed, and there were statistics to prove it,[16] but of course
there was a correlation between poverty, overcrowding and
alcoholism, too. The opponents of a German-style law claimed it
would be oppressive to poor parents, who were victims of their
environment.

In 1902 the NSPCC forwarded a draft bill for strengthening the
1894 Prevention of Cruelty to Children Act to the Lord Chief
Justice, Lord Alverstone, who, as Sir Richard Webster, had piloted
the 1894 measure. The draft included a clause making overlying an
offence, but it was omitted from the final version of the 1904 Act. It
was unlikely that such a clause could ever pass a Conservative-
dominated House, as it would imply a condemnation of drink,
which would embarrass the Tories' financial backers, the brewing
interests. In 1906, however, the Liberals, with their temperance
leanings, came to power. In that year the NSPCC, the Coroners
Society and the British Medical Association met to devise a draft
bill to deal with overlying and the injury to children from
unguarded fires. The bill, introduced by a child welfare activist,
T.A. Bramsdon MP, in March 1907 never got beyond a second
reading, but the Home Office Minister, Herbert Samuel, was
sympathetic and incorporated it in his Children's Bill in 1908. It
proposed that when an infant was overlain, the defendant was
presumed to be negligent and the onus was on her (or him) to
prove otherwise. If the defendant, in addition, was proved to be
drunk the penalty was more severe. The punishment was a fine
only; no prison. The clause received stiff and successful opposition:
Mr Akers-Douglas, a former Conservative Home Office Minister,
claimed it bore too severely on working-class families, as 'overlying

is largely due to the bad accommodation these people have' and that 'in many cases, it is mere accident; probably no person is more distressed than the mother'.

In the event Samuel had to be content with a diluted measure that passed as Clause 13 of the final Act. Overlying was an offence only if the defendant 'was at the time of going to bed under the influence of drink'. It did provide for up to three months' jail as a penalty, but the prosecution had to prove intoxication, and that the infant was '*in bed* with some . . . person over sixteen years of age'.[17]

The clause attracted immediate criticism: how could intoxication at the time of going to bed be proved? If several adults shared the bed, how could the culprit be identified? And a subsequent judicial ruling opened another gaping hole: the phrase 'in bed' meant precisely that. If the baby was overlaid on a couch or on the floor by an intoxicated adult, or if the adult flopped out over the baby lying *on top of* the bed covers, Clause 13 did not apply.[18]

Was the clause totally ineffective, as the NSPCC feared? Now, prior to 1908 suffocation inquests on infants were running at just below 1,500 a year, but there are signs of a perceptible fall both in inquests and in the Registrar General's suffocation death statistics just before the Act came into force.[19] Between 1908 and 1909 the fall is much sharper, and from 1909 to 1914 inquests ran at just over 1,100 a year, falling slightly in 1914. Now the coincidence with the implementation of the 1908 Act is so precise that I reckon that Clause 13 had some deterrent effect; though it is true that the incipient decline in alcoholism just prior to 1914 (see Chapter 2) may have played a part, too. The experience of the 1914–18 war and its aftermath shows that the 'demon drink' school was right all along. I shall tabulate two sets of figures for the infant death rates (up to 1 year old) from suffocation per 1,000 live births:

	Year 1913[20]	
	Legitimates	*Illegitimates*
London	2.54	5.39
County Boroughs (larger towns)	1.75	3.95
Rural Districts	0.62	1.83

	Year 1919[20]	
	Legitimates	*Illegitimates*
London	0.83	4.56
County Boroughs	0.83	2.81
Rural Districts	0.49	1.24

Now, we saw in Chapter 2 the dramatic beneficial impact of wartime restrictions on drink; in 1912 the death rate from alcoholism per 1,000,000 of the population was 138; in 1920 it was 64.[21] The very low incidence of suffocation in rural districts even before the war must be largely due to the milder ill-effects of drink there: between 1890 and 1909 the rate of convictions for drunkenness in the country areas was a third of what it was in manufacturing districts.[22] However, despite rural poverty and overcrowding, country babies were more robust, and the unfavourable level of urban suffocation may also be due to town children's generally poorer health and greater susceptibility to bronchial disorders.

The statistics raise other questions. Why were illegitimates so much more at risk? Why should an illegitimate child sleeping with its single mother have been more likely to suffocate than a legitimate child sleeping with both its parents? Illegitimate babies were the weakest; but were single mothers also more drunken? Or was there a deal of concealed infanticide in those 'suffocations'? And why did suffocation of illegitimates hold up particularly stubbornly in London at the end of the war?

The fall in drink consumption between the wars, and the sharp decline in suffocation inquests on infants in the same period are too closely associated for a link to be denied, though we should recall that there were fewer new-borns to suffocate and a trend towards sleeping babies in their own cots, too. In 1919 there were 459 inquests, that is 40 per cent of the 1913 level; in 1929 it was 238, and 1935 down to 134.[23]

20   The disappearance of baby-farming 1920–39

Curiously, it was only in the inter-war period, with the infanticide problem as familiar to the Victorians fading fast, that Parliament finally got round to completing changes in the law which infant life protection campaigners had urged for over sixty years; it is almost as though the legislature was simply writing a final address to a social problem that was well on the way to solving itself.

In 1922 an Infanticide Act at last got through, creating a non-capital offence distinct from murder.[1] A woman could be indicted for infanticide where 'by any wilful act or omission [she] causes the death of her newly born child' but at the time 'she had not fully recovered from the effect of giving birth . . . and by reason thereof the balance of her mind was then disturbed.' The punishment was as for manslaughter. An infanticide indictment did not preclude a jury from returning a murder or concealment verdict instead if they saw fit.

Unfortunately the Act did not define the time-limit of 'new-born'; a 6-week-old baby was adjudged not to be 'new-born' in 1927; nor a 3-week-old in 1936.[2] In 1936 a group of back-benchers introduced a bill extending the statutory limit definitely to 8 weeks where 'distress and despair' prompted a mother to kill her child. Mr Jagger MP, in introducing the bill, said there had been six 'tragic cases' of infanticide in the last twelve months where others had been formally sentenced to death, but subsequently reprieved, and the bill was intended to end this tormenting farce. Perhaps the worst recent case of legal cruelty he cited was that of an 18-year-old with a mental age of 11, who killed her baby of 18 months when the father stopped paying maintenance.[3] The bill got nowhere, but the Infanticide Act of 1938[4] specified an age limit of 12 months for the victim, and that is current law.

The infant still emerging from the womb remained legally unprotected until the Child Destruction Act of 1929.[5] This made the wilful killing of a viable child 'before it has an existence independent of its mother' punishable by a maximum of life

182

imprisonment. The age of presumed viability was set at 7 months.

It remains the law to this day (in England) that proof of separate existence is necessary to establish murder, manslaughter or statutory infanticide, but since the 1929 Act juries are empowered to return a 'child destruction' verdict instead, where separate existence is not proven. In fact child destruction is a very rare crime. Between 1929 and 1938 only two cases were known to the police in England and Wales, and the first of those was in 1937.[6]

Murder and infanticide figures in the criminal statistics do not by themselves indicate any dramatic decline in the vulnerability of babies between 1900 and 1939. In the mid-1920s murders of babies 0–1 and infanticides combined formed 34 per cent of all murder victims known to the police, and in 1938 (with infants below 1 having fallen to less than 2 per cent of the population since the late 1920s) the figure was 28 per cent. But in terms of absolute figures the problem was not large. The total number of murders (all age groups) in England and Wales hovered around 140–150 a year between the wars. After 1922 'infanticide' is distinguished from infant murder in the criminal statistics; between 1925 and 1929 there was an average of 37 infant murders (0–1) and 20 infanticides a year. During the 1930s this steadily declined; in 1938 there were 19 infant murders and 17 infanticides.[7] We can say that baby-killing by depressed or unbalanced mothers accounted for under half of all infant murders between the wars, but the figure held up more steadily than that for murder. Remember, though, that there were fewer babies around to dispatch in the 1930s than the 1920s; 780,000 were born in 1922 and 599,000 in 1935.[8]

If society is more violent in the 1980s than in the 1930s, infanticide trends have steadily gone the other way. With births at about 630,000 a year in the early 1980s,[9] the average number of homicides on 0–1-year-olds is at an all-time low at 26 a year.[10]

The year 1926 was a red letter one for legislation bearing directly or indirectly on the subject matter of this book: the Birth and Deaths Registration, Coroners and Legitimation Acts I have touched upon, but there were also passed the Midwives and Maternity Homes and the Adoption Acts.

The Maternity Homes Act[11] at last enacted nationwide the registration of lying-in homes that the Infant Life Protection Committee had called for in 1871, but the historical reason was not really connected with the traditional suspicions of midwives, for, as we saw in Chapter 14, the new trust in midwives was implicit in the terms of the 1926 Registration Act relating to stillbirth certificates.

The Home Office had been receiving periodic pleas from

coroners since the 1890s for the registration and inspection of lying-
in homes, but it was not until 1910 that a Home Secretary (then
Winston Churchill) took opinion on its desirability.[12] The Central
Midwives Board's view was that since uncertified midwives were
forbidden to practise from that year, and since local authority
inspectors had the right to enter lying-in houses to check on
midwives' qualifications, registration of the houses themselves was
unnecessary.

However, the National Insurance Act of 1911 changed the
situation. Women coming within the state scheme were entitled to
a lying-in allowance, and poorer women, who previously might
have unwillingly resorted, say, to a Poor Law infirmary, now used
the benefits to enter private maternity homes; lower-class homes of
unsatisfactory sanitary standards began proliferating, and they
were in need of close inspection. The LCC paved the way with a
requirement for registration in a local act, the LCC General
Powers Act of 1915,[13] but it was not until 1926 that registration
became national.

A declining national fertility, the large numbers of families bereft
of sons in the 1914–18 war, and the war's side-effect of stimulating
a temporary surge in unwanted illegitimate babies, created the right
supply and demand conditions for a boom in genuine 'adoptions'
after 1918, but the whole commerce was totally unregulated by
law. 'Adoptions' were arranged privately or through philanthropic
agencies like the National Adoption Society and the Homeless
Children's Aid and Adoption Society. Now we have seen that
adoptions so-called were no more than fosterings and the mothers
technically might be able to reclaim the child, subject to the court's
approval. In view of the post-war demand, government committees
sat between 1921 and 1926 (the Hopkinson and Tomlin Committees[14]) to examine the desirability of introducing formal legal
adoption, and this was recommended. The 1926 Adoption Act
applied to England and Wales only: a similar Scottish Act was
passed in 1930. It created a class of *de jure* adoptions to be
sanctioned by court order: the child became the adoptor's quasi-
natural offspring, unreclaimable by the natural mother. The Act
did not affect the traditional extra-legal adoptions, which were free
to operate as before, and there was no regulation of adoption
agencies or other private intermediaries.

The malpractices associated with inter-war adoptions were paler
and less crude than the Victorian abuses. It was no longer a
question of bogus adoptors taking the lump sum and then
supposedly killing off the infant as quickly as possible. Now the
abuses arose from the unsuitability of some adoptive parents, and

the failure of certain adoption societies, and more commonly private intermediaries, to check the applicants' circumstances and motives, sometimes with appalling consequences. The NSPCC had many case-histories. For example, from Wakefield in 1925: a 70-year-old man and his 56-year-old wife 'adopted' two small girls. When their deteriorating condition was observed by schoolteachers, the NSPCC visited the home and 'found the elder child staggering along with pails full of pig food . . . this child lived on bread and vegetables although the adults had meat, and was made to do long hours at heavy work'. The foster-parents admitted adopting her as cheap labour; the magistrate fined them £2 and the children were removed.[15]

Between 1930 and 1932 a woman operating as a private broker arranging official adoptions through the courts, charged the mothers up to £50 a time, and found clients by advertising anonymously in the press, using a box number. She was in the habit of sending the mothers threatening letters, demanding more money. A stable of infants was found on her premises kept in dirty and unsatisfactory conditions awaiting adoption, and she had failed to give notice to the local authority under the 1908 Children's Act; she was convicted twice in 1932,[16] but the Children and Young Persons Act of that year[17] put an end at least to one practice that helped shield such shady operators: anonymous box-number and letter-drop adverts were banned, and advertisers had to insert their own names and addresses.

In 1937 the Horsborough Committee, appointed to review the working of the 1926 Act, reported persistent abuses and unethical practices.[18] It referred to the practice of midwives in some maternity homes of arranging adoptions as a sideline, sometimes as a sympathetic service to clients, sometimes purely for money. In one case in 1935 a midwife was found to have placed a baby (charging £6 6s. 7d 'expenses'), in the home of an unemployed farm labourer and his wife, both of low intelligence.

The practices of charitable adoption societies, it felt, savoured too strongly of 'baby-farming' (this must be the last government report ever to use the phrase, which was now passing out of currency): they often demanded fees from mothers and adopters before the adoption was arranged, to ensure their income. The former, who might be desperate to unburden herself of the child, was vulnerable to excessive demands; fees from mothers, the Committee felt, should be discontinued, and fees from adoptors should be paid only after completion.

The pervading criticism was still the lack of adequate checking of adoptors' suitability by some societies and the private agents.

The ensuing Adoption of Children (Regulation) Act 1939[19] closed the loopholes and made baby-farming truly a thing of the past.

Adoption societies must register, and only registered societies and local authority children's departments could operate as agents; private agents (acting for payment) were banned; adoption advertising (whether seeking or offering children) was banned, except for advertising by registered societies and local authorities; this vital artery for the baby-trafficker had at long last been severed.

In the meantime, the 1908 infant life protection provisions had been applied with increasing effectiveness since 1920. By 1922 most Infant Protection Visitors were women.[20] In 1926 the Tomlin Report on Adoption could claim that the act 'has proved an efficient instrument for combating and has in fact largely eradicated, the mischief against which it was directed'. However (as the Ministry of Health reports of this period were also urging), Tomlin recommended the transfer of inspection work to health visitors of the local authority Maternity and Child Welfare Departments, who were better trained and equipped than Poor Law relieving officers to offer the child-minders constructive counselling. As long as Poor Law administration was separate from the county and borough councils this development was impeded. However, the Local Government Act of 1929, by absorbing the Poor Law into the general local authority, now allowed administrative flexibility. By 1931 of the country's 2,949 Infant Protection Visitors, 2,655 were health visitors, 193 were 'other female visitors' and there were only 101 male visitors.[21] With the stigmatising visits from a Poor Law official now removed, baby-minders were readier to come forward and notify voluntarily, and the Ministry of Health's Annual Report for 1931–2 noted with satisfaction an improvement in the 1908 Act's operation.[22] The Children and Young Persons Act of 1932 added some more safeguards: the protected age was raised to 9, and minders now had to notify authorities in advance of the actual reception of children. In fact by now the Victorian image of the baby-farmer was fast fading; the *Child's Guardian* last used the phrase 'baby-farming' in an English context in August 1926, and its last reported case of the bold-style abuses by a baby-minder was in January 1933.

Conclusion

The story of infanticide within the period covered by this book demonstrates that beneath the ethical veneer of his civilisation Man's real behaviour pattern is dominated by the fundamental law of nature, the instinct of self-preservation, and, where the pressure of his environment becomes intolerable, he will react ruthlessly and mechanically to restore the balance.

The death of 'surplus' or unwanted babies was a biological necessity at a time when birth control was scarcely understood, and it is only as the birth rate fell at the very end of the last century that the value of infant life correspondingly rose. It is this value today, at a time of an unprecedentedly low birth rate in the advanced world, that prompts our sympathy with the plight of starving children in Africa, where the birth rate is still rampant. But who knows if in the future this continued rapid growth of population will be perceived as a 'threat' to our own well-being; then we can be sure of an instinctive hardening of hearts and shutting of minds, as we consciously or unconsciously will Nature to take its course and restore the balance by eliminating the surplus.

In Britain in the 1980s it is no accident that the number of parental assaults on young children has increased as the level of unemployment has risen. When pressures increase, the young and helpless become ready victims and we must not delude ourselves that our instincts are anything but elementally animal whatever religious and ethical ideals we aspire to.

Notes and references

(Where authors' names only are given, and for abbreviations, consult Select bibliography and abbreviations.)

Chapter 1   Setting the scene

1   Newspaper cuttings digest NSPCC.
2   For seventeenth century see: R.W. Malcolmson; P. Hoffer and N. Hull; David Hume – *Commentaries on the Laws of Scotland* 1797 ed.
3   J. Brownlow(a); J. Brownlow(b); J.H. Hutchins; George Burrow Gregory, SC ILP 1871 Q 1736.
4   J.H. Hutchins.
5   J. Weeks; E. Shorter.
6   See M. Hopkirk for examples.

Chapter 2   Infant mortality: 'the waste of infant life'

1   P. Fryer; A. McLaren; J.A. Banks(a); J. Weeks; G.U. Yule.
2   M. Hewitt.
3   J.A. Banks(a).
4   I. Wickes.
5   M.W. Beaver. (The decline in gin-drinking following the Gin Act of 1751 must also have played a part.)
6   The term 'infant death rate' throughout this book will refer to the 0–1 age group, unless otherwise indicated.
7   I. Wickes.
8   Hereafter referred to as the NAPSS.
9   Reg-Gen BDM 1860: PP 1862 Vol. 17 pp. 98–9.
10   Reg-Gen BDM 1890: PP 1890–91 Vol. 23.
11   Reg-Gen BDM 1875: PP 1877 Vol. 25.
12   NCIM 1914 Herbert Lewis's Address.
13   A. Newsholme(a) (1923).
14   J.B. Curgenven(a).
15   H.R. Jones.
16   H.R. Jones.
17   M. Hewitt; W. Neff; L. Holcombe; I. Pinchbeck(a).
18   John Burns MP, Pres. Address NCIM 1906.
19   J. Campbell.

20 *Opium and the People* Harmondsworth, 1981.
21 NCIM 1914.
22 PP 1864 Vol. 28.
23 See Commission on Children's Employment PP 1867 Vol. 16 e.g. Rev. M.S. Jackson's ev.
24 PP 1845 Vol. 18.
25 Stanley Atkinson, *Drunken Parents and Child Neglect* NCIM 1908.
26 For history of infant feeding see I. Wickes; T.E. Cone; J.C. Drummond and A. Wilbrahim; F.B. Smith; A. Wohl; NCIM 1908.
27 31/32 Vic. Ch. 121 and see V. Berridge for history of use.
28 V. Berridge/ E.F. Harrison's ev. S.C. Patent Medicines PP 1914 Vol. 9 at Q 2971.
29 For history see N. Longmate; G.B. Wilson; G.P. Williams and G.T. Brake; B. Harrison; A. Newsholme(b).
30 Hereford, and see also note 25.
31 Hereford.
32 See e.g. Prof. G. Sims Woodhead NCIM 1906.
33 A. Newsholme(b).

Chapter 3   The economic and sexual vulnerability of women

1   For a general background see: I. Pinchbeck(a); M. Hewitt; L. Holcombe; G. Braybon; W. Neff; B.L. Hutchins.
2   J.D. Milne.
3   J. Burnett.
4   L. Holcombe.
5   W. Shaw.
6   J. Burnett.
7   B.L. Hutchins.
8   J.A. Banks(b).
9   For background on prostitution: J. Walkowitz; F. Basch; M. Pearson; E.J. Bristow; S. Marcus.
10 NAPSS Sess. 1873: discussion following Lowndes's address on Infanticide in Liverpool.
11 *Fraser's Magazine*, Nov. 1862.
12 M. Hewitt, based on Reg-Gen BDM report for 1886.
13 W. Acton – *Prostitution* 1857 and W. Bucke Ryan quoting *The Standard*.
14 'J.B.' – Brownlow(c).
15 W. Acton(a).
16 Cited in J. Walkowitz.
17 J.D. Milne.
18 PP 1919 Vol. 13. War Cabinet Committee Report on Women in Industry p.230 (see Dr J. Campbell).
19 F. Huggett, chapter on 'Fallen Women'.
20 Cited in R.W. Malcolmson.
21 For a full discussion of this theme see F. Basch; E. Trudgill; P. Thomson.
22 See e.g. *Saturday Review* 2/8/1856 – 'Breach of Promise and Marriage Morals'; 20/10/1866 – 'Seduction and Infanticide'.

Chapter 4   Bastardy and the Poor Law in mid-Victorian England

1 NAPSS Tr. 1867. Curgenven and Lankester in discussion following Ransome's address on the registration system.
2 J.B. Curgenven in note 1.
3 2/3/1867 p. 232.
4 ILPS Prospectus 1870.
5 P. Laslett for background.
6 See *BMJ* 2/3/1867 and 'J.B.' 1864.
7 Reg-Gen BDM relevant Annual Reports.
8 SC/ILP 1871 Vol. 7 Q 1044–50.
9 J.B. Curgenven(b).
10 Hansard: Lords debate: 23/7/1896. Bishop of Winchester (after Col. 418).
11 1937 Ann Report NCUMC.
12 See M. Blaug: *Jnl of Econ. History* June 1963 – 'The Myth of the Old Poor Law', for a critique of these opinions.
13 P. Fryer.
14 U. Henriques.
15 Dr Michael Rose.
16 I. Pinchbeck: *British Journal of Sociology* 1954 Vol. 5. 'Social Attitudes to the Problem of Illegitimacy' for history of the doctrine and Sir Edmund Head, 'Report on the Law of Bastardy with a Supplementary Report on a Cheap Civil Remedy for Seduction' 1840 for reference to it.
17 4/5 Will. IV Ch. 76.
18 Quoted in 'J.B.'.
19 2nd Ann Report P.L. Commissions PP 1836 Vol. 29 Pt 1.
20 E. Head. See note 16. Also Assistant Commissioners' Report: PP 1844 Vol. 19.
21 G. Wythen Baxter.
22 G. Wythen Baxter.
23 G. Wythen Baxter.
24 Hansard 10/2/1844 Cols 476–9.
25 7/8 Vict. Ch. 101 S. 2–9.
26 31/32 Vict. Ch. 122 s. 41.
27 G. Behlmer(a).
28 *The Times*: 13/7/1853 pp. 6, 7.
29 W. Acton(a).
30 *The Times*: 16/7/1853 p. 8.
31 'J.B.'.
32 SC PP 1909 Vol. 6.
33 F. Dawes.
34 PP 1861 Vol. 55 p. 37 – A Return of Summonses Issued etc. . . . 1845–59, under the 1844 Act.
35 PP 1840 Vol. 3, pp. 473 and 479 – draft Seduction Bill. Hansard 10/6/1840 Col. 967 et seq.
36 E. Head 1840. See note 16.
37 H. Smith (1838).
38 F.P. Cobbe 1864.
39 RCPL 1909.
40 Finer Report Appendix 5 pp. 120–21.
41 N. Middleton.
42 D. Roberts: *Historical Journal* 1964: 'How Cruel was the Victorian Poor Law?'
43 SC ILP 1871 Appendix 4. RCPL 1909 Majority Report Section 8.
44 SC ILP 1871 Uvedale Corbett's evidence. RCPL 1909 (Maj Rpt). H. Ashby.

45   SC ILP 1871. Uvedale Corbett's ev.
46   J. Rogers.
47   RCPL 1909 Min Rpt p. 772.
48   SC ILP: Appendix 5 and Corbett Q 4887–8.
49   G. Wythen Baxter.
50   2nd Ann Report P.L. Commiss. PP 1836 Vol. 29 Pt 1 pp. 563–6.
51   SC ILP 1871 Appendix 4, and at Q 3960.
52   Ibid.
53   E.g. Dr. Michael Rose's thesis, and Local Govt Bd Report PP 1874 Vol. 25. PP 1841 Vol. 21 – Return on nos of women and children on relief.
54   See e.g. L.G. Board. PP 1897 Vol. 36 pp. 303–5. Reports: PP 1901 Vol. 64 p. 233.
55   M.A. Crowther.
56   N. Middleton.
57   Acton(a).
58   U. Henriques.

Chapter 5   Infanticide and the mid-Victorian conscience 1830–70 (I)

1   Emma Wood: *Sorrow on the Sea* 1868 (Mrs Drury, the midwife).
2   F.W. Lowndes(a).
3   See e.g. John Barrow, *Travels in China* 1804. John Beck's chapter on Infanticide in *T.R. Beck* 1842 ed. John Cave Browne, *Indian Infanticide*, 1857.
4   PP 1837–8 Vol. 44 p. 329.
5   G.K. Behlmer(a). R. Sauer.
6   *The Times* 15/8/1861 p. 9.
7   E. Lankester 2nd Ann Report as Coroner for C. Middx, cited in A. Wynter; *The Lancet* 12/6/1869 p. 825.
8   SC ILP 1871 Appendix 1.
9   SC ILP 1871 Q 2071–2.
10   NAPSS Sess 1873: Infanticide in Liverpool.
11   See Gernon's ev. SC ILP 1871 Q 823.
12   J. Brownlow(b).
13   *Marylebone Mercury* 7/8/1858 p. 3.
14   *Marylebone Mercury* 18/4/1863.
15   *The Sun* 24/10/1895. See also F. Dawes for an account in the 1880s.
16   R. Sauer; *Marylebone Mercury* 26/9/1863 and 18/4/1863.
17   PRO H.O.45 6955 Old Series.
18   W. Burke Ryan 1862: GLC Record Office P 89/MRY 1/607/1–9: St Marylebone parish records. Nov 1861; Lowndes (note 10).
19   NAPSS Tr. 1864. J.I. Iken on the 'Undue Mortality of Infants . . .' etc.
20   See H. Jeanne Peterson, *The Medical Profession in Mid Victorian London* University of California Press 1978. Sir George Clark, *A History of the Royal College of Physicians* Vol. 2. D'Arcy Power, *British Medical Societies* 1939.
21   'Infanticide in its Medico-Legal Relations' 1856. The manuscript is housed with the Medical Society of London.
22   PRO H.O. 45/8044 (Old Series).
23   The story is told in Richard S. Lambert's *When Justice Faltered* 1935, and see *The Times* accounts of her trial 20/3/1865 and 29/7/1865.
24   J.B. Curgenven(b): (1869) where he said 'Baby farming is a phrase new to us until the last twelve months'; but the phrase was used in connection with Bartholomew Drouet's Tooting 'Baby-Farm' in 1848. See Chapter 6.

25 J.B. Curgenven(a) and at Q 1068 SC ILP 1871.
26 *Weekly Dispatch* 29/9/1867. *Pall Mall Gazette* 25/9/1867. *Sunday Times* 29/9/1867. *BMJ* 11/1/1868 and 16/1/1868.
27 See *BMJ* 24/10/1903 for obituary.
28 Minutes of Harveian Medic. Soc. 17/5/1866.
29 J.B. Curgenven(c) and (d).
30 The Home Office was to mislay this, and Dr Tyler Smith, Pres. of the Harv. Soc. seems to have mislaid his own copy (see *BMJ* 14/3/1868 p. 262; and Ernest Hart's ev. SC ILP 1871 Q 10–13). This report seems to be lost, but the Recommendations are extant – see e.g. SC ILP 1871 Appendix 2.
31 J.B. Curgenven(b).
32 E. Lankester(a).
33 G.K. Behlmer(b).
34 Before the NAPSS in 1858 he had given an estimated figure of at least 60,000 stillborns a year in Britain. In the Lords he raised query as to what action the government was prepared to take following the *BMJ*'s investigations (see *BMJ* 1/8/1868 p. 121) but was fobbed off with the answer that it was a police matter rather than one requiring additional legislation.
35 *BMJ* 14/3/1868 p. 262.

Chapter 6   Infanticide and the mid-Victorian conscience (II): the milk of human kindness

1   Daniel Cooper's ev. SC ILP 1871.
2   F.W. Lowndes(a).
3   C.S. Loch: SC ILP 1890 at Q 1257.
4   RCPL 1909 Min. Rept p. 788 et seq.
5   GLC Lambeth Bd of Guardian Minutes 1870 Vol. 15 La/BG/15.
6   N. Middleton; G.F. McCleary(a).
7   See J. Walkowitz; M. Hopkirk; Cooper's evid. before SC ILP 1871.
8   *The Lancet* 8/2/1882 p. 280.
9   NAPSS Tr. 1877, Charley's Address on Seduction Bills.
10 See Mrs Main's evidence SC ILP 1871 Q 4631 et seq.
11 Charley, note 9.
12 See Charley note 9, and NAPSS Tr. 1869 Herbert Safford's paper following Lankester's address on infanticide.
13 Hereford's ev. SC ILP 1871 for weekly rates.
14 Whitehead SC ILP 1871.
15 NAPSS Tr. 1874: Elder Cumming – on 'Neglect of Infants in large Towns etc.'
16 G. Newman.
17 RCPL Min. Rpt. p. 772.
18 See e.g. Safford in note 12; and Frances H. Low – 'A Remedy for Baby Farming' *Fortnightly Review* 1898 (Vol. 63).
19 11/12 Geo. VI Ch. 53. Child-Minders Act.
20 See N. Longmate for an outline account of this problem, and reference to Louisa Twining's Workhouse Visiting Society.
21 *Jnl of Workhouse Visiting Society* Nov. 1859.
22 *Fraser's Magazine* Sept. 1864: reprinted in1865 in her *Studies: Ethical and Social*.
23 See A.W.C. Brice and K.J. Fielding: 'Dickens and the Tooting Disaster' *Victorian Studies* Vol. 12 Dec. 1968.
24 For a history of boarding-out see Frances Zanetti, 1904 Transactions of the Fourth International Home Relief Conference. RCPL 1909 – Maj. Report from

p. 184 and Min. Rpt from p. 806. SC ILP 1871 – Appendix 4 for 1870 Regulation. W. Chance – *Children under the Poor Law* (1897). A.F. Young and E.T. Ashton: *British Social Work in the Nineteenth Century* (1956).
For the Scottish System see J. Patten Macdougall and Miss Aikman's addresses to the 1904 Fourth International Home Relief Conference. Figures from Zanetti, Macdougall, Aikman and 1909 RCPL in note 24.

25 I have drawn on numerous primary and secondary sources for the study of wet-nursing, and what appears here is highly condensed. The following list is a small selection but should provide a useful starting point. F.B. Smith; P. Branca; M. Livia Osborn, 'The Rent Breasts' in *Midwife, Health Visitor and Community Nurse* Sept. 1979 Vol. 15 no. 9. Jonathan Gathorne Hardy; I. Wickes; T. Cone; C.H.F. Routh; E. Cautley; David Forsyth. Other references appear separately.

26 SC ILP 1871 Q 1057 et seq.

27 For William Acton's scoffing reference to this see *BMJ* 16/2/1861 p. 183.

28 David Forsyth.

29 E. Cautley.

30 SC ILP 1871 Q 1334.

31 W. Whitehead's ev. SC ILP 1871.

32 See note 25. He does not quote a source for this figure, however.

33 See e.g. Whitehead SC ILP 1871 Q 3303 et seq.

34 *BMJ* 2/2/1861 Letter from Dr Graily Hewitt.

35 Newsholme(b) citing Dr Scurfield. Also see F.B. Smith for midwifery and nineteenth-century medical profession.

36 For monthly nurses' role see SC on Midwives Registration PP 1892 Vol. 14 at Q 108 and Dept. Comm. on Midwives' Act PP 1909 Vol. 33 at Q 6677.

37 John Robertson, *Observations on the Mortality and Physical Management of Children* 1827.

38 Its full name: Ladies National Association for the Diffusion of Sanitary Knowledge. Not to be confused with Ladies Sanitary Associations e.g. at Liverpool formed later in the century.

39 By 'SRP' almost certainly Miss S.R. Powers, Assistant Secretary of the Association.

40 F.B. Smith, Chapter 2.

41 ISC 1860 Statistical Section. The Royal Statistical Library has a bound copy of the Transactions.

42 *BMJ* 14/1/1861 p. 68.

43 *BMJ* 27/5/1871 p. 570 signed 'FRCP'.

44 Cited in Peter Fryer's Introduction to Acton's *Prostitution* (1968 edition).

45 *BMJ* 14/4/1860 pp. 293 et seq. See also Acton(a) p. 493 footnote.

46 *The Lancet* 3/4/1858 cited in Mrs Baines's address NAPSS Tr. 1859.

47 Ibid.

48 SC ILP 1890 George Barrow Gregory Q 770.

49 See Chapter 2, n. 26 for sources. Also Cautley; NCIM 1906 (Dr James Knight); DCPD 1904 (Dr Ralph Vincent).

50 For feeding bottles' history, see e.g. Forsyth; Wickes; Cone; F.B. Smith; Jean Bel Geddes, *Small World* 1966; and Ladies Sanitary Association Tracts (in British Library) for brand names of contemporary bottles.

51 Dr J.M. Rhodes at 1906 NCIM.

Chapter 7   Coroners, inquests and the exposure of infanticide

1   See SCDC for English and Scottish procedures. Also for background see: Brodrick Report on Death Certification and Coroners 1971 Cmnd 4810. J. Jervis *Jervis on Coroners* 7th ed. 1927. F.W. Lowndes *Reasons why the office of Coroner should be held by members of the Medical Profession* 1892. Samuel Squire Sprigge *Life and Times of Thomas Wakley* 1897.
2   Dept. Comm. on Coroners PP 1935–6 Vol. 8.
3   Coppock's ev. SC on FS Bill PP 1854 Vol. 7 Q 490 et seq.
4   *The Sun*'s investigation into Baby-Farming 1895 Oct-Nov.
5   SCDC: Hicks Q 1465 et seq.
6   SCDC Q 2608.
7   Dept. Committ. on Coroners 1st Report PP 1909 Vol. 15 Appendix 2; see Brodrick Report for 1885 directive to registrars.
8   SCDC Q 3872–3.
9   P. Wilson.
10 Samuel Farr *Elements of Medical Jurisprudence* 1815.
11 Drawn from PP 1861 Vol. 2 return of coroners' inquests in Metropolis 1856–60. PP 1863 Vol. 48: return of coroners' inquests on infants under 2 in E. & W. 1861–2.
12 G. Greaves.
13 PP 1870 Vol. 63 p. 525 (Jud. Stats.).
14 Based on comparison of mortality stats in the Registrar's Annual Reports with inquest stats in the *Judicial Statistics* for relevant years.
15 Ibid.
16 SCDC Q 2564.
17 G. Greaves.
18 6/7 Will. IV Ch. 89.
19 See e.g. A.S. Taylor(a) e.g. 1886 edition, and SC on Coroners PP 1910 Vol. 21 p. 16.
20 See Chapter 8 on Infanticide and the Law for a full discussion.
21 LCC formed in 1888, and London north of the Thames outside the City now legally separated from Middlesex.
22 I have not located all his reports, and I don't know how many were produced. Reference to his 2nd Report: see A. Wynter (Chapter on Child Murder). Reference to his 3rd Report: see J.B. Curgenven's article on Infanticide in *Sanitary Record* 15/3/1889. 4th-7th Reports: see NAPSS Sess. for appropriate years to 1871.
23 *Dictionary of National Biography* and G.K. Behlmer(a).
24 See Chapter 5 n. 17 for source.
25 Source, as for n. 23: Coroner Humphreys' reply to the Home Secretary.
26 *BMJ* 30/3/1861 p. 341.
27 NAPSS Tr. 1866 E. Lankester: 'Infanticide, with the best means . . . etc.' and SC ILP 1871 Q 2295.
28 Census 1861 Vol. 1.
29 PP 1862 Vol. 44: Inquest verdicts on 0–2-year-olds in London 1861.
30 This was a peak figure. Generally murders of 0–1-year-olds hovered around 58–70, but the general pattern holds true.
31 G.K. Behlmer(a). Graph p. 424, Middlesex as a whole accounted for 50%+ declining to about 35 per cent over the same period (source: *Judicial Statistics*, selected years).
32 Curgenven SC ILP 1871 Q 1446.
33 See n. 23.

34 Lankester's 6th Annual Report 31/7/1868.
35 See Lankester's 4th Report 1865/6, and PP 1862 Vol. 44 p. 331 Coroners' Inquest Verdicts on Infants in London 1861.
36 E. Lankester(a).
37 E. Lankester(b).
38 Lankester's 7th Ann. Report 1868/9.
39 Lankester's 7th Ann. Report 1868/9.

Chapter 8   Infanticide and the law 1803–70

1   43 Geo. III Ch. 58.
2   For a history of Infanticide Law see G. Greaves; D.R. Seaborne-Davies; W. Burke Ryan.
3   49 Geo. III Ch. 14.
4   Re-enacted in 1896 Short Titles (Scotland) Act. See Gerald H. Gordon *The Criminal Law of Scotland* 1978 edition.
5   Archbold *Pleading and Evidence in Criminal Cases*, cited by G. Greaves.
6   John H.A. Macdonald *A Practical Treatise on Criminal Law of Scotland* 1894 and John Dove Wilson.
7   Offences Against Person Act 9 Geo. IV Ch. 31.
8   D.R. Seaborne-Davies.
9   *Russell on Crime* Vol. 1. 12th ed. 1964 pp. 608–9 for these and other anomalies.
10 F.W. Lowndes(b).
11 G. Greaves.
12 R.V. Knights 1860 cited in J. Jervis-Jervis in *Coroners* 1927 ed. p. 159.
13 John Dove Wilson. Andrew Wynter *Curiosities of Toil* 1870 blamed the crinoline for helping girls to conceal their condition.
14 For an outline of medical proofs of live birth see e.g. G. Greaves; A.S. Taylor (e.g. 1886 edition); W. Burke Ryan; W. Cummin; W. Hunter; W. Hutchinson; T.R. Beck; A. Tardieu; P. Brouardel.
15 2nd Report Crim. Law Commissioners PP 1846 Vol. 24 under Homicide p. 27.
16 P.J. Bishop *A Short History of the Royal Humane Society* 1974.
17 See e.g. R.W. Malcolmson.
18 F. W. Lowndes(a).
19 J. Mackintosh.
20 A.S. Taylor(a) 1886 ed. The test was finally discredited scientifically in 1901 (see C. Polson and D.J. Gee).
21 See T.R. Beck 1825 ed.
22 A. Tardieu for this discussion and see also P. Brouardel.
23 See also C. Polson and D.J. Gee.
24 Cited in Acton(a).
25 His ev. before RCCP 1866.
26 NSPCC Annual Report 1890.
27 RCCP evid.
28 Report of RCCP.
29 *The Times* 27/12/1853.
30 R. Sauer.
31 W. Acton(a).
32 See P. Wilson for details and *The Times* 11/8/1849 and 18/98/1849.
33 RCCP Sir George Grey at Q 1456 to Q 1469.
34 See P. Wilson for details. C.A. Fyffe 'The Punishment of Infanticide' *Nineteenth Century* 1877 Vol. 1.

35   PP 1837–8 Vol. 44 p. 329.
36   PRO H.O.45/6955 (old series).
37   See D.R. Seaborne-Davies for a full analysis.
38   J.B. Curgenven(e) for outline of Prussian Law and Lankester. SC ILP 1871 at Q 3121.
39   W. Burke Ryan.
40   A. Tardieu 1868.

Chapter 9   Lifting the lid on midwives and baby-farmers 1868–71

1   See ev. of Hart and Wiltshire before SC ILP 1871 for background and *modus operandi* of the enquiry.
2   *The Times* 26/8/1867 p. 3 Col. 5.
3   *BMJ* 8/2/1868 p. 127.
4   Gernon's ev. SC ILP 1871.
5   *BMJ* 19/9/1868.
6   Wiltshire – SC ILP 1871 Q 277.
7   14/7/1870 p. 4.
8   Dod's Parliamentary Companion 1893 and 1895.
9   See evidence of Charles and William Cameron before SC ILP 1871.
10   Dates: 11th, 16th, 23rd Feb. 2nd, 9th, 16th, 23rd, 31st March. 7th April 1871.
11   W. Cameron's ev. SC ILP 1871. C. Cameron's ev. SC ILP 1871.
12   W. Cameron ev. SC ILP 1871.

Chapter 10   'Churchyard luck': midwives and murder

1   A. Wohl; J. Donnison for background.
2   J. Donnison for this feminist interpretation.
3   Volume 3, Chapter 2 et seq. 'Sorrow on the Sea'.
4   24/25 Vic. Ch. 100. See F.B. Smith; L.A. Parry; A. McLaren; B. Dickens; M. Potts; W. Burke Ryan for background.
5   SC on Midwives Act PP 1909 Vol. 3 Q 6007.
6   SC ILP 1871 Q 297.
7   SC ILP 1871 Q 4577 et seq.
8   P. Brouardel *Abortion* 1901.
9   SC ILP 1871 Q 4527 to 4563.
10   *The Sun* 31/10/1895.
11   *The Sun* 1/11/1895.
12   *The Sun* 5th and 12th Dec. 1895.
13   *BMJ* 1898 Vol. 1 p. 242.
14   *Curiosities of Toil* – Chapter on 'Child Murder'.
15   SC on Midwives Act PP 1909 Vol. 33: Dr A. Robinson at Q 2605.
16   SC ILP 1871 Q 2213-6.
17   See previous chapter: *The Times* 14/7/1870 p. 4.
18   W. Bathurst Woodman and Charles Meymott Tidy: *A Handybook of Forensic Medicine etc.* 1877 (citing findings of A. Tardieu); C.J. Polson and D.J. Gee *Essentials of Forensic Medicine* 1973. Ambroise Tardieu *Etude Médico-Légale sur l'Infanticide* 1868. Alfred S. Taylor(a) *Manual of Medic. Jurisprudence* 1886 ed.
19   E. Lankester NAPSS Tr. 1867 (following Dr A. Ransome's address on the Registration System).
20   A. Wynter *Curiosities of Toil*.

21 R. Parr(a) (both cases).
22 SC ILP 1908 Q 377, Motion's ev.
23 G.E. Male.
24 A.S. Taylor – e.g. 1886 ed. and later ed. He calls them 'suppositious births'. He supplies a list of notable 19th century court cases.
25 *BMJ* 8/2/1868.
26 A.S. Taylor – see 1920 and 1934 editions.

Chapter 11 The South London Baby-Farmers 1870

1 *BMJ* 1/8/1868 p. 121 (also to Mr Vanderbyl 14/3/1868 p. 262).
2 PRO Mepo 3/92 and 3/96.
3 M.A. Baines *A Few Thoughts Concerning Infanticide* n.d. but c. 1865.
4 See also M. Potts on the lack of logical Philosophy behind the abortion law.
5 4th Ann. Report as Coroner for C. Middlesex 1866/7. NAPSS Sess. 1867.
6 Gernon's ev. SC ILP 1871 Q 658–9.
7 SC ILP 1871 Q 224.
8 PRO Mepo 3/92.
9 This looks like a charge under s. 27 of the OAP Act 1861, but *The Times* account of her trial (see 27/9/1869) states that she received 5 years' penal servitude, when the Act prescribes a maximum of 3 years.
10 Sgnt Relf's ev. SC ILP 1871 Appendix I.
11 *The Times* 27/9/1869.
12 PRO Mepo 3/94 Papers relating to Mary Hall. Cummings's statement.
13 Other phonetic spellings in the contemporary accounts: Mrs Cassell, and Sergeant Relf.
14 See G.F. McCleary(a) and Gernon's and Relf's evidence before SC ILP 1871 and Appendix I.
15 Most of the following is based on accounts of the Margaret Waters trial: *The Times* 21/9/1870 and 23/9/1870. *South London Press* 24/9/1870. *Illustrated Police News* 8/10/1870, 15/10/1870. See also P. Wilson.
16 16/7/1870 Vol. II PP 66–7.
17 PRO Mepo 3/96 Miscellaneous papers re Baby-Farming. Document, 23/12/1870.
18 SC ILP 1871 Q 224. See note 6. Perhaps Relf was under pressure from his superiors to show results in view of the embarrassing number of babies' bodies found in P-Division.
19 J.R. Mayo's letter to the *Morning Advertiser* 6/10/1870.
20 Relf's ev. SC ILP 1871.
21 See note 18.
22 PRO Mepo 3/96 Supt. Gernon's memo 29/12/1873.
23 For events after the trial see: *Illustrated Police News* 15/10/1870. *South London Press* 8/10/1870 and 15/10/1870 and 29/10/1870. *Daily Telegraph* 12/10/1870. *Morning Advertiser* 12/10/1870 and 25/10/1870.
24 *South London Press* 29/10/1870.
25 *Illustrated Police News* 15/10/1870.
26 *South London Press* 15/10/1870 and *Morning Advertiser* 12/10/1870.
27 *South London Press* 29/10/1870.
28 PRO Mepo 3/96 police memos early Nov. 1870.
29 PRO Mepo 3/96.
30 SC ILP 1871. Relf's Report Appendix I.
31 Newspaper accounts also spell his name Loe, but 'Lowe' seems likelier. The

story is drawn from:
(a) *South London Press* 1870: 29/10; 5/11; 12/11; 19/11; 26/11; 17/12.
(b) *South London Chronicle 1870*: 26/11.
(c) *The Times* 1870: 14/12.
(d) Relf's evidence and Report for the 1871 SC ILP (Appendix 1).
(e) PRO Mepo 3/94 Papers relating to Mary Hall.
32 See Mary Ann Goddard's statement in 'Relf' at 31d.
33 'Relf' at 31d.
34 Two accounts conflict. Relf at 31d gives her period of service as Jan-March 1870. The SLP of 19/11/1870 gave it as February 1869, but Relf names another servant in the Halls' employ at that date.
35 Relf at 31d.
36 From *South London Press* 19/11/1870.
37 *South London Press* 19/11/1870.
38 PRO Mepo 3/96: papers relating to baby-farming 1870–77.
39 Note 38 Inspector Clarke's memo 23/12/1873.

Chapter 12   Infant life protection legislation 1870–90

1 I am giving the political moves only the sketchiest of treatments here. A fuller account is contained in G.K. Behlmer(b).
2 See Chapter 6.
3 SC ILP 1871 Q 1398.
4 PP 1871 Vol. 7.
5 *The Times* 2/8/1871 and see Hereford SC ILP 1871 Q 1907 et seq. As with Waters, she was only exposed because of paternal concern about an infant in the house.
6 35/36 Vic. Ch. 38.
7 3/9/1872.
8 B. Waugh(a).
9 See *The Sun* 16/12/1895 and SC ILP 1896.
10 For history of this see Alfred Spencer's ev SC ILP 1896 Q 23 et seq. See – *BMJ* 1/5/1880. Annual Report of MB of W for 1879 (PP 1880 Vol. 62) and Annual Report of MB of W for 1880 (PP 1881 Vol. 59).
11 See *BMJ* 30/8/1879 and 6/9/1879: *The Lancet* 23/8/1879.
12 P. Wilson.
13 *BMJ* 27/9/1879. *The Times* Sept. 1879, Oct. 29th (p. 12) and Oct. 30th (p. 10).
14 *The Times* 21/11/1879 (p. 10), 24/11/1879 (p. 9).
15 Lord Denbigh's, Hansard: Lords 9/1/1896 Col. 414 et seq. speech.
16 Annual Report MB of W for 1888 (PP 1889 Vol. 66).
17 *The Times* 28/5/1888 and 5/10/1888.
18 P. Wilson.
19 G.K. Behlmer(b).
20 See Hicks ev. 1896 SC ILP.
21 See Spencer, note 10.

Chapter 13   Bastardy, seduction and infanticide law reform 1870–1900

1 See Bills: PP 1872 Vol. 1 p. 135.
2 35/36 Vic. Ch. 65. Technical amendments were made by an Act of 1873 (36 Vic. Ch. 9).

3   SC ILP 1871 Q 1217; See also Gernon at Q 663.
4   Official figures for applications, and orders in the *Judicial Statistics* at that period
    may be an underestimate however. Then returns were compiled by the police
    who were less punctilious about them as they were classed as 'quasi-criminal'
    only. Information: Mr Scott, Home Office Criminal Statistics Office 1984.
    Statistics derived from Finer Report Part II p. 124.
5   See Mary James ev. SC BO Q 597.
6   Poor Law Conference 1889. Mr Vassie of Kensington Union; discussion
    following Louisa Twining's address on Unmarried Mothers in the Workhouse.
7   SC BO Mary James Q 584.
8   See Chapter 4.
9   For the bills (1873–5) see NAPSS Tr. 1877 Charley on Seduction Law (pp. 295
    et seq.). The 'Offences Against the Person Amendment Bills' of 1874 and 1875
    should not be confused with Charley's 1876 Bill of similar title to amend the
    Infanticide Law (see note 15).
10 Hansard: Commons 14/4/1875 Col. 917–8.
11 House of Lords PP 1881 Vol. 8. Also 1882 Vol. 7 and 1883 Vol. 9.
12 Curiously the marriage age remained at 12 for a girl and 14 for a boy until the
    Age of Marriage Act 1929.
13 PP 1892 Vol. 9 p. 389.
14 PP 1886 Vol. 53 p. 235. The no. of women serving commuted capital sentences
    for Infanticide: 18 of the 27 are in their twenties. P. Brouardel *L'Infanticide* 1897
    for French figures.
15 For an account of his efforts see W.T. Charley *Infanticide Law Reform* NAPSS
    Tr. 1877. The bills: PP 1873 Vol. 2; PP 1874 Vol. 2; PP 1875; PP 1876 Vol. 5
    p. 293 – 'Offences Against Person' Bill – NB See note 9.
16 Seaborne-Davies gives a comprehensive but incomplete round-up of such bills
    as they relate to infanticide, but he skimps Charley's bills and omits a bill of
    1914.
17 A.S. Taylor *Principles and Practice of Medical Juris.* 7th ed. 1920 Vol. 2 p. 236.
18 PP 1886 Vol. 53 p. 235: no. of women in prison on commuted capital sentences
    for infanticide.
19 *The Times* 28/3/1895 p. 14. See also *Spectator* April 1895 – 'The case of Amy
    Gregory'.
20 Algernon West 'English Prisons' *Nineteenth Century* Vol. 39 1896.
21 R. Parr(a) 1908.
22 Carl Heath *Some Notes on the Punishment of Death* 1908. For background see
    Elizabeth Orman Tuttle *The Crusade Against Capital Punishment in GB* 1961.
23 Seaborne-Davies wrongly states 1909 as the date of the last pre-war bill. Others
    were: PP 1910 Vol. 2 p. 431; 1911 Vol. 2 p. 713; 1913 Vol. 3; 1914 Vol. 3 p. 165.

Chapter 14   Cradle and grave: birth and death registration and infanticide

1   6/7 Will. IV Ch. 86.
2   Edwin Chadwick's Report on Interment in Towns PP 1843 Vol. 12.
3   17/18 Vic. Ch. 80.
4   37/38 Vic. Ch. 88.
5   NAPSS Tr. 1867 Discussion following Dr A. Ransome's address on
    Registration System.
6   Hansard 14/5/1874 Col. 274 et seq. Sclater-Booth.
7   See Chapter 4.
8   Brodrick.

9   Chadwick, note 2 (Appendix 10, Coppock's letter).
10 SC DC Rentoul at Q 3055.
11 SC DC: Dr Ogle Q 3924 also H.O.45/8044 (Old Series) 1867. Manchester Stat. Soc. to Home Sec.
12 Brodrick.
13 SC DC 1893–4. Final Report for stats. and Appendix 17 pp. 298–9.
14 SC DC Ogle at Q 4053 et seq.
15 SC DC. Appendix 14 Table 3.
16 SC DC Q 3896 Sir Charles Cameron, quoting the Medical Officer of Health.
17 G. Greaves 1863 (appendix). SC ILP 1871 Q 2127–8.
18 Horatio Nelson Hardy SC DC Q 2560 and Dr Ogle SC DC Q 3941 for such irregularities and abuses.
19 SC CLI PP 1890–91 witnesses' recommendations p. 3. Hicks-Commons SC FS PP 1888–9 Vol. 10 Q 4106 et seq.
20 Hardy SC DC Q 2556.
21 From *Child's Guardian* Aug. 1890.
22 *Child's Guardian* Nov. 1890.
23 See *Child's Guardian* March 1890 (Oxford coroner); March 1900 (LCJ at Northamptonshire Assizes).
24 PRO H.O.45/641 (Old Series).
25 SC DC Q 1345–7.
26 SC DC Hicks Q 1434.
27 PRO H.O.45/3600 (Old Series).
28 PRO H.O.45/641 (Old Series).
29 PRO H.O.45/3600 (Old Series).
30 A. Wynter 1870.
31 SC DC Q 1435 et seq.
32 Gernon-SC IILP 1871 Q 666–671.
33 Sanitary Section: Discussion 20/7/1860.
34 See PRO H.O.45/8044 (Old Series) for Manchester Stat. Soc. and Manchester and Salford Sanitary Association's address to Home Sec.
35 NAPSS 1858, cited in Burke Ryan.
36 Robert Reid Rentoul: SC on Midwives Registration PP 1892 Vol. 14. Q 397–Q 408.
37 See PRO H.O.45/3600 (Old Series) and H.O.45/8044 (Old Series) respectively.
38 34th Ann. Report Reg. BM & D 1873 PP 1873 Vol. 20 p. 1.
39 PRO H.O.45/8044 (Old Series). Liverpool Northern Medical Soc. to Home Sec. June 1869.
40 See J. Donnison for full story of midwives' registration.
41 See *The Lancet* 21/3/1891 p. 675; SC DC 1893–4 Rentoul's ev. at Q 3020; *Child's Guardian* Sept. 1893 p. 119.
42 See *The Lancet* and *Child's Guardian*, n. 41.
43 SC DC Q 1894–6 (Tatham's evidence).
44 J. Donnison.
45 Hansard: 17/3/1893 Col. 448; 20/3/1893; 27/3/1893.
46 Brodrick.
47 Brodrick.
48 G.F. McCleary(a); NCIM 1908 – Alderman Broadbent's address.
49 G. Newman.
50 His articles *BMJ* 14/2/1914 p. 356 & 25/4/1914 p. 902.
51 16/17 Geo. V. Ch. 48.

Chapter 15 Burial insurance and child murder (I)

1 Background research materials: P.H.J.H. Gosden *Self Help* 1973. H.A.L. Cockerell and E. Green *The British Insurance Business* 1976. Dermot Morrah *A History of Industrial Life Insurance* 1955. P.H.J.H. Gosden *The Friendly Societies in England 1815–75* 1960. Cornelius Walford *Insurance Cyclopaedia* 1876. Edwin Chadwick *Interment in Towns* PP 1843 Vol. 12. Benjamin Waugh 'Child Life Insurance' *Contemporary Review* July 1890. Pembroke Marshall 'Child Life Insurance: A Reply (to Waugh)' *Fortnightly Review* Vol. 48 Dec. 1890. Charles Hardwick *History etc. of Friendly Societies* 1893. B. Waugh *Results of Child Life Insurance* 1891 (NSPCC). P. Marshall's reply *Fortnightly Review* (Jan–June) 1891 p. 939. The *Preston Original Legal F.S.* ref: PRO H.O.45/5203. *A History of the Prudential Assurance Co.* 1880. In library of Chartered Insurance Institute London. *A Century of Service: A History of Prudential 1848–1948.* Annual Reports of Chief Registrar of Friendly Societies (P.Ps).
2 PRO H.O.45/10069/B5959 Papers relating to Child Life Insurance.
3 Lords SC CLI Ludlow's ev.
4 See SC CLI and 1854 SC FS.
5 PRO H.O.45/10069/B.5959 Papers relating to Child Life Insurance.
6 PP 1844 Vol. 17.
7 For the case see E. Chadwick (note 1): Appendix; *The Times* 23/10/1840; 3/11/1840; 4th, 5th, 6th Aug. 1841; Henry Coppock's ev. SC FS 1854.
8 *Child's Guardian*: Supplement August 1890.
9 *The Times* 18/1/1849 Anonymous, but bears all of Clay's hallmarks.
10 PRO H.O.45/5203 (Old Series).
11 *The Times* 12/5/1846 and 10/8/1846.
12 Clay's letter, note (9).
13 For the Essex Poisonings: see *The Times* 14th & 21st Sept. and 4th Oct. 1848. 25/7/1848 29/8/1848. Also Sarah Chesham case Annual Register 1851 p. 396.
14 His letter to *The Times* 14/2/1889.
15 *Child's Guardian* Aug. 1890 – citing ev. before SC CLI 1890.
16 PP 1849 Vol. 14.
17 13/14 Vic. Ch. 115.
18 *The Times* 11/4/1853. SC FS 1854 ev. of judge William Wightman; John Clay's 'Letter to William Brown MP' 1853.
19 *The Times* 10/12/1853. Clay's 'Letter' (n. 18).
20 For the following, up to passage of the 1858 FS Act. PRO H.O.45/5203 (Old Series). Hansard 10/5/1854 – debate on FS Bill. 1855 FS Act 18/19 Ch. 63. 1858 FS Act 21/22 Vict. Ch. 101.

Chapter 16 Burial insurance and child murder (II)

1 SC DC.
2 Dewey before SC CLI.
3 PRO H.O.45/B5959 papers relating to insurance of children's lives 1884–1907.
4 *The Times* March 6, 7, 8th 1873. P. Wilson, R.S. Lambert.
5 38/39 Vic. Ch. 60.
6 *The Times* 11/2/1878.
7 PRO H.O.45/B5959.
8 Waugh's letter in *The Times* 6/10/1888.
9 C-G. July and August 1888. Ch Reg. Report 1888 Vol. 102.

10 PP 1888 Vol. 12 and 1889 Vol. 10.
11 PP 1890–91 Vol. 11.
12 See Chapter 15 note 1 for references: also Waugh's NSPCC pamphlet 'The Results of Child Life Insurance' 1891.
13 See NSPCC Annual Report 1935–6.
14 See F. Schooling's Address: 'Insurance Record' Oct 12th 1906.
15 *The Times* 1889: 23/4, 10/5, 31/5, 4/6, 10/7, 24/10, 26/10. SC CLI Waugh's ev. Q 2093 et seq. SC FS 1889 Page X of Final Report. Mrs Winters died before the trial. Frost was convicted of forgery, for misrepresentation on the insurance documents.
16 For the bill see Ann. Report NSPCC 1890–91 Appendix J. Reaction to bill: Pembroke Marshall's 'Reply' Dec. 1890 – see note 1 Chapter 15.
17 See PRO H.O.45/B5959 File 21; and Child Life Registration Bills (Scotland) 1891 and 1893–4 Sessions instigated by Scottish SPCC.
18 PP 1895 Vol. 3 p. 245.
19 See H.O.45/B5959 File 47 and Hansard (Commons) 12/9/1895.
20 PP 1894 Vol. 79.
21 *Child's Guardian* Aug. 1890; and Waugh's ev. SC CLI at Q 2103 et seq.
22 *Child's Guardian* Sept. 1909 issue.
23 Cohen Report CMD 4376 (1934).
24 Acts 1948: Ch. 39 s. 1.

Chapter 17   Infant life protection 1890–1914

1 PP 1890 Vol. 5 p. 523. Hansard 1890: 17/3/1890 Col. 1081 et seq. Amended Bill PP 1890 Vol. 5 p. 529.
2 SC ILP 1890 Vol. 13. SC ILP 1896 Vol. 10. SC ILP 1908 Vol. 9.
3 Roodhouse *The Lancet*: 16/5/1891 p. 1114. Reeves – G.K. Behlmer(b).
4 W. Chance *Children under the Poor Law* 1897.
5 Onslow's Bill 1895. Lords Papers Bill 140 of 1895 Session. Denbigh's Bill – Lords Papers Bill 20 of 1896. NSPCC Safety of Nurse-Children Bill no. 74 of 1896 session.
6 Sources on Mrs Dyer: P. Wilson; Gaute and Odell *The Ladykillers* 1980; *The Times* 13/4 & 23/5/1896. P. Brouardel *L'Infanticide* 1897; Roy Palmer *Everyman's Book of British Ballads* (1980) for the ballad of Mrs Dyer.
7 60/61 Vict. Ch. 57.
8 SC ILP 1896 Deaconess Gilmore (Q 2200). SC ILP 1908 Ninian Hill Q 6.
9 SC ILP 1896 Isabel Smith Q 1086 et seq.
10 GLC Record Office: LCC San. and Sp. Purpose Committee Minutes 1890 – Ann. Report of I.L.P. Inspector.
11 Zanetti's address: 1908 NCIM. Also her ev. before 1908 SC.
12 Babey – 1890 SC ILP. Ninian Hill – 1908 SC ILP.
13 Waugh 1896 SC ILP at Q 1568.
14 RCPL 1909 Min Report pp. 772 et seq.
15 J.R. Motion SCILP 1908.
16 Babey SC ILP 1896. J. Ollis SC ILP 1908.
17 SC ILP 1908 ev. James Doyle.
18 RCPL 1909 Q 45, 957.
19 SC ILP – various: 1871–1908. R. Parr(a).
20 SC ILP 1896: Waugh & Hill. SC ILP 1908: Hill (Q6).
21 PRO H.O.45/10569/175825.
22 *The Lancet* 21/3/1891.

23 *BMJ* 27/5/1871.
24 W. Henderson SC ILP 1890.
25 SC ILP 1890 Hicks at Q 106.
26 See *The Lancet* 12/10/1867 (p. 467) for references.
27 *The Times* 14/12/1870.
28 *Child's Guardian* Dec. 1894.
29 R. Parr(a).
30 NSPCC Ann. Report 1891.
31 R.J. Parr *Child Adoption*: NSPCC Occasional Papers, n.d. but pre-1926.
32 P. Wilson; also R. Parr(a) and *The Lancet* 24/1/1903.
33 P. Wilson; *Cardiff Weekly Mail* 3/8/1907.
34 8 Edw. 7 Ch. 67.
35 Child Adoption Committee 3rd Report PP 1926 Vol. 9.
36 PRO H.O.45/10569/175825.
37 Letter from Clerk, Glasgow Parish Council 22/8/1911 – n. 36.
38 GLC Record Office LCC Public Control Comm. Minutes Vol. 11: meetings 14/10/1910 and Vol. 15 meeting 27/3/1914.
39 Ann. Report Min. Health for 1922–3 (PP 1923 Vol. 11).
40 Ann. Report Min. Health for 1924/5 (PP 1924/5 Vol. 13).

Chapter 18   Bastardy, eugenics and affiliation law reform to 1939

1 For background to eugenism: A. McLaren; J. Weeks. On Pearson see E.S. Pearson *Karl Pearson* 1938. For Pearson's views see e.g. *Nature and Nurture: the Problem of the Future* 1910. *Eugenics and Public Health* 1912.
2 For Saleeby's views see e.g. NCIM 1914 his address on the *Nurture of the Race*.
3 Saleeby *The Progress of Eugenics* 1914.
4 Marie Stopes *Contraception: Theory, History etc.* 1926.
5 RCPL 1909 Min. Rpt. p. 776.
6 *Westminster Review* – 'A Crime and its Causes' 1899 Vol. 151 (pp. 131–9).
7 For law see Guy Lushington *Law of Affiliation and Bastardy* 1928 ed. (ed. Albert Lieck). NCUMC pamphlets and annual reports in British Library. Finer Report 1974. For inter-war history of bastardy: Lettice Fisher *Twenty One Years and After* 1946 (short history of NCUMC); G.F. McCleary(a); N. Middleton; Pinchbeck and Hewitt.
8 H. Ashby.
9 See N. Middleton, and Annual Reports NCUMC from 1927 onwards.
10 See Ann. Report Min. of Health 1918–19 (PP 1919 Vol. 24) for a clue to this.
11 Ann. Reports NCUMC 1929 and 1937. Lena Jeger *Illegitimate Children and their Parents* 1951.
12 On Blood Testing see Ann. Reports NCUMC 1937–9 and N. Middleton. Also Lushington (note 7) compare 1928 and 1934 editions.
13 Ann. Report NCUMC 1937.

Chapter 19   Infant conservation 1890–1920

1 For background: see e.g. G.F. McCleary(b); A. Wohl; F.B. Smith; M.W. Beaver; W.G. Savage *Milk and Public Health* (1912); NCIM 1906 (A.K. Chaloner's address) NCIM 1908 (E. Pritchard's Address); Thomas E. Cone; NCIM 1914 (Dr Janet Campbell).
2 G.K. Behlmer(a) Graph p. 424.

3   Source – note 3; % of babies in pop. from sample Ann. Reports R.G. of BDM.
4   Crim Stats 1925; PP 1927 Vol. 25 p. 27.
5   R. Sauer.
6   SC ILP 1896 Appendix E.
7   See Bernard Knight *Sudden Death in Infancy* 1983.
8   *The Lancet* 1855 Vol. 1 p. 103.
9   7th Ann. Report as Coroner (year 1868–74) NAPSS Sess. 1870–71 p. 89.
10 G. Newman.
11 Reg. Gen. Report 1898; PP 1899 Vol. 16.
12 PP 1890–91 Vol. 23.
13 Herbert Samuel: Hansard 12/10/1908 Col. 54 et seq.
14 Andrew Graham Murray: SC DC 1893.
15 *Child's Guardian* Dec. 1895.
16 See e.g. *Child's Guardian* March 1909: LCC M.O. of H's study.
17 For Bramsdon's Bill and the passage of the clause in Herbert's Bill: *Child's Guardian* March and April 1907. Hansard 5/3/1907. PP 1908 Vol. 1 p. 403 – Children's Bill (original draft). PP 1908 Vol. 6 p. 739 – Standing Committee proceedings. Hansard – 1st Reading 1/2/1908. 2nd Reading 24/3/1908. Hansard 2/7/1908 report of Standing Committee. Hansard 12/10/1908 Cols 54 et seq. – Debate on Bill.
18 See Hansard 12/10/1908 Debate. *Child's Guardian* Feb. 1913.
19 There was a change in the presentation of the Reg-Gen's tables at this time. Suffocation deaths are only shown totalled for all ages, though infant suffocations were certainly the overwhelming majority of these. These, too, show a slight fall just before the Act came into force.
20 Sources Reg-Gen Report for 1913 (PP 1914–16 Vol. 9. Table 30). Sources Reg-Gen Report for 1919 (PP 1920 Vol. 11 (eleven) Table 17).
21 G.B. Wilson.
22 Newsholme(b).
23 Source: *Judicial Statistics* for the relevant years.

Chapter 20   The disappearance of baby-farming 1920–39

1   12/13 Geo. 5 Ch. 18.
2   R. v. O'Donoghue and R. v. Hale respec. See Seaborne-Davies.
3   Hansard 24/11/1936 Col. 234. PP 1936.7 Vol. 2 p. 936 Infanticide Bill.
4   1/2 Geo. VI Ch. 36.
5   19/20 Geo. V Ch. 34.
6   Crim Stats. PP 1939/40 Vol. 11 (eleven) p. 15.
7   Source *Criminal Statistics* relevant years. For % of 0–1-year-olds in early 1980s – Office of Pop Censuses and Surveys.
8   Reports of Reg-Gen BDM for relevant years.
9   *Population trends* (OPCS Spring 1984).
10 *Criminal Statistics* 1982 (CMND 9048).
11 16/17 Geo. V Ch. 32.
12 PRO H.O.45/10458/B19958.
13 5/6 Geo. V Ch. 103 Part 4 Clause 17.
14 PP 1921 Vol. 9; PP 1924–5 Vol. 9; PP 1926 Vol. 9. For background see Pinchbeck and Hewitt Vol. 2.
15 22/23 Geo. V Ch. 46 section 68: the provision was re-enacted in the Public Health Act 1936.

16 NSPCC Occasional Papers: R. Parr 'Child Adoption (Supplementary)' n.d. (post-1926).

17 From Horsborough Committee on Adoption Societies and Agencies 1937 (PP 1936–7 Vol. 9).

18 22/23 Geo. V Ch. 46 (s. 68): the advertising clause was re-enacted in the Public Health Act 1936.

19 See note 16.

20 2/3 Geo. VI Ch. 27.

21 PP 1931–2 Vol. 10.

22 Figures in Min. of Health Ann. Report for 1933–4, PP 1933–4 Vol. 12.

Select bibliography and abbreviations

W. Acton(a), 'Observations on Illegitimacy in the London parishes of St. Marylebone, St Pancras and St George, Southwark (1857)', *Jnl of Statistical Society of London*, Dec. 1859.

Hugh T. Ashby, *Infant Mortality* (1922).

J.A. Banks(a), *Victorian Values* (1981).

J.A. Banks(b), *Prosperity and Parenthood* (1954).

Françoise Basch, *Relative Creatures* (1975).

George Wythen Baxter, *The Book of the Bastiles* (1841).

M.W. Beaver, 'Population, Infant Mortality and Milk', *Population Studies*, 1973 (Vol. 27).

Theodoric Romeyn Beck, *Elements of Medical Jurisprudence* (various editions. 7th ed. 1842 with John Beck).

George K. Behlmer(a), 'Deadly Motherhood: Infanticide and Medical Opinion in Mid-Victorian England', *Jnl Hist. Medicine and Allied Sciences* 1979 (34).

George K. Behlmer(b), *Child Abuse and Moral Reform in England, 1870–1908* (Stanford University Press 1982).

G.K. Behlmer(c), 'The Child Protection Movement in England', Ph.D. thesis, Stanford University (1977).

Virginia Berridge (and Griffith Edwards), *Opium and the People* (1981).

Patricia Branca, *Silent Sisterhood* (1975).

Gail Braybon, *Women Workers in the First World War* (1981).

E.J. Bristow, *Vice and Vigilance* (1978).

'*BMJ*', *British Medical Journal*.

'Brodrick', Brodrick Committee on Death Certification and Coroners 1971, Cmnd 4810.

Paul Brouardel, *L'Infanticide* (1897).

John Brownlow(a), *Memoranda or Chronicles of the Foundling Hospital*, 1847 ed.

J. Brownlow(b), *History and Design of the Foundling Hospital*, 1858.

'J.B.' (Brownlow(c)) [almost certainly John Brownlow] *Thoughts and Suggestions, having Reference to Infanticide* (1864).

John Burnett (ed.), *Useful Toil* (1977).

Dr Janet Campbell, Memorandum to the War Cabinet Committee on Women in Industry. PP 1919, Vol. 31.

Edmund Cautley, *The Natural and Artificial Methods of Feeding Infants* (1897).

Walter Lowe Clay, *The Prison Chaplain (Memoir of John Clay)* (1861).

Frances Power Cobbe, 'The Philosophy of the Poor Law', *Fraser's Magazine*, Sept. (1864).

Thomas E. Cone, *Two Hundred Years of Feeding Infants in America* (Ross Laboratories, 1976).

M.A. Crowther, *The Workhouse System* (1983).

W. Cummin, *The Proofs of Infanticide Considered* (1836).

John Brendon Curgenven(a), 'The Waste of Infant Life' NAPSS Tr. 1867.

J.B. Curgenven(b), 'On Baby Farming and the Registration of Nurses' NAPSS Tr. 1869.

J.B. Curgenven(c), 'Belgian Laws regarding Illegitimates and Foundlings' NAPSS Tr. 1867.

J.B. Curgenven(d), *On the Laws of France relating to Illegitimate Children etc.* 1871.

J.B. Curgenven(e), 'Infanticide, Baby Farming and the ILP Act', *Sanitary Record* 15/3/1889.

Frank Dawes, *Not in Front of the Servants* (1973).

DCPD, Departmental Committee on Physical Deterioration. PP 1904 Vol. 32.

Bernard Dickens, *Abortion and the Law* (1966).

Jean Donnison, *Midwives and Medical Men* (1977).

J.C. Drummond and A. Wilbraham, *The Englishman's Food* (1956).

Finer Report, Report on One-Parent Families. PP 1974 Vol. 16, Part II Appendix 5.

David Forsyth, History of Infant Feeding from Elizabethan Times, *Proc. of Royal Soc. of Medicine* (Section Diseases in Children, c.1910–11).

Peter Fryer, *The Birth Controllers* (1965).

Dr George Greaves, Observations on Some of the Causes of Infanticide, *Trans. of the Manchester Statistical Soc.* Jan. 1863.

Jonathan Gathorne Hardy, *The Rise and Fall of the British Nanny*.

Brian Harrison, *Drink and the Victorians*.

U. Henriques, 'Bastardy and the New Poor Law': *Past and Present*, Vol. 37 (1967).

'Hereford', Bishop of Hereford's Committee Report: 'The Children and the drink' (1901).

Margaret Hewitt, *Wives and Mothers in Victorian Industry* (1958).

P.C. Hoffer and N.E.H. Hull, *Murdering Mothers: Infanticide in England and New England 1558–1803* (1981).

Lee Holcombe, *Victorian Ladies at Work* (1973).

Mary Hopkirk, *Nobody Wanted Sam* (1949).

Frank Huggett, *Life below Stairs* (1977).

William Hunter, *Observations on the Uncertainty of the Signs of Death in the Case of Bastard Children* (1783).

B.L. Hutchins, *Women in Modern Industry* (1915).

John H. Hutchins, *Jonas Hanway* (1940).

ILPS, Infant Life Protection Society.

Hugh R. Jones, 'The Perils and Protection of Infant Life', *Jnl of the Royal Stat. Soc.* March 1894.

R.S. Lambert, *When Justice Faltered* (1935).

Edwin Lankester(a), Address on Infanticide, NAPSS Tr. 1869.

E. Lankester(b), Infanticide, with Reference to the Best Means for its Prevention, NAPSS Tr. 1866.

Peter Laslett *et al.*, *Bastardy and its Comparative History* (1980).

LCC, London County Council.

Norman Longmate, *The Water Drinkers*.

Frederick W. Lowndes(a), Address on Infanticide in Liverpool, NAPSS Sess. 1873.

F.W. Lowndes(b), On the Destruction of Infants Shortly After Birth, NAPSS Tr. 1876.

G.F. McCleary(a), *The Maternity and Child Welfare Movement* (1935).

G.F. McCleary(b), *Early History of the Infant Welfare Movement* (1933).

John Mackintosh, Concealed Pregnancy, Infanticide, Legitimacy and Rape, supp. to Dr Charles Denman's *The Elements of Practical Midwifery* (1838).

Angus McLaren, *Birth Control in Nineteenth Century England* (1978).

R.W. Malcolmson, 'Infanticide in the Eighteenth Century' in *Crime in England 1550–1800* ed. by J.S. Cockburn.

George Edward Male, *An Epitome of Juridical and Forensic Medicine* (1816).

Stephen Marcus, *The Other Victorians* (1967).

Nigel Middleton, *When Family Failed* (1971).

J.D. Milne, *The Industrial Employment of Women in the Middle and Lower Ranks* (1870).

NAPSS, National Association for the Promotion of Social Science. Tr. = Transactions. Sess. = Journal and Sessional Papers.

NCIM, National Conference(s) on Infant(ile) Mortality: 1906, 1908, and 1914.

NCUMC, National Council for the Unmarried Mother and her Child.

NSPCC, National Society for the Prevention of Cruelty to Children.

Wanda Neff, *Victorian Working Women* (1929).

George Newman, *Infant Mortality – A Social Problem* (1906).

Arthur Newsholme(a), *Vital Statistics,* ed. 1889, 1899 and 1923.

A. Newsholme(b), Report to the Local Government Board on Infant Mortality. PP 1913 Vol. 32.

'*NBDM*', North British Daily Mail.

OAP Act, Offences against the Person Act 1861.

PP, Parliamentary Papers [Hse of Commons, unless otherwise stated. Volume nos are given in Arabic numerals].

Robert Parr, *The Baby Farmer – An Exposition and an Appeal* (1908).

L.A. Parry, *Criminal Abortion* (1932).

Michael Pearson, *The Age of Consent.*

Ivy Pinchbeck(a), *Women Workers in the Industrial Revolution* (1930).

Ivy Pinchbeck(b) and Margaret Hewitt, *Children in English Society* (2 vols) (1969, 1973).

C. Polson and D.J. Gee, *The Essentials of Forensic Medicine* (1973).

Malcolm Potts *et al., Abortion* (1977).

PRO, Public Record Office.

Reg. Gen. BDM, Registrar General – Births, Deaths and Marriages.

Joseph Rogers, *Reminiscences of a Workhouse Medical Officer* (1889).

Michael Rose, 'Admin. of the Poor Law in the West Riding of Yorkshire 1820–55', D.Phil. thesis (Oxford) (1965).

C.H. Routh, *Infant Feeding and its Influence on Life* (1860 and subsequent ed.).

RC, Royal Commission.

RC CP, Royal Commission on Capital Punishment. PP 1866 Vol. 21.

RC FS, Royal Commission on Friendly Societies 4th Report. PP 1874 Vol. 23.

RC PL 1834, Royal Comm. on the Poor Laws. PP 1834 Vol. 27.

RC PL 1909, Royal Comm. on the Poor Laws. PP 1909 Vol. 37. Maj/Min Rpts = Majority/Minority Reports.

R.S. Soc., Royal Statistical Society.

William Burke Ryan, *Infanticide: its Law, Prevalence and History* (1862).

R. Sauer, 'Infanticide and Abortion in Nineteenth Century Britain': *Population Studies* 1978 Vol. 32.

D.R. Seaborne-Davies, 'Child Killing in English Law' in *English Studies in Criminal Science* Vol. IV (1945) by L. Radzinowicz and J.W.C. Turner.

SC, Select Committee.

SC BO 1909, Select Committee on Bastardy Orders PP 1909 Vol. 6.

SC CLI (Hse. Lords), Select Comm. on Child Life Insurance. PP 1890–91 Vol. 11.

SC DC, Sel. Comm. on Death Certification Pp 1893–4 Vol. 11.

SC FS 1854, Sel. Comm. on Friendly Societies Bill. PP 1854 Vol. 8.

SC ILP, Sel. Comm. on Infant Life Protection:

1871 – PP 1871 Vol. 7
1890 – PP 1890 Vol. 13
1896 – PP 1896 Vol. 10
1908 – PP 1908 Vol. 9.
William Shaw, *An Affectionate Pleading for England's Oppressed Female Workers* (1850).
Edward Shorter, *The Making of the Modern Family* (1978).
F.B. Smith, *The People's Health 1830–1910* (1979).
Revd. Herbert Smith, *An Account of the Situation and Treatment of the Women with Illegitimate Children in the New Forest Workhouse* (1838).
Ambroise Tardieu, *Étude Médico-Légale sur l'Infanticide* (1868).
Alfred Swaine Taylor(a), *A Manual of Medical Jurisprudence* (various editions, 19th/20th centuries).
Patricia Thomson, *The Victorian Heroine* (1956).
Eric Trudgill, *Madonnas and Magdalens* (1976).
Judith R. Walkowitz, *Prostitution and Victorian Society* (1980).
Benjamin Waugh(a), 'Baby farming', *Contemporary Review* 1890 pp. 700–714.
Jeffrey Weeks, *Sex, Politics and Society* (1981).
Ian Wickes, 'A History of Infant Feeding', *Archives of Diseases in Childhood* 1953 vol. 28.
G. Prys Williams and G.T. Brake, *Drink in Great Britain 1900–1979* (1980).
Raymond Williams, *The Long Revolution* (1965).
G.B. Wilson, *Alcohol and the Nation 1800–1935* (1940).
John Dove Wilson, Suggestions for Amending the Criminal Law of Infanticide, NAPSS Tr. 1877.
Patrick Wilson, *Murderess* (1971).
Anthony Wohl, *Endangered Lives* (1983).
Andrew Wynter, *Curiosities of Toil* [Chap. on Child Destruction] (1870).
G. Udney Yule, *The Fall in the Birth Rate* (1920).

Index

abortion, 86, 87, 93-5, 171, 174
abortifacients, 6, 7, 86, 95, 134
accoucheuses, 88, 94
Acton, Dr William, 18, 19, 21, 43, 54
Acts of Parliament: Adoption Acts
(1926, 1930), 79, 173; Adoption of
Children Regulation Act (1939), 186;
Affiliation Law, 26; Bastardy Act
(1868), 29; Bastardy Act (1872), 115,
170, 172; Bastardy Law (1874), 23,
30, 31; Birth and Death Registration
Acts: (1836), 36, 120; (1854), 121;
(1874), 22, 16; (1926), 122, 135, 183;
Child Destruction Act (1929), 182;
Children's Act (1908), 158, 167, 168,
179; Children and Young Persons Act
(1932), 168, 185, 186; Contagious
Diseases Acts (1864, 1866), 43;
Coroners Act (1887), 53, 123;
Coroners Act (1926), 57; Cremation
Act (1884), 89; Dangerous Drugs Act
(1920), 12; English Registration Act
(1874), 121; Food and Drugs Act
(1875), 12; Friendly Society Act
(1793), 136; Friendly Society Act
(1850), 144-6; Friendly Society Act
(1855), 145, 146, 150; Friendly
Society Act (1875), 123, 147, 150,
155; Industrial Assurance and
Friendly Society Act (1948), 158;
Infanticide Acts (1922, 1938), 182;
Infant Life Protection Act (1872), 110
et seq.; Infant Life Protection Act
(1890), 159; Infant Life Protection
Act (1897), 161, 168; LCC General
Powers Act (1915), 184; Legitimation
Act (1926), 173; Licensing Act
(1910), 57; Local Government Act
(1888), 57; Local Government Act
(1929), 186; Lunacy Act, 108;

Maternity and Child Welfare Act
(1918), 172; Maternity Homes Act
(1926), 183; Medical Act (1858), 41;
Medical Register Act (1858), 120,
121; Midwives Act (1902), 85;
National Insurance Act (1911), 184;
National Insurance Act (1946), 158;
Notification of Births Act (1907), 134,
175; Offences Against the Persons
Acts, 70, 86, 93, 110; Poisons and
Pharmacy Act (1868), 12; Poor Laws,
24 *et seq.*, 46 *et seq.*, 116; boarding out,
46 *et seq.*, 159; Poor Law Amendment
Act (1844), 28, 30; Prevention of
Cruelty Acts (1889, 1894), 13, 125,
151, 155, 156, 179; Sanitary Act
(1886), 57; Scottish Adoption Act
(1930), 184; Scottish Registration Act
(1854), 121; Seduction Act (1840),
30; Trade Union Amendment Act
(1876), 150
adoption: fostering adoption
advertisements, 80, 98, 165, 167
Ady, Dr James, 87
affiliation, laws, orders and summonses,
26, 109, 110, 115, 116, 173
age of consent, 110, 115-17
Akers, Douglas, 179
alcohol, misuse of, 9, 12
alcoholism, *see* diseases
anaesthesia, 41
Arnold, Mrs J., 113
Aspinall, C., 68, 178
atelectasis, 72
atrophy, *see* diseases

Babey, Samuel, 111, 113, 162, 163, 165
baby disposers, *see* baby traffickers
baby dropping, 40, 68
baby dumpers, *see* baby traffickers